PRICE REFORM IN CHINA, 1979–86

Price Reform in China, 1979–86

Jiann-Jong Guo
Associate Professor
National Taiwan University, Taipei, Taiwan
and Executive Secretary General
Institute of International Affairs, Taiwan

M
St. Martin's Press

First published in Great Britain 1992 by
THE MACMILLAN PRESS LTD
Houndmills, Basingstoke, Hampshire RG21 2XS
and London
Companies and representatives
throughout the world

This book is published in Macmillan's *Studies on the Chinese Economy*
General Editors: Peter Nolan and Dong Fureng

A catalogue record for this book is available from the British Library

ISBN 0–333–52644–9

Printed in Great Britain by
Billing and Sons Ltd
Worcester

First published in the United States of America 1992 by
Scholarly and Reference Division,
ST. MARTIN'S PRESS, INC.,
175 Fifth Avenue,
New York, N.Y. 10010

ISBN 0–312–06819–0

Library of Congress Cataloging-in-Publication Data
Guo, Jiann-Jong, 1957–
Price reform in China, 1979–86 / Jiann-Jong Guo.
p. cm.
Includes bibliographical references and index.
ISBN 0–312–06819–0
1. Price—Government policy—China. 2. Price regulation—China.
3. China—Economic policy—1976– I. Title.
HB236.C55G86 1992
338.5'0951—dc20 91–24332
CIP

To my parents, and Ms S. Y. Lai and
Ms I. W. Tsai

Contents

List of Figures and Tables

Figures

Tables

Preface

This book attempts to analyse the fundamental theoretical and practical issues of producer and procurement price reform in China between 1979 and 1986. The Chinese government has tried to transform its high degree of price control in a rigid command economy to partial price control in a socialist market economy. The reform patterns adopted to achieve this goal are adjustment, liberalisation and a combination of both, and the price reform was taking place simultaneously with a reform of the whole economic system.

Yet price reform neither successfully rid itself of the vestiges of a command economy, nor developed the full characteristics of a decentralised market economy. Rather, it developed unique and contradictory features representative of both planning and market economies. Nevertheless, the new pricing system has achieved its goal to some extent in terms of stimulating output and balancing supply and demand for some commodities. The pricing system has developed from a single fixed pricing system to a mixed one, and the role of price has laid greater emphasis on 'resource allocation' than on 'accounting' and 'income distribution'.

This book is an outcome of five years of research. I am grateful to Dr Peter Nolan for his encouragement to publish the results. I must record my debt to Professors Gordon White and Adrian Wood, Fellows of the Institute of Development Studies at the University of Sussex, whose supervision and help made completion of this work possible. My thanks to Jack Gray and Dr Joseph Dahms, who both kindly let me use their information. I am also indebted to Dr David Dyker and Dr Akio Takahara, with whom I had useful discussions on the political and economic reforms in China and East Europe. I would like to express my deep sense of gratitude to economists in the State Price Bureau, the National Price Association, and the People's University of China; and also to the managers, officers, and technicians of enterprises, for their valuable help during my visit in 1985 and 1986.

I would like to acknowledge the Committee of the Vice-Chancellors and Principals of the United Kingdom, which provided me with a one-year Overseas Research Award. I would also like to express my appreciation for the financing awarded to me by the Dudley Seers and Leche Funds. I remember with deep gratitude the private financial assistance from my friends and colleagues. I also gratefully acknowledge the help of Joerge Dyrkton who carefully went through the manuscript and made suggestions on stylistic changes.

In the introductory chapter (Chapter 1), a theoretical framework for analysing the research objectives is constructed. This is followed by an introduction of the socialist pricing system and price reform in the historical and international context. Chapter 2 discusses the characteristics of Chinese price reform, including the goals, methods and time frame. Chapter 3 tackles administrative price formation. Chapter 4 deals with effects of price adjustment on total output. Chapter 5 studies effects of price reform on output composition. Chapter 6 studies the development of the new pricing system – the dual pricing system. Chapter 7 deals with enterprise-responsiveness to price changes. Chapter 8 draws some conclusions concerning the achievements and problems of the price reform, and future development and obstacles are also considered.

JIANN-JONG GUO

List of Abbreviations and Publication Titles

Acronyms of Bodies

CASS	Chinese Academy of Social Sciences
CCP	Chinese Communist Party
CESRRI	China Economic System Reform Research Institute
CMEA	Council for Mutual Economic Assistance
CPI	Consumer price index
FPO	Federal Post Office (Yugoslavia)
IDS	Institute for Development Studies
MPM	Means of production market (*Shengchan Ziliao Shichang*)
MTC	Material trading centre
NPC	National People's Congress
NPC	National Price Commission (*Guojia Wujia Weiyuan Hui*)
SEC	State Economic Commission (China)
SPA	Social Price Act (Yugoslavia)
SPB	State Price Bureau (China)
SPC	State Price Commission (USSR)
TESDRC	Technological, Economic and Social Development Research Centre at the State Council

Publication Titles

Caimao Jingji	*Financial and Trade Economy*
Dongnan Henchen	*Southeast Information*
Gongchang Guanli	*Industrial and Business Management*
Jiage Lilun Yu Shijian	*Price : Theory and Practice*
Jiage Lunwen Xuanji	*Selected Compilation on Prices*
Jingji Chankao	*Economic Reference*
Jingji Diaocha	*Economic Investigation*
Jingji Guanli	*Economic Management*
Jingji Ribao	*Economic Daily*
Jingji Yanjiu	*Economic Research*
Jingji Xue Zhoubao	*Economic Weekly*

Jong Qen Lian Luntan	*Young Economists' Journal*
Ming Bao Yuekan	*Ming Bao Journal*
Nankai Xuebao	*Nankai Journal*
Nongye Jishu Jingji	*Agricultural Technical Economics*
Renmin Ribao	*People's Daily*
Zhongguo Gongye Jingji Xuebao	*China's Industrial Economics Journal*
Zhongguo Gongye Jingji Yanjiu	*China's Industrial Economic Study*
Zhongguo Shehui Kexue	*Social Sciences in China*
Zhongguo Nongye De Gonghuai Chengjui	*The Great Achievement of China's Agriculture*

1 Historical and International Context

1.1 INTRODUCTION

Since 1978 the Chinese government, like many others worldwide, has pursued a policy of economic liberalisation – moving away from a high degree of state control towards a competitive market.[1] The goal of this economic reform programme has been to find an automatic, market-oriented mode of economic coordination which would avoid many of the costs associated with more direct political management of economic life: distortion and inefficiency, suppression of initiative, and concentration of power in the State to the detriment of managerial and individual self-determination and choice (Moore and White, 1987). Price reform, part of the liberalisation programme, is regarded as one of the important keys to reforming the economic system.

In this chapter we construct a theoretical framework suitable for analysing the reform of producer and procurement prices and investigating the background of development of the post-reform pricing system in China. We also review the East European and Soviet price policies and the pre-1978 Chinese experience.

1.2 SOCIALIST PRICING

The socialist pricing system can be examined using either a positive or a normative approach. The positive approach is used to explain or describe the nature of economic activity. It is objective, limited to cause-and-effect relationships of economic activity: it is concerned with the way economic relationships are.[2] The normative approach is concerned with what ought to be, and inevitably involves value judgements. We have adopted the positive approach in this analysis but also consider various normative views.

A. Socialist Price Theory

The theoretical debates on the socialist pricing system revolve around whether a socialist society can find a mechanism to conduct its economic affairs efficiently, especially with regard to the allocation of resources. One question of particular importance concerns what type of pricing mechanism should be employed. There are three major schools of thought on this issue: the planning position, the market position, and the position of 'optimal' price. Each of these positions is discussed below.

Planning Position

People holding this position view the price system in socialist countries as an instrument used to achieve both social and economic goals during the transition to communism. However, it is considered only a temporary phenomenon, to be discarded in the phase of communism.

Economists such as Bukharin, Preobrazhensky, Bettelheim, Chen Boda, Sweezy, Meek and Dobb, all claim that prices cannot be abolished until society has been completely transformed to a higher stage of communism.[3] Prices will then be required by the central planners only for accounting purposes. The original functions of prices – to allocate resources and balance supply and demand – will be restricted in a socialist society and will eventually be replaced by a planning mechanism. The role of prices, thereafter, is to serve as a channel for political intervention in the economic realm, particularly when such intervention cannot be conveniently carried out in another fashion (Bettelheim, 1978 : 229).

How is a socialist price system formed during the transition period? According to Bettelheim, it cannot be directly derived from the current production relations. It can be built up only by knowing the direction of the development of society, and then proceeding with an analysis of the production-relations characteristic of social formation (Bettelheim, 1978 : 227–34). Price should express the social conditions of production and the requirements for changing the economic and social structure (Bettelheim, 1978 : 184). The use of prices as instruments of economic control requires many deviations of price from value to promote efficient enterprise operation, recognise supply and demand factors, promote or discourage consumption of certain goods, and so forth.

In a socialist society, according to this position, it is incorrect to assume that prices should balance supply and demand. This task should instead be accomplished by the quantitative planning mechanism. The so-called 'law of planned proportional development' can be used to balance structural proportions, such as those between consumption and accumulation and those between different types of industries, as well as dealing with the issues of income distribution. According to this view, the planning mechanism can conduct economic affairs efficiently and is superior to the market mechanism.

Market Position

Some economists, such as Mises (1920), argue that an efficient allocation of resources cannot be achieved with socialised means of production. They assume that capitalism and optimal resource allocation go together. 'Where there is no free market, there is no pricing mechanism', and 'without a pricing mechanism, there is no economic calculation' (Mises, 1920). If there is no way to determine the economic efficiency of production or investment decisions, then rational economic calculation is infeasible. Thus, socialism is bound to fail.

The weakness of this position lies in the identification of the absence of private ownership of the means of production with the impossibility of a rational socialist pricing. This view is too simplistic, and unable to stand up to the provision of a theoretical framework demonstrating the compatibility of rational pricing and socialised ownership of the means of production, such as the Lange-Lerner model, discussed below.

Other economists, such as Robbins (1934) and Hayek (1935), also argue the impossibility of socialist pricing from a more practical aspect, the problem of implementation.[4] Hayek (1935) believes it is infeasible that planners could find a solution for the millions of simultaneous equations which make up the general-equilibrium system of a planned economy.

'Optimal' Price Position

By contrast, some economists have argued that the public ownership of the means of production and the absence of a free-market mechanism will not impede rational calculation (Csikos-Nagy, 1975 : 12). According to this position, rational prices can be arrived at on a competitive and decentralised basis.

The Lange–Lerner solution refutes both the impossibility and impracticability position by arguing that the State can carry out the required price adjustment functions, suggesting that a planned economy could mimic a market system by instructing state-owned enterprises to respond to announced prices in a profit-maximising way (Lange, 1936–7).

The essence of this 'solution' is that all prices are fixed by a process of trial and error until an 'equilibrium price' is found at which current supply is equal to current demand. If, at a set of announced prices, a commodity or factor were in surplus, its price would be lowered; if it were in deficit, its price would be raised. In this way, equilibrium prices can be achieved by successive approximations without either the simultaneous solution of millions of equations or the private ownership of the means of production and competitive markets. Only observation of supply and demand movements and appropriate price readjustment is required. This trial and error process is similar to the *tâtonnement* described by Walras. One important feature of the Lange–Lerner model is that its production managers are compelled to make their output and investment decisions on the basis of these accounting prices, which they cannot influence.

Lange's decentralisation model has some weaknesses (Feuchtwang and Hussain, 1983 : 13). It assumes that a central planning bureau can find equilibrium prices through a process of trial and error. It neglects the problems which might occur while the central planning bureau is groping for the set of equilibrium prices. It also assumes that enterprises behave according to the rules and regulations of a perfect market system, which is arguable even in a capitalist economy. This model has been attacked by some Marxist economists such as Dobb (1955), Sweezy (1949), Baran (1957) and Bettelheim (1978), who favour centralised decision-making.[5] Dobb argues that the price system can not be used as an automatic optimum-finder and that all major decisions affecting economic development must be taken by a central planning body (Dobb, 1955 : 86).

These three positions mainly deal with questions of whether price mechanisms can function in a socialist country. Their purpose is neither to provide a description of how a socialist price system actually works, nor to give a systematic explanation of how socialist countries reform their pricing systems.

B. Socialist Prices in Practice – Three Patterns

Prices are used for three major purposes: accounting, income distribution, and resource allocation. What role the prices should play in a society is determined by the particular form of political and economic systems which occur in different historical development phases.

Different socialist pricing policies and systems are determined by three forms of socialist economic systems: 'a heroic–enthusiastic economic system', 'a construction and consolidation of a bureaucratic-hierarchical command economy', and 'a less centralized market socialism' (Kornai, 1985). According to these three socialist economic systems, three patterns are formulated to describe actual socialist pricing systems and price reforms. They are the total price control in a revolutionary economy, the high degree of price control in a bureaucratic–hierarchical command economy, and the partial price control in a 'less centralized market economy'.

Pattern One: Total Price Control in a Revolutionary Economy

In this pattern, most prices are controlled or frozen by the government to avert inflation, to achieve equity, and to fulfil political and social objectives. The pricing system in the 'heroic–enthusiastic economic period' is only temporary; it cannot be sustained for an extended period.

Pattern Two: High Degree of Price Control in a Bureaucratic–Hierarchical Command Economy

In this pattern, the central planners try to maintain moderate price stability and equity, but exercise less control than in the first pattern. Prices are mainly used for accounting and income distribution and have only a minor role in resource allocation. As in the first pattern, the use of price as an instrument of economic control causes prices to deviate from value and gives rise to state subsidies and hidden inflation. Nevertheless price determination for some commodities is decentralised, with local governments controlling less important prices and black market prices existing peripherally.

Price reform in this pattern is based on an adjustment method; it requires neither a reformation of the entire economic system, nor an adoption of the market mechanism. Price reforms take place by letting some prices be determined by the local authorities (decentralisation), or by setting prices according to a new formula or technique.

Pattern Three: Partial Price Control in a 'Less Centralized Market Economy'

In this pattern, price reform takes place simultaneously with a reform of the whole economic system. The main objective of price policy is to improve economic efficiency through improved resource allocation; price stability and equity become secondary matters. In this pattern, price reform incorporates two aspects: improvement of the administrative method of price formation for certain important prices through the adoption of new formulae and better calculation techniques; and the adoption of the market mechanism for other prices. These two reform methods, adjustment and liberalisation, are used in economic systems undergoing transformation from a command to a mixed economy. An additional objective of price reform in this pattern is to improve enterprise responsiveness to price changes.

Although the above three patterns occur at different historical phases, they describe static situations. The actual development of a socialist pricing system and price reform is more sophisticated and dynamic. The development of a socialist pricing system with its cycles of decentralisation, recentralisation and liberalisation can be considered as movements back and forth between these three pricing patterns.

In the next section of this chapter we apply these three patterns in describing the development of the pricing system in a number of socialist countries. The East European experience is reviewed and the Chinese point of view concerning the lessons to be learned is examined.

1.3 EAST EUROPEAN EXPERIENCE

A. Soviet Union

The pricing system in the Soviet Union began in a way described by Pattern One above, when it was in the War Communist period. During the NEP of the 1920s the system changed to a Pattern Three type. The 1968 reforms and the post-1968 system can be described as belonging to Pattern Two.

The traditional Soviet pricing system was used by the central authorities as a means of realising planning goals (Bornstein, 1966). Prices were mainly used for distributing national income and accounting (Wilczynski, 1972). Producer prices were based on average production costs *less* rent and capital charges.[6] Prices remained unchanged for long periods – five to fifteen years in some cases.

Retail prices were only vaguely related to producer prices since they were set to adjust demand to planned supply to ensure equilibrium in the consumer goods market (Wilczynski, 1972); retail prices were changed more frequently than producer and procurement prices. Insulation of retail prices from producer prices was achieved primarily through highly differentiated turnover taxes or subsidies. Consequently, consumers' preferences had little influence on production except when acknowledged by central planners, who would then either adjust producer prices or reallocate resources.

Wilczynski (1972 : 77) provides a picture of the sheer bulk of the work involved in price determination by the planning board. For example, in the mid-1960s the State centrally fixed 100,000 prices for articles of clothing and 107 different prices for fishing hooks. These prices were all centrally determined in Moscow according to detailed descriptions of the product and the materials used. There were over 10 million kinds of goods at the time, and so administering prices presented many difficulties: 'As the government was not omnipotent; it could not keep in hand every price' (Kornai, 1980 : 355–8). Moreover, since prices in some sectors yielded higher profits than in others the old pricing system caused problems in terms of revenue imbalances between industries unrelated to differences in economic efficiency.

The traditional system was criticised by Soviet reformers since prices of producer goods did not reflect their value; prices did not furnish correct signals to planners and enterprise managers; and the shortcomings of these prices impeded the effective use of value targets for the control and evaluation of enterprise operations (Bornstein and Fusfeld, 1970 : 112–13).[7]

In 1968 a price reform took place. It was aimed at replacing the traditional 'cost plus' formula of price-setting by a 'production price' which involved a uniform (15 per cent) rate of profit on capital for different commodities and industries (Xu Yi, 1982 : 53–4) (Xu Yi is Director of Research, Institute of Finance, Ministry of Finance, China). Some writers expected that such a change would entail an 11–12 per cent increase in wholesale prices of industrial products (Bettelheim, 1978 : 199). This proposal, the reformers believed, might solve the problem of disparities in industrial prices. Moreover, the new system of profitability could be an important indicator of enterprise efficiency.

The price reform in the Soviet Union was conducted by the newly formed State Price Committee (SPC), which was under the State Planning Commission. The price system remained highly centralised in the post-reform period. The SPC itself fixed prices for important producer and consumer goods, including 75–80 per cent of the value of output of heavy industry and about 50 per cent of the value of output of the light and food industries (Bornstein, 1970 : 118). In addition to SPC price-setting, price committees in local republics set prices covering nearly 20 per cent of the value of output in heavy industry and over 40 per cent of the consumer goods industry. Enterprises could set prices themselves only for goods not controlled by higher authorities (Bornstein, 1970).

Some Soviet economists considered the price reform as unsuccessful since prices still did not play a role in resource allocation (which was accomplished by quantitative directives), and since profitability was still not a criterion of enterprise efficiency. The formula used for price-setting – production price – remained cost-oriented and neglected demand as a basic element of value and price.

The goal of a uniform rate of profit on capital of 15 per cent for all industrial departments was never achieved (Xu Yi, 1982 : 53–4). The rate of profit on capital varied: in 1968 it was 8.2 per cent in the coal industry, 15 per cent in the metallurgy of ferrous and non-ferrous metals and in the extraction of oil and gas, 14.2 per cent in machine-building, 20 per cent in the timber industry, 15 per cent in the chemical industry, 10 percent in electric power production, and 19.2 per cent in ferrous metal (Xu Yi, 1982 : 54; Bettelheim, 1978 : 199).

Profit rates varied for a number of reasons, one being the problem posed by the mutual substitutability of certain products whose prices had to be linked to adjust supply and demand. One such typical case was that of 'fuel and power' products like coal and oil (Xu Yi, 1982; Bettelheim, 1978). Since it was deemed necessary to keep certain prices stable, enforcing a uniform profit rate would have involved huge subsidies and thus placed an impossible financial burden on the State (Xu Yi, 1982).

The reform of producer prices carried out in Soviet industry did not simplify the conditions for price-setting. According to Xu Yi (1982), the lessons for China were, first, that a uniform rate of profit was infeasible in practice. Second, price reform should be aimed at attaining a rational ratio of profit rates for different industries. Xu Yi believed that the Soviet style of price reform was not suitable for China, and economists such as Chen Baoshun and Liang Wuxia supported Xu Yi's view.

B. Yugoslavia

In Yugoslavia, the pricing system changed from a Pattern Two in the 1949–50 period to somewhere between Patterns Two and Three in the 1950–65 period and to a Pattern Three type post-1965.

In the 1950s, Yugoslavia abolished the Soviet type of state administrative management system and adopted an approach to economic and social development rooted in the complementary principles of debureaucratisation and mass participation (Prout, 1985). These two principles constituted the ideological basis of Yugoslav market socialism. The system of self-managed enterprises embodying the concepts of 'worker collectives', 'socially-owned industrial assets', and 'surplus value accounting' was established. At that time, prices and foreign exchange controls were also relaxed. Since then, Yugoslavia has become a market-oriented country relying mainly on the market mechanism (Prout, 1985; Milenkoritch, 1971 : 90–101).

Following the break with Stalin there were three distinct periods in the development of the Yugoslav pricing system.[8] During the first period (1952–65) there were fixed, ceiling and free prices. Price reform followed the principle of debureaucratisation. However, the State directly fixed producer prices for important producer goods, including 32.1 per cent of the value of output of industry in 1958, 67 per cent in 1962, and an average of 60 per cent between 1962 and 1965 (ibid.).

The second period from 1965–79 was one which witnessed swings between centralisation and decentralisation of price control. The reform of producer prices, which began in July 1965, attempted to correct recently developed distortions between the prices of manufactured goods and the prices of agricultural goods, raw materials and infrastructure goods and services. At the same time, the State devalued the dinar to assist in aligning domestic prices with those prevailing in world markets (Prout, 1985).

This reform was designed to allow most prices to be determined according to supply and demand. However, due to the severe inflationary pressures which afflicted the economy this policy was not carried out. The state was forced to control or supervise 80 per cent of industrial producer prices, and most important commercial and agricultural prices (Lu Nan, 1985).

In 1972, the Social Price Act (SPA) was passed; it declared new criteria for price-setting and allowed producers and consumers to negotiate prices within the confines of the inter-republican agreement (Prout, 1985). This new policy indicated two stages of price determination. In the first stage, if producers desired to increase prices for their products, at least two-thirds of both the producers and the consumers of that product were required to agree to the increase. The agreement had then to be authorised by the appropriate economic chamber. In the second stage, the producers had to inform the Federal Price Office (FPO) of price increases one month in advance of planned implementation. If there was no objection from the FPO then the new price could be implemented. Under the SPA two-thirds of products had free prices, 57 per cent of which were industrial goods as of 1972.

In 1974, the State ratified the SPA, and strengthened the inter-republican agreement to provide a set of guidelines for the conclusion of inter-firm self-management agreements. Again, it emphasised the importance of the application of market criteria in price-setting.

During the third period, 1980–5, the authorities attempted to implement more fully the principle of debureaucratisation. In 1980 the FPO was abolished and replaced by Federal and Republican Price Communities. These Price Communities contained representatives of both producers and consumers in each sector; they determined prices after consultation with relevant offices. The main criteria for price setting were demand and supply conditions, world prices, liquidity and profitability considerations and the promotion of priority sectors (Prout, 1985; Lu Nan, 1985).

In 1985 the government passed the Fundamental Law of Social Price Control and Supervision. According to this, there are three main categories of prices: fixed prices, representing about 10 per cent of goods and services, including electricity, oil, telephones, transportation, etc.; negotiated prices between producers and consumers, representing about 30 per cent; and free prices, representing the remaining 60 per cent (Lu Nan, 1985).

The Yugoslav case had several outstanding features. First, the government had less power over price determination than in the Soviet Union and Hungary (discussed below). Second, free and negotiated prices were the most common. Third, enterprises had more autonomy in price determination than enterprises in other socialist countries. This highly decentralised system was regarded as a 'relatively free pricing system for a socialist society' by Lu Nan (1985).

According to Chinese economists in both the State Price Bureau and the People's University of China, the Yugoslav case was also inappropriate for China (interviews conducted by the author in

1985). First, it could cause a serious inflation problem. Second, it required an immense number of meetings between sellers and buyers. Lu Nan (1985) indicates that there were more than 240,000 people attending price negotiation meetings in Yugoslavia each day in 1985. Third, implementation of such a system would shatter the power of the central government. The first and third factors were the main reasons for the Chinese decision not to accept such a system.

C. Hungary

One of the conclusions of the Hungarian debate on the pricing system was that 'in an administrative system the rational orientating function of prices can assert itself only to a very limited extent' (Csikos-Nagy, 1971 : 147). Price reform in Hungary focused on the issue of what functions the price system should perform, rather than by what formulae prices should be determined (as in the Soviet Union), or who should set the prices (as in Yugoslavia). The goal of the Hungarian reform was to allow the market mechanism to have free play in determining some prices rather than setting all prices by administrative methods (Csikos-Nagy, 1971 : 148).

Price reform in Hungary followed the dual principles that national economic planning was necessary for purposeful economic development, and that without a market mechanism there could be no rational economic organisation (Csikos-Nagy, 1971). The price reform was aimed at building a hybrid system of price determination, utilising both a controlled price sector and a freely negotiated price sector (Nove, 1983; Csikos-Nagy, 1971). The system was based on the idea that in a 'less centralized market socialist system', the advantages of socialism (such as the abolition of exploitation, the socialisation of major economic decisions, full employment, rapid economic growth and social security) could be combined with the advantages of the market (such as the elimination of shortages and queues, the efficient use of intermediate products, innovation and rapid technical progress and attention to personal consumption) (Ellman, 1979 : 54; Nove, 1983). Theoretically a less centralised market socialism could open the possibility of establishing a relatively rational and efficient pricing system in terms of resource allocation.

Price reform was launched in Hungary in 1968. The prices of 'sensitive' commodities – some consumer goods and basic industrial inputs – were fixed by administrative fiat. Less sensitive commodities were subject to maximum, floating prices. Prices of most machines and semi-manufactures were freely determined (Nove, 1983; Csikos-Nagy, 1971).

The respective proportions of these three types of price in 1978 were 16 per cent of prices fixed, 46 per cent floating and 38 per cent freely determined (from an unpublished report circulated to researchers at the State Price Bureau). The proportion of freely determined prices grew steadily from 23 per cent of the total in 1968, to 38 per cent in 1978, 55 per cent in 1984 (*Financial Times*, 2 November 1984), and 58 per cent in 1985 (Lu Nan, 1985).

One major problem associated with the 1968 reform was that producer prices were reformed but relative retail prices were unaltered (Wilczynski, 1973 : 87). Consequently, the level of producer prices increased, and the gap between them and retail prices widened (Csikos-Nagy, 1979).

In 1980, a new 'competitive price' policy was announced (Lu Nan, 1985). It was designed to harden the firm's financial budget system by adjusting Hungarian domestic prices to foreign trade prices in convertible currencies (Kornai, 1983 : 226–34; Balana, 1982). This policy required a greater freedom of trade, especially for imports (Nove, 1983 : 125). Prices of one-third of industrial products were determined by this policy after 1980 (Lu Nan, 1985). This new price policy resulted in an introduction of a different type of state intervention. The government monitored the profit rates prescriptions for price calculations, causing a more artificial relationship between firms and the new pricing system (Kornai, 1983 : 230).

Further price reform, aimed at adjusting more domestic prices to world market prices, occurred in 1985. A new system of 'real competitive market prices' was put into practice. Its purpose was to reduce price subsidies from the State by unleashing the forces of competitive market prices. About 70 per cent of industrial products prices were determined by world market prices (Lu Nan, 1985).

Some problems arose in the Hungarian experience. Since competitive prices adjusted to world markets, prices became more vulnerable to the world market situation. In 1973, for example, Hungary suffered heavy economic losses due to the explosion in international oil prices (Csikos-Nagy, 1979 : 11). Another problem was the continuing deviation of producer prices from the retail prices in the post-reform period. If the State were to try to adjust these two kind of prices into a more rational relationship, the price level would then increase significantly and would intensify the problem of inflation (Lu Nan, 1985).

D. Summary of the East European Experience

Three different types of pricing systems resulted from different patterns of price development and reform: first, a centralised pricing system arose in the Soviet Union, the former German Democratic Republic, Czechoslovakia, Bulgaria and Romania; second, a hybrid system developed in Hungary and Poland; and finally a relatively free pricing system arose in Yugoslavia (Lu Nan, 1985). Price reforms in both Hungary and Yugoslavia moved in the same direction – that is, they attempted transformations from Pattern Two (a high degree of price control in a bureaucratic–hierarchical command economy) to Pattern Three (partial price control in a less centralised market economy). However, the fundamental methods of reform differed. Yugoslavia emphasised price determination by producers and negotiation between producers and users. Hungary put more emphasis on international pricing as an important criterion for price reform.

These three types of pricing systems still suffered some shortcomings: divergence of fixed prices from social costs[9] (Soviet Union, Hungary and Yugoslavia); neglect of consumer demand and inadequate reflection of differences in quality (this problem occurred mainly in the Soviet Union, and to a lesser extent in Hungary and Yugoslavia); widespread price differentiation[10] (mainly in the Soviet Union); economic distortions[11] (in Hungary and Yugoslavia); weak state enterprise response to price changes[12] (mainly in the Soviet Union, and less so in Hungary and Yugoslavia); and finally, serious problems of inflation, especially in Yugoslavia.

The problem of inflation was more serious in Yugoslavia than in Hungary. In Hungary the inflation rate averaged between 8 and 8.5 per cent in the 1979–85 period. By Chinese standards, this rate was quite high, but better than that of Yugoslavia. The inflation rate in Yugoslavia rose rapidly after reform: 10 per cent in 1970, 17.9 per cent in 1971, 13.8 per cent in 1972, 21.3 per cent in 1973, 29.5 per cent in 1974, and 17.5 per cent in 1975. It exceeded 40 per cent annually between 1980 and 1984 (Lu Nan, 1985).

The Chinese government, reviewing the East European experience, found the high rate of inflation entirely unacceptable. Vice-Director Qiao of the Price Research Institute of the State Price Bureau stated, 'When inflation is as serious as in Yugoslavia, then it is not merely a problem of economy, but also of social and political factors. We would not like to follow their case and will try to avoid it in our reform' (interviews with Qiao Rongzhang, 1985).[13] The problem of inflation was one of the most important factors affecting the Chinese choice of the direction and method of price reform. It is one of the reasons why China declined to use the Yugoslavia model.

1.4 CHINESE EXPERIENCE TO 1978

The price system prevailing in China in the post-1950 and pre-reform period was not the product of one comprehensive and consistent model or one particular theory. It was rather a mixed and duplicated consequence of the adaptation of historical prices (pre-liberation period), of the Soviet Union's system of price management, and China's own development strategies during different development periods (inverviews with Han Zhirong and Guo Gengji, 1985 and 1986).

Following a long period of serious inflation, in 1951 and 1952 the Chinese Communist government implemented various means of price formation aimed at bringing down the rate of increase of market prices.[14] After 1952, when the problem of inflation was under control, the government went further towards constructing a socialist pricing system. It was an imitation of the Soviet price management system; the government transferred certain industrial and agricultural prices into 'administered' or 'regulated' prices, and simultaneously cut the tie between producer and retail prices for important commodities, such as chemical fertiliser and cotton.[15] This separation of producer and retail price was not the result of applying coherent principles to different situations, but rather of decisions taken in various directions in response to the requirements of different periods.

Starting in 1953, the State adjusted prices for different goods according to various *ad hoc* political, economic, and social considerations. These criteria varied over time, even for the same product.

According to Zhu Chengping (interview, 1985) and Liu Xuming (interview, 1985), the Chinese pricing system developed in a dynamic way. It involved changes in the institutional framework of price determination, the forms of prices, price policies, and price functions. It can be divided into four pre-reform periods: the recovery period (1949–52); the first Five-Year Plan (1953–7); the Great Leap Forward and economic adjustment period (1958–65); and, finally, the period of the Cultural Revolution and reconvergence (1966–78).

A. 1949–52

The 1949–52 period witnessed the building up of the socialist price management system. The government's main objective was to consolidate the economy. Consolidation included recovery from war devastation, stopping inflation and breaking the political and economic power of the petty bourgeoisie who might oppose the State's power and interests in the long term (Perkins, 1966).

During this period, one of the most important economic policies was to stabilise prices. While bringing inflation under control,[16] the State gradually moved toward a position of dominance in the retail markets of certain key commodities and in the greater part of the wholesale market (Perkins, 1966). The government built up its new price management network in this environment of stabilised and controlled prices.

The Ministry of Trade and its local divisions were responsible for market prices in 1950. However, in September 1952, the power of price management was transferred to the Ministry of Commerce (*Shangye Bu*) and its local divisions. Two types of prices existed in this period: fixed and free. The scale of the former was quite small. The state controlled approximately 10 per cent of agricultural prices in 1950 and 25 per cent in 1951. The state set procurement, wholesale and retail prices for a limited number of important commodities such as cotton yarn, cotton cloth, grain, coal, salt and sugar.

Free markets still dominated at the time, and the State did not rush to close them down. Perkins (1966) argued that this was due to the lack of a feasible alternative such as an already established strong state commercial network. Moreover, the State was aware that the recovery of agricultural output and industrial production needed the free market, if only for a short period.

One problem which occurred in this period was price inflexibility. Prices fixed by the central government could not be adjusted to local situations. As a result, in some localities, the fixed price for grains was 10–12 per cent higher than the market price.[17]

B. 1953–7

This was a period of gradual centralisation of the pricing system. In this period the socialisation of the economy and the establishment of the planning mechanism were largely completed. The paramount goal of price policy was price stability. Responsibility for price management continued to rest with the Ministry of Commerce. The Ministry was empowered to issue directives, regulations and recommendations to subordinate bodies; its tasks included supervision of procurement and market prices for key agricultural commodities, drawing up of general principles and procedures to govern price determination, and price-setting for certain goods. At the local level, the China Specialised Company (*Zhongguo Zhuanye Gongsi*) and the local Bureau of Commerce took responsibility for price management.

In 1956, an institutional change in price management occurred. The state delegated the management of urban and rural market prices to both the Ministry of Commerce and the National Supply and Purchasing Cooperative Bureau (*Quanguo Gongxiao Hezuo Zongshe*). In the summer of the same year, a bureau of price management, the Price Commission, was established at local levels in each province, city, and county. Each local Price Commission was under the supervision of the head of the province or city. The purpose of this new system was to unify price management.

Heavy industrial prices were determined after 1953 by a system copied from the Soviet Union. The Cost and Price Bureau of the State Planning Commission administered these prices. The system was quite flexible due to loopholes in the price management system and because of the need to encourage industrial output. Private enterprises, private and public joint ventures, and small and middle-sized state enterprises also had autonomy to set prices for their own products. The percentage of the value of output of the means of production manufactured by private enterprises and traded in free markets was 30 per cent in 1953 and 9 per cent in 1955 (interview, 1985).

There were three forms of price in this period: first, free pricing for 'small' manufactured products, and agricultural local special products (*tu te chan*); second, floating prices, applied to 'big' manufactured products by private enterprises. Prices of this type could be floated within a certain range, based on the fixed price of the same product. The third type was the fixed price. Since the State employed a system of advanced-purchase contracts,[18] fixed prices were applied to important agricultural products and to about 1000 industrial and consumer goods.

The system of advance-purchase contracts, fixed prices and planned purchase[19] succeeded in stimulating agricultural output and encouraging the sale of production to the State. For example, both the production and marketing of cotton in 1952 were at least double that of 1950 (Perkins, 1966).

However, the government did not have the intention of using price policy as a long-run solution to problems of inadequate agricultural production. 'The principal purpose of shifts in relative prices, therefore, was only to restore production of particular products to a more normal level (the prewar level usually being taken as the main point of reference). Once that level was reached, other methods, mainly increasing unit-area yield, were be employed' (Perkins, 1966). The price mechanism was regarded as a short-run solution while the planned purchase system and other administrative methods were considered long-run solutions to the output problem for agricultural goods (Perkins, 1966). The situation changed in the post-reform period and the government tried to use the price mechanism as a long-run solution to the problem of inadequate agricultural production in the post-1979 period.

The positive side of the mixed pricing system in the 1953–7 period was, first, that the institutional network functioned quite well according to the principle of 'united leadership and management at various levels' (*tongyi lingdao, fenji guanli*). Second, the mixed pricing system was quite flexible. Fixed prices were conveniently used by the planning system to allocate resources. Floating and free prices performed other roles, such as balancing demand and supply in various markets to the benefit of individuals, enterprises and economic development as a whole (Liu Xuming, interview, 1985).

According to Liu Xuming, the negative side of the pricing system in this period was that the government controlled too many prices. In addition to the first and second categories[20] of agricultural goods and important industrial goods, the State also supervised the prices of a third category of agricultural and consumer goods. Under these circumstances, the market mechanism was gradually eliminated.

Although the pricing system in this period encountered some difficulties it was still regarded as a good model in China's post-liberation history. Some reformers believed that the current price reform should learn something from the 1953–7 period. Actually, some of the mechanisms introduced in the current reform, such as floating prices and negotiated prices, were borrowed from this period.

C. 1958–65

This period started as an experiment in the relaxation of price control, though prices were later recentralised.[21] One result of the planned decentralisation of the pricing system was a transfer of autonomy of price management to local governments. In June 1958, the price management system was effectively decentralised by decentralisation of the management autonomy of approximately 800 state enterprises from Peking to provincial governments.

The prices of agricultural products in categories one and two were supervised by both central and local governments. The price management authority for category three goods and some agricultural goods of category two was given to the local authorities. The prices of industrial products, except for key commodities such as cotton cloth, cotton yarn, coal and oil (which were still determined by the central authorities) were handed down to local authorities (interview, 1985).

During the decentralisation experiment the economic crisis of the Great Leap Forward occurred, resulting in a fall in industrial and agricultural output, a fall in living standards, and inflation. The supply of consumer goods reached only 88 per cent of the 1960 level. Prices on the free market averaged more than three times the retail prices in the state stores in 1961 (Wang Zhenzhi *et al.*, 1982). The index of retail prices was 23.4 per cent higher in 1962 than 1960 (1952 = 100). The index of procurement prices of foodstuffs was 32.5 per cent higher in 1962 than 1960 (1957 = 100) (*China Statistical Data of Trading Prices*, 1952–1984). Producer prices of the means of production rose by 5 per cent, retail prices of agricultural means of production by 13 per cent in 1962 (interview, 1985; 1957 = 100).

No analysis of how much the decentralisation of the price management system contributed to the problem of inflation exists. However, information indicates that incorrect implementation of the decentralisation policy at the local level had negative effects on the economy. Some local price management authorities raised prices according to their own interests. For example, in 1961 in Harbin, the price of a converter was increased by 33 per cent by the local authorities to prevent the factory (Harbin Circuit Changer Factory) from going bankrupt due to poor management. This price increase affected the production cost of a KO3 voltage transformer. The price increase of the KO3 pushed up the production costs of other goods such as those manufactured at the Harbin Electric Cooker Factory (10 per cent increase). Inevitably, the prices of the products in the Cooker Factory increased as well.

This was the first serious inflation in China since 1952, and it caused the government to recentralise the price management system in March 1962. In the same year, the National Price Commission (NPC) (*Guojia Wujia Weiyuan Hui*) was established. The network of price control, from top to bottom, was tighter than ever before. Most prices were set by the NPC except for those of a small number of agricultural commodities of category three. According to statistics based on 14 large and middle-size cities, the value of sales in free market was only 2 per cent of total sales between 1962 and 1963. This type of situation continued until 1966.

In the 1958–65 period, free prices were not completely eliminated; however, they were too small to affect the economy. Negotiated prices still existed for small, durable goods such as scissors and toothbrushes. The price management system was firmly administered, and the functions of the price system were reduced and weakened to a large extent.

D. 1966–78

In this fourth period, the administrative pricing system from central to local level was either disrupted (1966–8), or totally controlled. To avoid price instability during the turmoil of the Cultural Revolution, the Central Committee of the CCP and the State Council announced a crucial price policy in August 1967[22] which declared that the irrational prices and price differentials existing in urban and rural areas should not be dealt with until a later stage of the Cultural Revolution. This announcement was followed by a virtual price freeze. No price readjustment were took place during this period, and free markets were placed under strict control (Robinson, 1976).

In the period between 1966 and 1968, the mass political movement affected the whole administrative system – including the price management system. Most of the staff in the NPC were sent to the countryside for 're-education through labour'. In 1969, the NPC was abolished. The only bureau in charge of prices was the State Planning Committee of the State Council.

After 1969, certain prices were adjusted. The price trends for retail, procurement, and producer prices moved in different directions. The retail prices of daily consumer goods and the agricultural means of production (such as the prices of medicine, coal, trucks and chemical fertilisers, decreased). The retail price index for 1976 showed a drop of 2.1 per cent from that of 1965 (Bettelheim, 1974 : 366; Robinson, 1976 : 3–23). In contrast, procurement prices of certain agricultural goods increased several times during this period:

Table 1.1 Price index 1965–76

Year	Index of industrial prices	Index of worker's living costs	Index of industrial producer price	Index of agricultural procurement price	Index of of industrial goods supplied to agriculture
1965	120.4	120.3	87.7	154.5	107.9
1966	120.0	118.9	84.0	161.0	104.8
1967	119.1	118.1	83.0	160.8	104.0
1968	119.2	118.2	81.2	160.5	103.7
1969	117.9	119.3	78.4	160.3	102.2
1970	117.6	119.3	75.0	160.4	102.0
1971	116.7	119.2	74.6	163.1	100.5
1972	116.5	119.4	74.1	165.4	99.9
1973	117.2	119.5	73.8	166.8	99.9
1974	117.8	120.3	73.1	168.2	99.9
1975	118.0	120.8	72.8	171.6	99.9
1976	118.3	121.1	72.6	172.5	100.0

Source: *China Trade and Price Statistics, 1952–1983*, China State Statistical Bureau (1984).

agricultural goods in 1966, peanuts, hogs, and cattle in 1970, sugar and beans (10 per cent) in 1971, 13 kinds of foodstuffs in 1973, cattle (14.74 per cent) in 1974, and 24 kinds of livestock in 1975. The index of agricultural procurement prices in 1976 showed an increase of 18 per cent over 1965 (see Table 1.1). This brought income increases to peasant households of 700 million yuan in 1969, 100 million in 1970, 1 billion in 1971, and 500 million in 1972 (interview, 1985).

Producer prices of industrial goods decreased several time during this period: −1 per cent in 1967, −1.8 per cent in 1968, −2.8 per cent in 1969, −3.4 per cent in 1970, −0.3 per cent in 1975, and −0.2 per cent in 1976. Typical cases were the metallurgical and chemical fertiliser industry: producer prices in the metallurgical industry decreased an average of 10 per cent every year between 1966 and 1976.[23] Price adjustments, downward or upward, were aimed at attaining price stability and closing the price 'scissors'.[24]

In this period there was only one kind of price – a fixed price. An insignificant black market existed. Production was determined by the political line, therefore prices themselves were secondary expressions of the political line. Under such circumstances, prices were useful only for accounting and income distribution.

In the 30 years from 1950 to 1979, the forms of producer and procurement prices, and the system of price management, underwent many changes. The price management system was gradually centralised from the 1950s to the time of the Cultural Revolution; the task of the price offices was to administer and control prices, rather than plan them.

The form of prices determined by the gradually centralised management system was changed from a hybrid price system (in the 1950s) to a fixed price system (in the late 1970s). In terms of resource allocation, prices became secondary to the planning mechanism. The next section reviews the shortcomings of the pricing system, and its negative effects on the economy.

E. Shortcomings and Diagnoses

Shortcomings

Four key shortcomings of the pre-reform pricing system were identified by politicians and economists after 1979:

1. Disparities between purchasing (producer) and sales (retail) prices. In many cases, such as the agricultural sector, retail prices were not much higher than purchasing prices, and in some cases they were even lower (Tian Jiyun, 1985; Wang Zhenzhi *et al.*, 1982 : 229). This caused financial losses and required heavy subsidies from the State.[25] This situation also occurred with some industrial goods. The price of chemical fertilisers, for example, was kept low in order to stimulate agricultural output and to subsidise peasant income.[26]
2. Disparities among industrial prices (a problem of irrational price ratios).[27] Part of the value (profit) created by one industrial department was transferred to another through unequal exchange.

   Profit margins varied widely from one industry to another. The differences can be seen in an analysis of the 1979 financial accounts of 60,000 industrial enterprises belonging to 85 industries across the country. Some 38 of these industries were operating at a 'middling' profit margin – between half and double the average. The other 47 industries had dramatically varying profit margins (Wang Zhenzhi *et al.*, 1982).[28]

   This situation led to other inter-industry problems. On the one hand, it dampened the initiative of workers in industries with low profit margins, resulting in the underdevelopment of these industries.[29] On the other, it overstimulated growth in industries with high profit margins.[30] This situation created problems in the distribution of profits among different industries and enterprises and undermined the State's objective to prioritise the fuel, power and raw material industries.

The price disparities also made it difficult to appraise the performance of industrial departments. Under the irrational pricing system, enterprises lacked initiative to improve their performance. In particular, enterprises with low profit margins made no effort to improve, since they could not catch up with the highly profitable enterprises and their losses would be covered by the State (Wang Zhenzhi *et al.*, 1982).

3. Another shortcoming of the pre-reform price system, mentioned by the Vice-Prime Minister, Tian Jiyun, was that prices did not reflect quality differences. Low-quality products often had high prices and high-quality ones had low prices. Enterprises were able neither to expand the production of superior goods nor to scale down the production of overstocked, inferior goods. This shortcoming was a primary factor dampening the drive to improve quality, increase variety, and create new products, as the case study of the bicycle factory in Chapter 5 demonstrates.
4. The use of costs rather than capital as the basis for computing industrial profit understated the contribution of capital (Cheng, 1982 : 250; Hare, 1983 : 208). Prices of relatively capital-intensive branches of industry tended to be too low, and the incentive for an enterprise to use capital efficiently was quite weak (Hare, 1983 : 208).

   This pricing system lead to inefficiencies in resource allocation, since enterprise reaction to input and output price changes was very weak. Enterprise survival did not depend on profitability.[31] These problems were very much the same as those which existed in pre-reform periods in the East European countries.

Diagnosis

These problems of the pre-reform period were recognised by most politicians and economists. However, their causes received differing diagnoses.

Some economists claimed that the problems of the inefficient pricing system were not caused by the socialist central-planning model of the pricing system, but rather by defective implementation of the system. For example, prices were set according to incorrect formulas, profitability was not used as the main indicator of enterprise efficiency, price adjustments were mainly based on political rather than economic considerations, and so on.

Other economists believed that the cause of the problems lay not only in the defective implementation of the fixed pricing system but also in the economic system *per se* adopted from the Soviet Union. In other words, the problem was the high degree of price control in a 'bureaucratic–hierarchical command economy'. Due to the differing diagnoses of the problems of the pre-reform period, different price reform packages were proposed by Chinese politicians and economists. They affected price reform in terms of its goals, methods, content and time frame. In Chapter 2, a number of the reform packages proposed for implementation in China are presented.

2 From Adjustment Towards Liberalisation

2.1 GOALS OF PRICE REFORM

A. The Goal Narrowly Defined

The narrowly defined goal of price reform was to transform the main function of the price system from that of accounting to that of resource allocation for most, but not all, industrial and agricultural goods.

A number of Chinese economists have written about the purpose of price reform on a theoretical level.[1] The key points of their arguments can be summarised as follows: the price system should be used to increase or decrease output, lower production costs and match supply and demand;[2] prices should be used to affect enterprise behaviour in terms of efficient management and rational financial decisions;[3] prices should be used to rationalise income redistribution among individuals, enterprises and the State;[4] and prices should rationalise capital investment.[5]

Most Chinese economists considered these four aspects as equally important. However, a few (Xu Yi, 1982; Xue Muqiao, 1981; and Tian Yuan, 1986) have highlighted the contradictions between the role of allocation and the role of distribution, and between the role of efficient allocation and price stability.

Tian Yuan (Director of the Price Division at the Economic, Technological and Social Research Centre of the State Council) argued (1986) that prices have three functions in socialist countries: accounting, income distribution and resource allocation. The function of income distribution contains more 'messages of political considerations' (*zhengzhi xinxi hanliang*) than the function of efficient allocation, which possesses mainly 'messages of economic considerations' (*jingji xinxi hanliang*). The main problem of the traditional price system was that the prices of many commodities contained more 'messages of political considerations' than 'messages of economic considerations'. As a result, price policies were mainly concerned with the problems of income distribution and price stability: prices reflected neither commodity values nor the relation of supply and demand.

The traditional system was thus regarded as inefficient and irrational (Third Plenary Session of the 12th Central Committee of the CCP, 1984). Therefore, according to Tian Yuan and others, the purpose of price reform was to strengthen the function of resource allocation and gradually to reduce the importance of the role of income distribution. This view was shared by Dai Guanlai and Jia Xiuyan (1985 : 73), who insisted that 'the role of resource allocation is fundamental and the role of income distribution is secondary in socialist countries'.

The theoretical interpretation of the roles of price which began in 1985 (when the Market Reformers became influential in policy-making) was strongly influenced by the concept of equilibrium in supply and demand. Since that time, the direction of price reform has been dominated by the Market Reformers and has been aimed at 'enabling prices to reflect and regulate supply and demand' (Liu Guoguang, 1986; Zhang Weiying, 1985).

Liu Guoguang, Vice-President of the Chinese Academy of Social Sciences, argued that the former price mechanism was an essential part of China's original, highly centralised economic structure, characterised by administrative coordination and management of materials and equipment. He believed that the main functions of traditional prices were limited to serving as a statistical means of measuring the use value of a product; and as a tool for the distribution of national income – that is, concentration of the country's financial resources on its priority projects by manipulating price ratios and differentials. No consideration was given to the use of prices as measures of economic performance, as stimuli to technical advancement or as a means of directing the allocation of resources (Liu Guoguang, 1986).

Liu and other economists insisted that the ultimate goal of price reform (in the narrow sense) was to establish a system where 'the price structure would no longer be merely an accounting tool or an instrument for the distribution of national income, but, rather, a measure of economic efficiency, a means of stimulating technical advance, and a gauge of both supply and demand to guide the allocation of national resources' (Liu Guoguang, 1986).

It is very difficult for researchers outside China to ascertain whether the revision of the economic theory of the role of price promoted the change of price policies, or vice versa. However, price policies did change during this period of transition toward 'market socialism'.

Two main policies – price stability and reducing the 'price scissors' (*jiandao cha*) – were revised in coordination with the new economic structure (Xiao Zhuoji, 1980; Huang Da, 1981). A policy of 'basic stability' was adopted in China in 1982 to replace the old policy of 'absolute stability'.[6] The concept of 'basic stability' meant that the government was willing to accept an inflation rate between 3 and 6 per cent. The term 'price scissors'[7] was abolished and the phrase 'unequal exchange in prices between agricultural and industrial sectors' was used in government documents and academic reports from 1985 onwards. This implied that the government had admitted that it wanted to obtain large-scale investment funds from the agricultural sector by means of exchange relations. The State thus sold manufactured goods at high prices to peasants, and paid low prices for crops.

In the reform period, prices were to be used mainly to signal relative costs, needs and scarcities to enterprises and households; guide production and improve quality; and guide expenditure and investment decisions in economically appropriate directions. 'Its aim was to encourage competition between enterprises facing roughly the same conditions, promote the development of the forces of production and improve economic efficiency'.[8]

B. The Goal Broadly Defined

The purpose of price reform, in a broad sense, was to ensure the success of the whole post-1979 economic reform programme.[9] The government indicated in 1984 that 'various aspects of the reform in economic structure, including planning and wage systems, depend to a large extent on reform of the price system' (State Council, 1984). Price reform and the economic reform package were thus closely interwoven.

Profound changes were taking place in the economy. The scale of central planning for production was narrowed in both industry and agriculture.[10] The means of production market, the labour market, and the capital market were officially acknowledged, and expanded rapidly. At the same time, the government maintained the rationing system (*Zhongguo Shehui Kexue*, no. 2, 1986 : 29–53). According to the 'Reform Decision' of 1984, more autonomy and incentives were given to local government, to enterprises, and to workers. Firms were given greater responsibility in production and sales management, and were permitted to keep a higher portion of their excess profit (Koziara and Yan, 1983). Firms' incentives based on the fulfilment of obligatory targets were modified, first through this profit retention scheme, and later, by the contract management responsibility system.[11] Wage reform brought the introduction of a new wage system, which linked wages and enterprise profit and succeeded the old system of centrally-fixed wages.[12] All these changes indicate that China's economic system was undergoing a transformation from a bureaucratic–hierarchical command economy to a less centralised market economy, and thus required a new, concordant price system.

The government announced that successful price reform would require both a reform of the price system – that is, a reform of price functions (*jiage tixi*) – and of the price control system (*jiage tizhi*) (reform of the price control system refers to a reform of the State's power of intervention in price control). Irrational prices were due to the highly controlled management system; reforms of the latter were thus prerequisite to reforms of the former. Members of the Third Plenary Session decided in 1984 that 'China must reform the overly centralised system of price control, gradually reducing the scope of fixed prices and appropriately enlarging the scope of floating prices and of free prices'.

2.2 POSITIONS ON PRICE REFORM

The purposes of price reform in the broad sense were accepted by most politicians and economists in accord with either Chen Yun or Deng Xiaoping. The disagreements which occurred concerned the means of achieving the more narrowly defined goal. Disputes arose concerning where to start first, what methods to use, how fast to gear the pace of reform, and whether the main form of the new price system should be planned, free or floating.

The technical problems of price reform inspired theoretical debates and created conflicts among political groups, and these groups can be classified according to their theoretical positions and political interests. One group, called the Centralisers,[13] who considered the price problem as simply one of price formation, were located mainly in the Ministry of Finance itself and also in its associated Research Institute. A second group, by far the largest in number, called the Administrative Decentralisers, believed that the inefficient price system was caused by both the method of price formation and the nature of the highly hierarchical command economy. Most of this group's members were based at the Economic, Technological and Social Development Research Centre at the State Council, the State Price Bureau and its Research Institute, and the Department of Cost and Prices of the Institute of Finance, Commerce, and Supplies at the Chinese Academy of Social Sciences (CASS). A third group, identified as Market Reformers, believed that the problem of the price system was rooted in the administrative control system. They were largely based at the Economic Structure Reform Commission and its Research Institute but also included some young economists at the Institute of Industry and Economics at CASS. Each group not only had its own theoretical propositions of price reform, but was also involved in making and implementing price reform policies.

A. Centralisers

The economists and politicians, who agreed with Chen Yun's theory that the planned economy should be fundamental and predominant and that the market-regulated economy should be supplementary, insisted that price reform be based on the principle of 'overall balance in finance, credit and materials supply'.[14] That is, when it is necessary to adjust price ratios, the extent and scale of such adjustments must be determined on the basis of an overall balance in financial and material resources so as to avoid any inflation which might result when price increases exceed the financial and material resources (Xu Yi *et al.*, 1982).

According to the Centralisers, reform of the price system was important, but the policy of relative stabilisation of prices could not be neglected, since it was vital in preserving the unity and stability of the political situation and encouraging the enthusiasm of the workers and peasants in production. They therefore proposed the tactic of 'large-scale planning and a small free market' (*dajihua xiao ziyou*), for price reform (Xu Yi *et al.*, 1982 : 234).

B. Administrative Decentralisers

This group believed that construction of a rational socialist price system should be based on the theory of value. Prices could be determined either by the State or the market, depending on the importance of the commodity to the economy. If the State fixed prices, then the way to find the right price was to use the 'price of production'.[15] This type of state price determination was termed a 'conscience application of the law of value to price-setting' (White *et al.*, 1983 : 45).

Some of the economists and politicians of this group, who were involved in the work of price-setting for the central government, were aware of the difficulties and limitations of fixing prices for a large number of commodities. They emphasised the importance of decentralisation of price control in the reform programme. They proposed that price-setting autonomy (even for some of the category one commodities such as construction materials and energy) be decentralised to the local level during the period of the seventh Five-Year Plan.

C. Market Reformers

The Market Reform position, mainly held by the young economists of the Economic Structure Reform Commission and its Research Institute, believed in the theory of market determination. They advocated that the price mechanism be an objective law, free of political intervention or administrative control. They felt that the way to 'get prices right' was to eliminate price control and to let prices be determined by enterprises according to the law of supply and demand. They regarded the administrative method of price determination as the main obstacle to a rational price system.

From 1979 to 1983, conflict over the technical problems of price reform occurred mainly between the Centralisers and the Administrative Decentralisers. By 1984, the Market Reform position had become very influential in both ideology and politics. Since then, disputes related to price reform have occurred mainly between the Administrative Decentralisers and the Market Reformers.[16] These two groups did not have serious disagreements over price reform of category two and three commodities. Their main controversy concerned commodities of category one, such as construction materials and energy.

2.3 PRICE REFORM PACKAGE DEBATES

The disputes among these three groups concerning the technical problems of price reform focused on several issues: first, the methods of price reform; second, the principles of price formation; third, the

Table 2.1 Three different theoretical and political positions on price reform

	Centralisers	*Administrative Decentralisers*	*Market Reformers*
Price functions	Accounting Income distribution	Resource allocation[1] Income distribution	Resource allocation
Principle of price-setting	Average production Cost	Price of production	Supply and demand
Main form of new pricing	Fixed price	Floating price	Free price
Agents of price determination	Central government	Central, local government and firms	Firms
Methods of price reform	Adjustment	Adjustment and liberalisation	Liberalisation
Time frame of price reform	7–10 years small steps	5–7 years medium steps	3–5 years big steps

Note: 1. According to the Administrative Decentralisers, prices should play a fundamental role in resource allocation and their income distribution function should be secondary.

Sources: Survey and interviews, 1985–6.

form of the new price system; and fourth, the time frame for price reform (see Table 2.1). These four issues are elaborated below.

A. Methods of Price Reform

Three methods of price reform were proposed. Adjustment was suggested by the Centralisers according to the principle of 'large-scale planning and a small free market' (Xu Yi *et al.*, 1982). The official definition of adjustment stated that 'prices for commodities which have a great bearing on the national economy and the people's livelihood – those under the State's mandatory plan, the major means-of-production, farm and sideline products of the first and second categories, and daily necessities – be adjusted step by step under a unified state plan, so that these prices gradually become more rational' (Tian Jiyun, 1985; Xu Yi *et al.*, 1982 : 226–233).[17]

The second method, proposed by the Market Reformers, was called liberalisation. It called for the State to cease controlling prices and allow market forces to operate substantially.[18]

The goal of applying this method of price reform was not to find a solution involving a combination of plan and market, but rather, to let market forces dominate. Both Li Yining (1986) and Zhang Weiying (1985) criticised the concept of 'using governmental power to solve economic difficulties', and blamed economic inefficiency on the administrative control system. They proposed letting market forces be felt first and fully, and felt that relying on market adjustment was much more effective than arbitrary and impractical administrative measures.

The liberalisation method was judged effective by a group of investigators at the Institute of the Reform of the Economic System. Under this method, the quality of commodities and the management capacity in enterprises improved; the price responsiveness of enterprises sharpened; and a buyer's market arose for some commodities. The investigators claimed that liberalisation should be further applied to reform the price system of the means of production and to solve the problems of capital and labour (Wang Xiaoqiang *et al.*, 1985).

A third method, involving the use of both adjustment and liberalisation separately for different goods (depending on their importance in the economy), was proposed by the Administrative Decentralisers, who disagreed with both the Centralisers and the Market Reformers.

The Administrative Decentralisers attacked the Market Reformers, claiming that a completely competitive market as posited in equilibrium price theory simply cannot exist in reality. They argued that only two things happen in a market: constant fluctuation of prices in accordance with changes in supply and demand, and constant changes in supply and demand in accordance with price fluctuations. Such prices are definitely not equilibrium prices. They are merely prices forced upon one of the parties – either the seller or the buyer. A forced balance is achieved by means of sacrifices on the part of either the seller or the buyer; cyclical imbalances in production and consumption; vast fluctuations of price; and social waste (Tian Yuan *et al.*, 1986; Yamanouchi, 1986 : 11; Wang Zhenzhi and Wang Yongzhi, 1986 : 51–8).

Those holding this view insisted both that the completely competitive market was infeasible and that the State was not omnipotent. They, therefore, proposed that price reform could not rely solely on the method of adjustment, nor on the method of liberalisation but, rather, on a combination of both.

B. Price Formation and Determination

The three methods of price reform affected price formation and price determination.[19] The Centralisers and the Administrative Decentralisers favoured having the State set prices while the Market Reformers preferred to let enterprises set prices.

The Centralisers claimed that prices of category one and two commodities should be fixed by the State according to the principle of average production costs. Prices were to be calculated by multiplying the cost of production by a factor which allowed a certain standard of profitability (Xu Yi, 1982; Bettelheim, 1978).[20]

The Market Reformers argued that fixing prices on the basis of cost plus average profit rate would be simply 'a new bottle containing old wine', with no significant improvement in price determination. Since they viewed the basic functions of price as first, assuring a balance between supply and demand and, second, bringing about a rationalisation of the industrial structure, they felt price was best decided by enterprises.[21]

The Market Reformers insisted that the State should exercise no control over prices at any time for any reason, except for cases of natural monopolies such as railways, telecommunications and public services. The state should supervise the general price level rather than regulate the prices of more than 100,000 items.

The Administrative Decentralisers argued that some prices should be set by the State while other prices should be free, depending on the importance of the commodities to the economy. Prices of commodities in categories two and three should be managed by local governments, negotiated between buyers and sellers, or exchanged freely in the market. However, prices of category one commodities, especially industrial goods, should be fixed by the State according to the law of value so as to reflect both 'value' and the relationship between supply and demand (Hu Changnuan, 1982).[22] Problems in price formation and determination led to further problems related to the main form of the new price system.

C. Main Form of the New Price System

Although the proposals put forward by these three groups concerning the methods of price reform differed, yet they agreed that the new price system should be a mixed one including fixed, negotiated, floating, and free prices. Controversy arose as to which of the four types of prices should dominate.

The Centralisers insisted that planned prices should be fundamental, with floating prices playing a supporting role and free price a subsidiary one (Xu Yi, 1982 : 225–43). Their ideal model was the system in effect during China's first Five-Year Plan. However, Liu Guoguang criticised this model, claiming that it did not make a real break with the traditional fixed price system.

The Administrative Decentralisers proposed that the main form of the new price system should be neither completely market prices nor planned prices, but rather floating prices, supported by market prices, with fixed prices trailing behind.[23]

The floating prices were criticised as inheriting the nature of the fixed price system and, thus, being an inefficient tool for guiding the allocation of national resources (Liu Guoguang, 1986). The main problem involved how to decide on a price range which could mesh with the fluctuations of the market.

The third group, the Market Reformers, claimed that market prices should play the principal role, while floating and planned prices took a subsidiary one. They suggested that for free prices to flourish, certain conditions must be met: first, that enterprises involved in commodity exchanges have independent economic interests; second, that no tendency towards monopoly exist; third, that the market be a buyer's one; and fourth, that there be a workable channel for money circulation (a capital market) and an efficient banking organisation (Liu Guoguang, 1986; Diao Xinshen, 1986).

D. Time Frame of Price Reform

Market Reformers favoured implementing price reform in large steps, hoping to complete the reform in three to five years. The Centralisers preferred small steps, and planned on a seven- to ten-year horizon. The Administrative Decentralisers believed in taking medium steps and planned on a five- to seven-year horizon.

Zhang Weiying, one young, well-known economist of the Market Reform persuasion, observing recent economic development and the goals of the four modernisations, called for the abandonment of the rigid price system as soon as possible. He said:

> If a country is to pay attention not only to fairness, but also to efficiency; not only to the distribution of wealth, but more so to the production of wealth; not only to people being fed and clothed, but more so to seeing that they are enjoying an increasingly rich and colourful life; and if the country no longer adheres to a policy of giving priority only to the development of certain departments, but to a policy for an even development of the whole economy; and if it is no longer satisfied with turning in on itself but wants to open its door wide and go out into the world, catching up with the development trends of history, then that country must give up its rigid fixed price system without the least hesitation and replace it with a flexible market price system (*Social Sciences in China*, no. 4, 1985).

Those who shared this persuasion noted that price reform in large steps could cause inflation and other political and economic problems. However, they felt it was a cost that China should pay since it would be lower than the economic losses caused by continuing the irrational price system (an economic loss estimated to be nearly 2 billion yuan per year). They also considered that the main obstacle to implementation of price reform in large steps was not financial but, rather, political.

This optimistic view held by the Market Reformers regarding the financial aspect of price reform was rejected by the Centralisers. Since state finance had been continuously in the red from 1979 to 1984, they argued that it was impossible to proceed with price reform without first taking financial constraints into account. They insisted that price reform in small steps was more appropriate for China's economic situation.

The Administrative Decentralisers were aware of both the urgent need for price reform and the financial difficulties. They, therefore, adopted a more realistic position and insisted that neither the small step nor the large step would succeed. They believed that since traditional prices were seriously distorted small steps would have little effect; that since China was reforming the whole economic structure, a simple unleashing of market forces might produce a period of speculation and chaos inimical to efficiency; and that enterprise capacity to bear rapid price changes was weak. They argued that, under such circumstances, price reform for category one

Table 2.2 Three stages of price reform

Stage	*Reform Methods*	*Category of commodity* I	II	III	*Characteristics of economic system*
1979–82	Adjustment	*A*	*A*	*A*	Planned economy
1982–4	Adjustment parallel with liberalisation for different goods	*A*	*L*	*L*	Planned economy parallel with market
1984–6	Adjustment and liberalisation for the same commodity	*AL*	*L*	*L*	Planned economy intermixed with market

Notes: *A* denotes adjustment. *L* denotes liberalisation. *AL* denotes adjustment and liberalisation. Definitions of adjustment and liberalisation are provided by Vice-Premier Tian Jiyun (1985). The *AL* pattern is interpreted by Liu Guoguang (1986); Dai Yuanchen (1986); and Hua Sheng *et al.* (1985, 1986). The features of the dual economic system (plan intermixed with manner) are discussed in Hua Sheng *et al.* (1986). Koziara and Yan (1983) have a detailed description of the classification of these three categories.

Source: Interview with the State Price Bureau, 1985 and 1986.

commodities should involve a preliminary phase of adjustment by administrative means and only later involve liberalisation. They felt that prices of commodities in categories two and three could be liberalised immediately.

The divergent proposals of price reform provided by these three groups – including methods of reform, principles of price determination, the form of the new price system, and the time frame of reform – affected the different stages of post-1979 price reform.

2.4 THREE STAGES OF PRICE REFORM

The 1979–86 price reform in China can be divided into three stages (see Table 2.2). The remaining sections of this chapter contain a general discussion of these stages, and case studies of coal, steel, cotton, bicycles and chemical fertilisers.

Table 2.3 The first stage: adjustment

Year of adjustment	*Commodities*
1979	1. Increases in procurement prices of 18 major farm products (including cotton); 24.8 per cent weighted average increase
	2. Increase in retail prices of 8 major foodstuffs e.g., pork 33 per cent and eggs 32 per cent
	3. The Fourth Ministry of Machinery Industry set price ceilings for four electronics products
	4. Increase in producer prices of coal, mineral products, iron and steel; the price of coal was raised by 5 yuan per ton
1980	1. The floating price system for 16 machinery products was introduced by the First Ministry of Machinery Industry, it allowed firms to lower producer prices by as much as 20 per cent based on the fixed prices
1981	1. Price cut on mixed polyester-cotton fabric by 10 per cent
	2. Price hike on cigarettes by 0.27 yuan, 0.08 yuan or 0.02 yuan per package respectively, according to quality
	3. Price hike on alcoholic beverages

Sources: *People's Daily* (25 October 1979); *Jingji Ribao* (18 January 1983); Ishihara (1983); Liu Guoguang (1986).

A. 1979–82

In the first stage, 1979–82, the government implemented price reform by means of the adjustment method (*tiao de moshi*) applied to all types of commodities (see Table 2.2) (Xu Yi, 1982).

In 1979, after the third Plenary Session of the 11th Party Central Committee, the Chinese government effected a major increase in state procurement prices for 18 major farm products. Grain prices rose 20 per cent for mandatory quota procurements and an additional 50 per cent for above-quota procurements. Edible oil prices increased by 25 per cent and 50 per cent respectively, and cotton prices rose 15 per cent and 30 per cent (see Table 2.3).

The price policies in this stage were designed to 'encourage production of agricultural and mining products, to cut down profit margins and, hence, output of certain industrial products, and to maintain stable living costs for urban residents' (Chen Nai-Ruenn and Hou Chi-Ming, 1986 : 820). These policies caused the general price level to increase. 'The extent of China's total inflationary pressure may have reached 4.7 percent in 1979, 8.5 percent in 1980, and 12.2 percent in 1981, while the official retail price index showed open inflation of 2 percent, 6 percent, and 2.4 percent respectively'[24] (Chen Nai-Ruenn and Hou Chi-Ming, 1986 : 823).

B. 1982–4

The second stage of price reform, starting in 1982, involved 'adjustment parallel with liberalization'[25] (*tiaofang bankuai moshi*). Prices of commodities in category one were adjusted by the price authorities upward or downward for different reasons, while prices of category two and three goods were liberalised. Liberalisation introduced free prices and, thus, enabled some enterprises to set prices for their goods (Dong Fureng, 1986 : 297).[26]

In 1982, the State Council approved the 'Report on the Gradual Relaxation of Controls over Prices of the Minor Commodities and Permitting of Prices to be Determined by the Market', designed by the State Price Bureau. Control over the prices of 160 different types of commodities was abolished and the price-setting autonomy was given to enterprises (*Price: Theory and Practice*, no. 6, 1983 : 43). One year later, a new policy, 'The Further Relaxation of Controls over Prices of Minor Commodities', decontrolled prices of a further 350 types of minor commodities (a detailed list may be found in *Price: Theory and Practice*, no. 6, 1983).

'The Policy of Completely Abolishing Control of Prices of Minor Commodities' was announced by the State Price Bureau in October 1984. To date, no detailed information about this policy exists. We believe it handed price-setting autonomy for most light and textile commodities of categories one and two to enterprises. During this stage, the State continued to play the primary role in price determination as the State Council and the Standing Committee of the National People's Congress (NPC) announced the policy of 'Provisional Regulations on Price Control'.[27] Inflation due to price liberalisation and the expansion of rural and urban markets continued to be a real concern[28] (see Table 2.4).

C. 1984–6

The third stage began at the end of 1984. A more complicated and sophisticated method, a combination of adjustment and liberalisation (*tiaofang tongyi moshi*) was adopted by the government (Tian Yuan *et al.*, 1986; Hua Sheng *et al.*, 1985). It applied only to commodities in

Table 2.4 The second stage: adjustment parallel with liberalisation

Reform methods	*Commodities*
Liberalisation (*Year*)	
1. 1982	Liberalising price control of 160 minor commodities
2. 1983	Liberalising price control of another 350 minor commodities
3. 1984	Liberalising price control for the majority of the light and textile commodities in categories one and two
4. 1985	Liberalising price control for secondary foodstuffs
Adjustment (*Year*)	
1. 1982	Elimination of premium payments for over-quota purchases of oil-bearing crops and tobacco
2. 1983	a. Price out on synthetic textiles; cut of 28 per cent on polyester-cotton yarn; price hike on cotton production by an average of 20 per cent b. Price cut on light industrial and electronic products
3. 1984	Introduction of floating prices for cotton cloth (up to 20 per cent above fixed prices), washing machines and refrigerators (up to 10 per cent above fixed price)
4. 1984	Adjusting state purchase and sale prices for grain in rural areas
5. 1985	Price increase for urea (10 per cent)

Sources: *Price: Theory and Practice* (1983); Nambu (1985); Liu Guoguang (1986).

category one such as construction materials and energy. This method was employed when these commodities were in shortage; when the system of resources allocation could not be completely abolished; and when fixed prices were too low to be adjusted rapidly.

The third stage began when the State Council announced its policy of 'Ten Regulations of Autonomy Decentralization to State Enterprises', allowing state-owned firms to sell above-quota production to the market. This new system of self-sale (*zi xiao*) allowed firms to set the prices (20 per cent above or below list prices) for above-quota production.

However, in 1985, the State abolished the 20 per cent floating range limit for above-quota production,[29] and thus firms were permitted freely to set prices for above-quota production (see Table 2.5).

Table 2.5 The third stage: a combination of adjustment and liberalisation

Year	*Reform methods* (*type of price*)	*Commodities (yuan /ton)* *Wire stock*[1]	*Foundry pig iron*
1983	Fixed price (adjustment)	677	258
1984	Fixed price for quota output (adjustment)	756	326
	Floating price 20 per cent above or below fixed prices for above-quota output (adjustment)	1000	450
1985	Fixed price for quota output (adjustment)	816	376
	Free price for above-quota output (Liberalisation)	1800	590

Note: 1. Wire stock of size no.6.5–8.

Source: Information collected from Hebei province in our survey, 1985.

According to the 1985 policy of 'Relaxation of Price Control', the State adjusted the quota price of steel from 756 to 816 yuan per ton. The government also allowed the price of above-quota steel to be determined by the market. The free price was twice as high as the planned price (see Table 2.5). This dual pricing had both negative and positive effects in production, circulation, and distribution; these issues are further discussed in Chapter 6.

2.5 PRICE REFORM IN FIVE COMMODITIES

In this section we investigate which reform methods were applied to each of the five commodities of our study: cotton, steel, coal, chemical fertilisers and bicycles.

Table 2.6 Application of reform methods to five commodities, 1979–86

Year	*Reform methods*	*Cotton*	*Steel*	*Coal*	*Chemical fertilisers*	*Bicycles*
1979–82	Adjustment	Yes	Yes	Yes		
1982–4	Adjustment parallel with liberalisation				Yes[1]	Yes[2]
1984–6	Combination of adjustment and liberalisation	Yes	Yes	Yes	Yes	

Notes: 1. Adjustment for producer prices of bicarbonate of ammonia, liberalisation for urea prices. 2. Adjustment for good-quality bicycles, liberalisation for inferior-quality bicycles.

Source: Interview with the State Price Bureau, 1985 and 1986.

A. Cotton

Price reform in the cotton sector mainly used the method of adjustment. The price of cotton was adjusted upward three times and downward once in the 1979–86 period in order to encourage, and then discourage, cotton production.

Prior to 1985, the State kept tight control over cotton products through a system of unified purchase and distribution. In 1985, the State abandoned this system and introduced the contract purchase system. According to the provisions of this system, the State would purchase only contracted volumes of cotton at set prices in the harvest season; output above contracted volumes could be marketed by the peasants or sold to the State at 'protective prices' which were set by the State at rates lower than quota prices.

In principle, the reform method for the price of cotton was transformed, under a 1985 policy, from adjustment to a combination of adjustment and liberalisation (see Table 2.6). In practice, however, the price of cotton in the free market was lower than both the quota price and the 'protective price'. Not surprisingly, farmers preferred to sell above-quota cotton to the State at 'protective prices'.[30] Thus, the main reform method for the cotton price remained adjustment.

Chinese economists and the government itself viewed the cotton sector as a successful example of using the price mechanism to regulate output.

B. Coal

From 1979 until 1984 coal prices were reformed by adjustment. A combination of adjustment and liberalisation was used from late 1984 onwards. The price of coal was increased by 5 yuan per ton in 1979. The government added premiums to above-plan purchases and recognised sales at 'negotiated prices' in 1982 so as to help the majority of coal mines come out of deficit (Nambu, 1985). Negotiated prices averaged twice the level of fixed prices in 1985. By the end of 1984, coal transactions at planned prices and at negotiated prices were almost equal. This dual price policy (simultaneous fixed and negotiated prices) stimulated the output of coal substantially and eased the coal supply problem of 1985 and 1986 (Interviews with Chen Dezun, November 1985, January 1986).

C. Steel

The reform methods used to revise the prices of steel products were the same as those for coal. The first method, adjustment, was applied for resolving the irrational price ratios between various products in the steel industry.[31] In 1985, the third method, a combination of adjustment and liberalisation, was employed to promote the output of steel. Large firms were permitted to sell their over-plan iron and steel output at negotiated prices. Small firms had no quota obligations, and thus could sell all their output at negotiated prices.[32]

D. Chemical Fertilisers

The reform of chemical fertiliser prices started in 1982 with the second method, adjustment parallel with liberalisation, and then in 1985 changed to the third method, a combination of adjustment and liberalisation. In 1982, control over producer prices of bicarbonate of ammonia manufactured by small factories was abolished. The fixed price of urea, produced by big factories, was increased by 50 yuan per ton in 1984. From 1985 onwards, the price of quota production of urea was administrated by the State Price Bureau (adjustment) and the price of above-quota production was determined by enterprises (liberalisation). The dual price of urea was officially sanctioned.

E. Bicycles

Between 1982 and 1984 the price of bicycles was reformed according to the second method (see Table 2.6). Prices of high-quality bicycles, in shortage since 1980, were controlled by the government. In 1984, the State Council approved the policy 'Implementation of Expansion of Production of Ming Pai Bicycles' which allowed prices of good-quality bicycles to be adjusted upward, by 5 to 15 per cent fixed prices.

The state simultaneously relaxed its control over the price of inferior bicycles manufactured by small and medium-sized factories. The price of these inferior products could be negotiated between buyers and producers (some local price authorities still supervised producer prices of inferior bicycles).

2.6 SUMMARY

The goal of price reform in China was quite clear. The government tried to create a new system which would allow prices to play a more fundamental role in resource allocation, and yet still allow the government to control the prices of certain important goods.

There were three different ideological and political groups involved in the debates on how to accomplish this goal. The debates on the reform package among the Centralisers, the Administrative Decentralisers and the Market Reformers centred, first, on methods of price reform, second, on price formation and determination, third, on the main form of prices and, finally, on the time frame of price reform. The 1979–86 reform was an outcome of the conflicts among these three different ideological and political groups. The process of price reform can be divided into three stages.

In the first stage, 1979–82, the method of adjustment proposed by the Centralisers was employed for all commodities. The economic system remained largely a planned system. In the second stage, 1982–4, the method of adjustment parallel with liberalisation for various goods, proposed by the Administrative Decentralisers, was adopted. Price adjustment was applied to commodities in category one, price liberalisation was applied to commodities in categories two and three. The planning system and the market existed side by side.

In the third stage, 1984–6, the method of a combination of adjustment and liberalisation suggested by the Market Reformers was applied to individual commodities in category one. In this period, fixed prices and free prices existed for the same goods and, thus, contradicted each other.

One important outcome of the application of the different reform methods was that various forms of prices simultaneously existed: fixed prices, floating prices, negotiated and free prices. In 1983 free prices covered only approximately 4 per cent of the items in domestic trade in cities (White, 1983). However, the situation rapidly changed and this percentage increased to 50–60 per cent in the 1985–6 period.[33] Correspondingly, state-controlled prices applied to only approximately 40–50 per cent of the value of output in 1985–6. This was partially due to the reduction in the number of industrial products subject to mandatory planning from 120 to 60 in 1984 (Perkins, 1986) and the appearance of dual pricing in 1985. This dramatic change indicates that the trend of Chinese price reform was to move away from a system of a high degree of price control in a bureaucratic–hierarchical command economy toward a system of partial price control in a less centralised market economy. The reform began with price adjustment and moved towards price liberalisation.

3 Administrative Prices in Theory and Practice

Chapter 2 studied the general problem of price reform in terms of its purposes, political and ideological positions, methods and stages of reform. Chapter 3 deals with the administrative method of calculation and determination of producer prices, from both the theoretical and practical aspects.

Inefficiencies in the administered pricing system in China arose at each of the three stages. The first stage, price calculation, required an accurate formula, which was worked out by lower-level administrators or enterprises and handed to higher authorities for approval. The problem at this stage was whether cost price, value price, production price, world price, or some other price should be used. One other problem which arose was whether a uniform formula for price-setting should be used for all commodities. Even if price calculation at the first stage was based on a rational formula, and price-setting was correct and close to 'value', it was still subject to distortions in the second stage.

The second stage was the administrative process of price determination at higher-level institutions where institutional conflicts could, and did, occur. At this stage, the determination of the actual price was likely to be a political and economic compromise among institutions or between institutions and enterprises. The third stage was the process of policy implementation which often encountered difficulties related to the capacities of different levels of price bureau. In this chapter we focus mainly on problems of the first and second stages.

3.1 PRICE FORMATION PRINCIPLES

The importance of having a proper theoretical formula for administrative price formation has been emphasised by Chinese economists. Xue Muqiao, in the 1960s, argued that the lack of correct formulas would affect the economic accounting of state enterprises, as well as the evaluation of enterprise achievements, income distribution, and allocation of resources (Chen Nai-Ruenn, 1966 : 39).

Before economic reform, the debate on prices focused on the question of how prices should be calculated. It was taken for granted that prices should be administratively determined, and the issue of price function became subordinate to the issue of price calculation.[1] Perfecting a formula which could accurately express production costs was thus regarded as a purely technical calculation problem. It was posed without reference to the political and economic structures or the possibility of changing them – in other words, it was believed that the socialist policy of fixed pricing could be improved and made efficient without changing the political and economic system. The Chinese economic literature contains many debates about the correct formula, and how to perfect it. The theoretical debate before 1979 can be divided into two periods.[2] In the first, that prior to 1960, controversy centred on certain practical issues of price policy.

The first issue concerned pricing policies for heavy industrial goods. Producer prices, set by the State in the period of the first Five-Year Plan were higher not only than prevailing world market prices but also the relative prices of the same goods in China before the communist takeover[3] (Chen Nai-Ruenn, 1966; Perkins, 1966). The policy of high prices for heavy industrial goods, on which the State's revenues depended, generated the first theoretical price-setting debates in 1956 and 1957.[4]

The second issue was related to the problem of pricing new products. New products were priced according to test-manufacturing expenses incurred during the final stage of product development. It was argued that test-manufacturing expenses of new products were exceedingly high, therefore they would exaggerate the gross value of industrial output.[5] For example, a 6000 kilowatt engine for steamships was priced at 1,320,000 yuan when first manufactured in Shanghai in 1955, but was reduced to 380,000 yuan the following year (Chen Nai-Ruenn, 1966).

Another controversy arose over regional price disparities, caused by incorrect methods of price-setting. For some products regional price disparities were so wide that they could not be explained merely by transportation costs and trade profits.[6] Irrational regional prices certainly had adverse effects on production and distribution, and certain economists thus suggested that these large price differentials should be adjusted.[7]

In this period, no agreement was reached on theoretical proposals to resolve the above-mentioned problems. Principles of rational price-setting for heavy industrial goods and new products were not clearly conceptualised. For some commodities, real price changes took place only after compromises between institutions were reached.[8]

After 1961, the price debates entered a second phase and Chinese economists started to focus their attention on a formula for price formation of industrial and agricultural products (Lin, 1981; Chen Nai-Ruenn, 1967; Rieman, 1967). They were inspired by recognition of the defects of the existing system, and attempted to formulate a rational socialist pricing system (Chen Nai-Ruenn, 1966; Hu Changnuan, interview, 1985).

The key issue in this debate concerned how profit should be calculated, and on what basis the surplus product should be applied in the price formula: $P = c + v + s$ (where: P stands for price, c for fixed capital, v for wages, raw materials, etc., and s for profit).[9] The debate was between proponents of using labour cost, cost of production and capital as bases for profit markup respectively.[10]

A. Markup on Labour Cost

The Labour Cost school of thought, represented by Wang Zhiye (1962) and Bai Hong (1964), insisted that the distribution of surplus product in the economy be proportionately based on labour costs or the wage bill (Lin, 1981 : 25). Their formula for price-setting was: $P = c + v + (v(S/V))$ (where S and V stand for total surplus value product and the total wage fund in the national economy, respectively).[11] Calculating surplus product value for society according to the national average wage–profit ratio (S/V) was in keeping with the basic theory that only labour created value.

According to Bai Hong, the advantage of this type of price formula was that it would properly guide consumption – that is, encourage consumers to consume commodities produced with relatively less labour (Rieman, 1967). However, this approach was criticised by opponents such as Yang Hongdao, on the grounds that it made labour-intensive products expensive and capital-intensive products cheap, and thus discouraged technical progress (Lin, 1981 : 25). It was also argued that this method was based on a narrow interpretation of the Marxist Labour Theory of Value and that it was supported by only a few economists.

B. Markup on Cost of Production

The second school of economists, which included Yang Hongdao, Zhang Wen and Zhao Liguang, proposed to distribute the surplus product according to the costs of production, which included both labour and non-labour costs, that is: $P = c + v + (c + v)\ (S/(C + V))$[12] (where C stands for the cost of material inputs; and V stands for the total wage bill; $(c + v)S/(C + V)$ represents the average profit rate of a particular product).

This school claimed that by taking both labour and material costs into account, the above formula provided a more objective basis for pricing than labour cost alone, and that its use would help to economise not only on labour costs but also on material outlays (Chen Nai-Ruenn, 1966; Lin, 1981 : 25–6). Since the cost of production constituted a major part of value, price calculation, according to this formula, would generally be close to value (Ibid.).

The Cost of Production school was criticised by the Labour Cost school on the grounds that if price-setting were based on the cost of production formula it would encourage enterprises to use expensive materials in production, thereby increasing their output value; the same product could be priced differently due to differences in the degree of vertical integration in the production process – hence, the higher the degree of vertical integration, the higher the profit to producers (Chen Nai-Ruenn, 1966; Lin, 1981 : 26).

The third school, which advocated using capital as the basis for calculating profit, also attacked the Cost of Production school's formula on the basis that the role of capital – particularly fixed capital – was not treated adequately.

C. Price of Production

The third school believed that 'the proportion of fixed capital to labour in an enterprise has considerable effect on labour productivity and that proportional distribution of surplus product should take into account past labour stored up in fixed capital' (Chen Nai-Ruenn, 1966).

This school, which emerged in 1963, presupposed a constant return to capital and proposed the formula of 'price of production', $P = c + v + rk'$ (where k' stands for the average total capital invested in the production of each unit of the product and r stands for the ratio of S to k (total capital invested in the economy)).[13] Economists such as

Yang Jianbai (1963), Ho Jianzhang and Zhang Ling (1964) advocated that the average rate of profit calculation be based on total capital, a method derived from Marxist doctrine[14] (Lin, 1981 : 26). They also argued that 'Socialist society required large-scale production characterized by a high degree of social integration of labour, intensified division of social labour and intimate relationships among various branches of production.[15] Capital was therefore important in socialist economic development. Furthermore, both centralised planning decisions and factory-level decisions needed to be made primarily on the basis of profitability.

The advantage of this formula of price-setting was that it ensured investment efficiency and helped economise the use of scarce capital (Yang Jianbai, 1963; Ho Jianzhang, 1964). It also provided an effective measure for evaluating enterprise performance and selecting investment projects.[16]

This proposal was regarded as most radical, and it attracted more attention than the others. Not surprisingly, it was also subject to harsher attack. One important criticism of this school was that production price policies would result in increased profit rates for heavy industrial goods relative to light industrial and agricultural goods. This would accelerate the growth of heavy industry by making it easier to finance new investment, thus contradicting the official policy of encouraging light industry and agriculture. One other criticism of this school's thought was that profitability should not be the sole criterion used to evaluate the effectiveness of investment; other investment criteria, such as the basic economic laws of socialism, 'the law of planned and proportionate development of the national economy', the needs of society, and other political and economic requirements were equally, if not more, important (Rieman, 1967; Chen Nai-Ruenn, 1966).

Controversy over price formation in the second period was not resolved. There was no theoretical solution commonly accepted by the three schools.

3.2 PRE-1978 PRACTICE

A. Academic Opinions

According to the Chinese economic literature, the determination of a commodity's planned price at producer and procurement levels was, in practice, based on the cost-plus formula in the pre-reform period (Xu Yi *et al.*, 1982 : 59; Hu Changnuan, 1982 : 24; 112).

The average-cost-plus principle was adopted for price calculation. Producer and procurement prices were calculated on an average branch-production cost basis, plus a profit margin,[17] and taxes proportionate to producer and procurement prices (Hu Changnuan, 1982 : 112; Chai, 1986 : 3).

Costs of industrial goods included the manufacturer's expenses for raw materials, intermediate products, supplementary materials, fuel, power, payments to workers and staff, workshops, management, and capital depreciation (Wang, 1980 : 74; Chai, 1986 : 3). Rental and capital charges were excluded from costs, though interest charges on bank loans were included. Depreciation charges did not include charges for obsolescence (Chai, 1986 : 3).[18] The cost of production, calculated in this way, constituted the economic basis for setting commodity prices.

The planned price of a commodity at the producer, wholesale, and retail levels was decided only after determining the costs of production and distribution (transportation), profit markup, and taxes. The technical procedures of price-setting at different levels have been detailed by Cheng (1982 : 223–56) and Wang (1980 : 74–88).

B. General Experience

Was the formula of cost-plus markup actually widely and strictly applied to price-setting in the pre-reform period, as the Chinese economic literature indicates? Economists outside China have rejected this assertion and alleged that, in practice, 'there appear to be no uniform rules for setting either industrial producers or agricultural procurement prices' (Chen Nai-Ruenn, 1966), and that cost-plus pricing was not widely or strictly applied (Wang, 1980). Instead, actual price-setting was determined by varying criteria (Chai, 1986; Chen Nai-Ruenn, 1966; and Wang, 1980).

The cost-plus formula, when applied, encountered difficulties. This was partly because the Soviet average-cost-plus principle, introduced in China in the early 1950s, was found inapplicable in many cases, and partly because the principle itself had many defects (Chen Nai-Ruenn, 1966 : 39). This view was supported by another economist, Wang (1980), almost 15 years later. Wang's study tried to explain why planned prices diverged from value. He argued that planned price-setting did not follow a particular formula such as the cost-plus markup for most commodities.

Wang argued that planned prices, mechanically derived from the cost-plus formula, could not approximate commodity values 'unless the costs of production and distribution used as the bases of computation were reasonable and accurate, and relevant demand factors were adequately taken into account'. There was an additional problem of a price adjustment time lag between planned costs (base price) and actual costs, and thus an accurate cost basis for price planning was usually not available. The planned costs of production used in the cost-plus formulas as the basis for planning producer, wholesale, and retail prices of industrial commodities were supposed to change only once every three to five years. However, actual production costs changed every year and season since production capacities, degree of utilisation, input prices, and the efficiency of production management varied over time (Wang, 1980 : 79).

Another factor which caused the divergence of planned costs (base prices) from actual costs of production was that increases in planned prices were not proportionate to increases in production costs. Wang (1980) argued that theoretically, if the actual unit costs of production (and of distribution when relevant) were used in the cost-plus formula as the base for fixing producer, wholesale and retail prices, these prices would logically change at the same rates as the costs of production or prices at the preceding level, if there were no change in tax rates or planned profit rates. Even though changes in tax and planned profit rates were rare in 1950s and 1960s, most official producer, wholesale and retail prices were not changed at the same rates as their respective costs of production and prices at the preceding level (Wang, 1980).

Chen Nai-Ruenn in the 1960s, and Wang and Chai in the 1980s, faced limited availability of information on actual price-setting and yet reached the same conclusion: that the cost-plus formula had not been universalised in pricing practice. Rather, 'it had been limited to a relatively small number of commodities in certain selected years and then to a given distribution stage, say the producer or wholesale stage' (Wang, 1980).

According to our 1985 interviews, it appears that before reform there was no uniform rule for setting industrial producer, or agricultural procurement prices. Commodity prices were determined according to the model cost method; the deduction method; the individual factories actual cost method; and historical price data.

The first method, model cost, was based on model firms, believed to be representative of all firms producing the same product. Their average production costs were computed as the basis for pricing. Profits per unit of product were calculated in relation to cost or capital. The second method, deduction, was used to find producer and procurement prices by deducting distribution costs and trade profits from retail prices. The third method, actual costs of individual factories, was applied to new products and those manufactured by only a few factories. According to this method, prices were determined primarily at the experimental cost level, and also by the actual costs of a particular enterprise; this type of price could be cut when production costs fell. The fourth method, employed mainly for the purpose of adjusting prices, used historical prices as a basis. 'Historical prices' referred to the price prevailing between 1930 and 1936, a period of relative price stability (a view of price stability criticised by Liu and Yeh, 1965). This method was regarded as the simplest, and was used to determine the price level of many daily staples between 1950 and 1953.

The above four methods were all applied in price-setting prior to 1956. After the socialisation of the industrial sector in 1957, only the first and third methods were employed to calculate the 'base' or 'cost price' for price-setting and adjustment. Producer prices of industrial producer and consumer goods and procurement prices of agricultural goods were normally arrived at by modifying the base prices (Chai, 1986). Various factors, discussed below, caused actual prices to differ from base prices. In the next section of this chapter we consider price formation for five commodities in the pre-reform period.

C. Pre-1979 Price Formation for Five Commodities

Cotton

The procurement price of cotton was set according to deduction and historical price methods. State purchase prices for agricultural products were determined by deducting estimated distribution costs and trade profits from prevailing market retail prices (interview, 1985). This was confirmed by the State Price Bureau, who pointed out that the price ratio between cotton and grain in the 1930s was also taken into account.

In 1950, the State announced a price ratio of 1:10.1 for cotton and grain (one jin (= 0.5 kilogram) of cotton exchanged for 10.1 jin of grain). The 1950 relative price of cotton was higher than the 1949 price ratio of 1:6 and the 1930s price ratio of 1:7.4. The high price of cotton encouraged peasants to grow more, and cotton output increased to 1.3 million tons in 1952. This level was 300 per cent higher than the 1949 output, 0.44 million tons, and 53.6 per cent higher than the output of 1936.

The output of cotton in 1952 not only eased tension in domestic demand, but also transformed China from a cotton importer to a country self-sufficient in cotton. At the end of 1952, the State decided to reduce the price of cotton to 'balance' the price ratio of cotton to grain. The price ratio considered 'best' was that which prevailed in the 1930s. The procurement price of cotton was reduced from 91 yuan per 100 jin to 86 yuan per 100 jin in Zhejiang Province in 1953 (see Table 3.2). The ratio of profit to cost for cotton decreased from 20.3 per cent in 1951 to 17 per cent in 1952 and to 14.6 per cent in 1953. This immediately affected national cotton output; output decreased 9 per cent from 1.3 million tons in 1952 to 1.17 million tons in 1953 and to 1.06 million tons in 1954. The area sown to cotton was reduced by 7.1 per cent from 83.64 million mu in 1952 to 77.7 million mu in 1953 (1 mu = 0.0667 hectare).

To ensure cotton output, the State Council announced a policy of planned unified purchase and supply in 1954. In addition, a new price ratio of cotton to grain was fixed by the Central Financial and Economic Commission in March 1954; the price of cotton was determined by averaging the prices of the previous four years (1950–53).

In 1954, the increase in the price of cotton led to a 5.44 per cent increase over 1953 levels in area sown. Total output decreased from 1.17 million tons in 1953 to 1.06 million tons in 1954, due to bad weather. It has been claimed that the price of cotton was increased again in 1955; however, we gathered no evidence to support this statement. From 1955 to 1978, the price of cotton increased only three times: in 1963, 1972, and 1978 (see Tables 3.1, 3.2 and 3.3). In the post-1954 period, the price ratio of cotton to grain, the balance of supply and demand, and government policies regulating income distribution by affecting the terms of trade between agriculture and industry each affected cotton prices. The first and third factors were the most important (interviews with the local price bureau in Zhejiang Province, 1985).

Coal

In 1950 there was no uniform producer price for coal in China; prices varied by area. Producer prices were based on the prevailing pro-

Table 3.1 Cost and procurement price of Grade 3, 27 cm ginned cotton, 1952–83 (yuan/100 jin)

	1952	*53*	*54*	*57*	*62*	*65–70*	*75*	*76*	*77*	*78*	*79*	*80*	*81*	*82*	*83*
Cost[1]	46	n.a.	n.a.	57	72	62	92	108	103	100	95	92	99	84	75
Procurement price	86	n.a.	88	88	88	92	104	107	107	120	133	154	147	150	153

Note: 1. National average production costs. Information on procurement price, 1954–62, was collected from the southern part of China, national average procurement price in this period could be 2 to 4 yuan per jin higher than the prices in the north. Price here excludes the higher price of above-quota cotton.

Sources: The cost structure between 1952 and 1980 is from Xu Yi (1982 : 79; 129). Cost-price structure of cotton from 1980–3 is based on our interviews, 1985.

Table 3.2 Procurement price of ginned cotton in Pinghu, Hangzhou and Jinhua, Zhejiang Province, 1950–79 (yuan/100 jin)

Product Grade	*5*	*3*	*5*	*3*	*5*	*3*
Year	*Pinghu*		*Hangzhou*		*Jinhua*	
1950	87					
1951	91					
1952	91					
1953	86					
1954[1]	88		87			
1955–62	88		87			
1963	91		90		89[3]	
1964–71	91		90		89	
1972[2]		104		104		104
1973–7		104		104		104
1978		115		115		115
1979		132		132		132
1980		145		145		145

Notes: 1. In 1954 the State nationalised the price of cotton. 2. In 1972, the State changed the name of Grade 5, 7–8 inch to Grade 3, 27 cm, and increased its price. 3. Before 1960 there was no cotton in the Jinhua area.

Sources: Interviews with the Zhejiang local Price Bureau, 1985.

Table 3.3 Cost structure of Grade 3, 27 cm ginned cotton, Pinghu area, 1973–80 (yuan/100 jin)

	1973	*1974*	*1975*	*1976*	*1977*	*1978*	*1979*	*1980*
Production cost after tax	85	64	68	91	83	66	84	77
Procurement price	104	104	104	104	104	115	132	145

Note: The information on cost structure of cotton for Pinghu country was available only from 1973.

Sources: Interviews with the Zhejiang local Price Bureau, 1985; interviews with the Zhejiang local Price Bureau, 1985.

ducer price of a particular mine, or the average producer price of several mines in the area. For instance, in the Northeast, the producer price of coal was based on the producer price of the Shenyang Coal Mine; this price was not determined by a theoretical formula but rather by historical prices.

The non-unified coal-pricing system existed from 1950 until the policy of 'The Management of the Producer Price of Coal' was announced by the National Price Committee (*Guojia Wujia Weiyuan Hui*) in 1965 (see Table 3.4). Prior to 1965, price adjustments took place in different areas based on changes in production costs, quality, and regional price disparities. This caused large differences in regional wholesale prices.[19]

Starting in 1965, the State used the average production cost of all state-owned coal mines (excluding cooperative and small village coal mines) as the basis for unified producer prices. Profit was calculated on an average cost of production basis (see Table 3.4). There were no further price adjustments for coal until 1979 (there is more detail on this topic in Chapter 4).

Steel

The producer price of steel from 1950 to 1952 was based on historical prices – that is, prices which varied by city. In 1953, the first year of the first Five-Year Plan, the producer prices of steel were set by the State according to the average production costs of 3 to 5 large steel mills, such as Anshan and Bunchi (conducted and managed by the

Table 3.4 Price–cost structure of coal in China, 1952–80 (yuan/ton)

Year	*Cost*[1]	*Producer price*[3]	*Tax*[2]	*Profit*	*Ratio of profit to cost (%)*	*Ratio of tax to cost (%)*
1952	9.00	11.46	0.86	1.60	17.78	27.33
1957	10.90	12.05	0.90	0.25	2.29	11.28
1960	9.17	14.97	1.20	4.60	50.00	63.24
1962	17.28	15.20	n.a.	n.a.	n.a.	n.a.
1965	15.77	18.00	1.44	0.79	5.00	14.14
1970	13.47	18.00	1.44	3.09	22.94	33.63
1971	13.60	18.00	1.44	2.96	21.76	32.35
1972	14.08	18.00	1.44	2.48	17.61	27.84
1973	14.51	18.00	1.44	2.05	14.13	24.07
1974	17.14	18.00	1.44	–0.58	-3.38	5.02
1975	15.86	18.00	1.44	0.70	4.41	13.49
1976	16.70	18.00	1.44	–0.14	–0.84	7.78
1977	16.61	18.00	1.44	–0.05	–0.30	8.37
1978	16.12	18.00	1.44	0.44	2.73	11.66
1979	17.78	22.10	1.77	2.55	14.34	24.29
1980	20.00					

Notes: 1. The actual cost and price per ton of coal was modified by Chinese economists. 2. The tax rate was 7.5 per cent before 1958 and was increased to 8 per cent in the tax reform of 1958. 3. The producer price of 1962 was based on my own calculation, it may be 0.2 to 0.5 yuan lower than the actual figure. According to Chinese economists, data for the 1960s was inaccurate for several reasons: first, statistics were used as 'a weapon of class struggle' before 1979 and, second, China did not have a sound statistical collection system at that time.

Sources: *Economic Research Data*, vol. 2 (1981 : 11), quoted in Xu Yi (1982 : 164).

central government). The fixed price was only applied to products manufactured by state-owned large and medium-sized steel mills. It was applied to products manufactured at the Wuhan Iron and Steel Mill, which began production in 1955, and also to the 119 new types of steel products produced by several large and medium-size steel and iron mills during the first eight months of 1962 (interviews, 1985). Prices of products manufactured by small, collective steel mills were set by local price authorities. Generally, the producer prices of steel products fluctuated every year between 1953 and 1955.

In 1956, the producer price of steel was adjusted downward (see

Table 3.5 Producer price index of industrial goods, 1952–7 (yuan/ton)

Commodities	*1952=100*				
	1953	*1954*	*1955*	*1956*	*1957*
Coal	102.4	104.2	106.4	105.5	105.7
Steel and iron	98.3	96.1	93.3	74.5	75.4

Sources: The Collection of Commercial Statistical Data 1950–1957, China State Statistical Bureau (1958 : 39).

Table 3.6 Wholesale price index of iron and steel, 1952–7 (yuan/ton)

	1952	*1953*	*1954*	*1955*	*1956*	*1957*	*1957 against 1952 (%)*
Iron	100	88.9	95.3	88.2	85.2	85.2	–14.8
Steel plates	100	78.4	75.4	62.3	61.0	61.0	–39.0

Notes: In the period between 1950 and 1955 goods were priced in old Renminbi (old currency); in 1955 the government introduced new Renminbi – 1 new yuan was equal to 10,000 old yuan.

Sources: *A Collection of Shanghai Price Information and Related Materials Before and After Liberation, 1921–1957*, Shanghai People's Publications (1958:516–25).

Tables 3.5, 3.6 and 3.7), and then kept stable until 1958 when the State increased its power to ration key producer goods (235 commodities were rationed in 1956 and 285 in 1959).[20] The downward adjustment of producer prices of steel products during the first Five-Year Plan was mainly due to the increase in productivity. Production costs in the industrial sector decreased by an average of 5 per cent per year in this period. This 1956 adjustment of steel prices became the basis of further adjustments only for products manufactured by state-owned, large and medium-sized mills.

In 1958, a new 'local and temporary pricing system' was applied to the output of the small, backyard furnaces. During the Great Leap Forward such furnaces were encouraged so as to stimulate a rapid expansion of steel and iron output. Since small-scale, semi-modern furnaces produced poor-quality products at high cost, the State felt that the fixed price system should not be applied, and instead, immediately introduced 'local and temporary pricing'.[21]

Table 3.7 Producer prices of different types of steel (yuan/ton)

Steel	*Sizes*	*1953*	*1954*	*1955*	*1956*	*1957*	*1957 against 1953 (%)*
Steel products	25mm	530	530	385	385	385	–27.4
Carbon steel	7–13 & 19–20mm	950	950	950	759	759	–16.3
Small steel round bars		Average 625			440		

Note: The producer price of small steel round bars was 530 yuan per ton in 1980.

Source: Interview, 1985.

Bicycles

In the 1950s, producer prices of bicycles were determined either by experimental costs or by actual costs of individual factories. The state did not try to employ uniform producer, wholesale and retail prices based on the model cost method. At that time there were few bicycle factories, and the output of bicycles was low; only 14,000 sets were produced in 1949 and bicycles were imported in the 1950s.

Each type of bicycle, as Table 3.8 indicates, had its own producer and wholesale and retail prices which were set according to production costs. A uniform tax rate was laid down by the State prior to price-setting. However, profit rates were set differently by the central government for large enterprises and by local authorities for small factories.[22] In some cases, profit rates were determined by factors other than economic considerations.

The problem of setting profit rates for different bicycles stemmed not from the first stage of price formation – calculation, but from the second stage – determination. Administrative price determination involved conflicts, not only between enterprises and price authorities but also between institutions (this is discussed further in the final section of this chapter).

Chemical Fertilisers

Between 1950 and 1952, the producer price of agricultural chemical fertilisers was adjusted according to historical prices. Such prices

Table 3.8 Cost–price relationship of four types of bicycles, 1982 (yuan/set)

Location	*Type*	*Total output*	*Cost structure*					*Producer Price*	*Wholesale Price*	*Retail Price*
			Cost	*Tax*	*Ratio (%)*	*Profit*	*Ratio (%)*			
Tianjin	Red Flag No. 01	2 100	77	16	15	14	18	108	120	137
Guangzhou	Five Ship PA13	1 019 000	91	17	15	8	8	117	129	147
Beijing										
	PA12	100 000	118	21	15	0.98	0.8	140		158
	No. 3	60 000	117	22	15	8	7	148		165

Notes: The tax ratio was based on producer prices. The profit ratio was calculated according to production costs.

Sources: Interviews with BBF, 1985.

Table 3.9 Producer prices of urea, 1962–84 (yuan/ton)

	1962–5	*1966*	*1967–70*	*1971–83*	*1984*
Producer price	1000	540	400	350	410
Retail price	n.a.	660	500	450	510

Note: These producer prices were fixed by the central government and applied across the nation.

Sources: Survey and interviews with Professors Hu Changnuan and Ye Shangpong, 1985.

were relatively high. In order to encourage mechanisation in agriculture and to stabilise the relationship between the peasants and the government, a policy of constant price reductions for chemical fertilisers was adopted in 1953 (see Table 3.9).

The price of ammonium nitrate was cut 16 times, from 590 to 220 yuan per ton, in the 19 years between 1953 and 1972. The price of urea was cut several times, from 1000 yuan a ton in 1962 to 350 in 1971 and then remained constant for more than 10 years (see Table 3.9). One effect of this policy was that the use of chemical fertilisers more than doubled, from 31.19 jin (15.9 kilogram) per mu at the beginning of 1970s to 70.4 jin (35.2 Kilogram) per mu in 1978.

After 1956, the producer prices of chemical fertilisers were fixed at two levels. The price of 'important' chemical fertilisers such as urea,

Table 3.10 Producer price of ammonium carbonate in Zhejiang Province, 1966, 1967 and 1979–82 (yuan/ton)

	1966	*1967*	*1979–82*
Costs	92	110	111.59
Producer price	124	124	140.00
Retail price	140	140	156.00

Note: These prices were set by the local government.

Sources: Our survey in *Zhejiang* Province, 1985.

Table 3.11 Producer price of ammonium carbonate in Hebei Province, 1969–85 (yuan/ton)

	1969–80	*1981*	*1982*	*1983*	*1984*	*1985*
Producer price	150	150	155	155	155	155
Retail price	170	182	182	190	195	165

Note: These prices were fixed by the local authorities.

Sources: Based on interviews, 1985, with the no. 1 Changzhou Small Chemical Fertiliser Plant in Hebei Province.

produced by large firms, was set by the central government. The price of less important chemical fertilisers such as ammonium carbonate, produced by small firms, was fixed and managed by local price authorities. Prices varied according to region (see Tables 3.10 and 3.11).

Some Chinese economists have argued that the price determination and adjustment of this product was based on concerns about peasant income. But, according to Liu (1971), the market price of ammonium sulphate between 1956 and 1957 was almost three times greater than its average cost; its transfer price was 1.6 times higher than the cost. Chinese farmers paid a higher price for ammonium sulphate relative to rice than farmers in other rice-producing Asian countries: the Chinese ratio was 2.54 units of rice for one unit of ammonium sulphate, while in India, Japan and Thailand the exchange ratios were below 1. The Chinese ratio was 10 times higher than that of Japan.

In the 1960s, this pricing system brought profits to most fertiliser enterprises.[23] However, the situation changed in the 1970s. A large number of enterprises, especially small and medium-sized ones, occurred losses in the 1970s and in the reform period.[24] Government subsidies were consequently increased.

D. Summary of the Five Commodities

The main features of the price formation of these five commodities can now be summarised below.

First, in the 1950s producer and procurement prices were formulated according to different criteria, including political, economic, and historical factors. There was no single uniform principle applied to price formulation or adjustment in the pre-reform period.

Second, the fundamental problem of price formation in the first stage (calculation) was that it was not based on any scientific method or algorithm. The administrative price system therefore started on a problematic basis.

Third, the criteria of demand and supply, quality and development of new technology and products were hardly taken into account in price formation and adjustment prior to 1979.

These factors, according to the view of Chinese economists, resulted in an irrational pricing system, where prices reflected neither value nor the relation of supply and demand. The administrative method of price setting thus required reform.

3.3 PRACTICE DURING 1979–86

A. Theoretical Proposals

Since 1979, Chinese economists have put forward eight proposals for the price formation of basic (not actual) prices (Yu Xingfa, 1984 : 36–50). Three of the proposals – value price, cost price, and production price – were similar to those discussed in the 1950s and 1960s. One newly proposed method, the triple channel, was theoretically immature. Four other proposals appear also to have influenced Chinese economic thinking.

Of these four latter proposals, the two-channel price (*shangqiu jiage*), which related part of the surplus to wages and another part to current capital, and the combination price (*zhonghe lirun lu*), which related part of the surplus to wages and another part to both current funds and fixed production funds, were both studied in the Soviet

Union and Hungary in the 1960s (Bettelheim, 1978 : 202–4). They were introduced in China after 1979.

The third of the four proposals advocated value-added prices where prices were intended to consist of material costs (including depreciation) and value-added. The value-added of each product was to be calculated by allocating the economy's total value-added (wage and non-wage) among individual products in proportion to the labour employed in their production (Chai, 1986 : 21).

The final proposal, equilibrium price, was derived from mathematical programming techniques and general equilibrium models (Lou Jiwei and Zhou Xiaochuan, 1984 : 13–20). According to this principle, prices should reflect not only costs but also demand. This type of price is similar to the western concept of a scarcity price.

Actually, these proposals for changing the method of price formation were developed in three phases between 1979 and 1986. In the first phase, 1979–83, theoretical thinking about price formation was dominated by the concept of how the government could perfect the formula of price-setting so as more accurately to express value. The theoretical disputes of this period were centred on a choice between the principles of cost-price proposed by the Centralisers (Xu Yi *et al.*, 1982) and production price advocated by the Administrative Decentralisers (Hu Changnuan, 1982; He Jianzhang and Zhang Zhuoyuan, 1981; Chen Dezun, interview in 1985). By the end of 1982, production price had won the support of a majority of those in academic and political circles, and dominated the thinking about administrative price-setting.

In the second phase, 1983–5, the production price proposal was challenged by three other proposals: combination price,[25] two-channel price,[26] and equilibrium price,[27] put forward by economists among the Administrative Decentralisers; the latter two proposals became influential in economic thought. It appears that the above four principles were not widely applied to price setting in practice (interviews with economists from universities, and different levels of the Price Bureau, the Chinese Academy of Social Science and the Price Research Centre at the State Council in 1985). This was due to their theoretical shortcomings, disagreements on application, and a strong challenge from the Market Reformers. For example, the popular two-channel price, $P = C + V + V\ (S\ 0.30\%/V) + k\ (S\ 0.70\%/K)$ (where 30 per cent of the surplus goes to wages and 70 per cent to capital funds), is still theoretically controversial.[28] (In this formula k represents average fixed and working capital per unit of the economy, and *K* represents the total fixed and working capital in the economy). There is not yet a satisfactory theoretical explanation for such a division of surplus.[29] A similar problem existed for the combination price method. It lacked a theoretical justification for both the proportional allocation of the 'social wage' and the profit rate applicable to production funds. Both economists and politicians disagreed with the application of these proposals.

The unsolved problems of administrative price-setting encouraged the Market Reformers to break with the traditional thought that the State could perfect the formula of price-setting. They advocated eliminating administrative price-setting as the best way to get the price right. Their criticism focused on the capacities of institutions for price determination (the second stage) and implementation (the third stage), rather than on the problem of calculation (the first stage). Their position led to the third phase of the theoretical debates, beginning at the end of 1984.

B. Implementation: 1979–86

The reform of the fixed-price system did not follow any one blueprint in the 1979–86 period. The theoretical proposals discussed above had little influence on actual price-setting.[30] The majority of fixed prices were adopted from the previous pricing system; some were adjusted upward or downward according to varying criteria.

One criterion taken into account for price adjustment was the level of international prices. Imported commodities, having no domestic equivalent and no set supply price, had prices set by converting the c.i.f. price to yuan and adding a markup.[31] Commodities imported through the Foreign Trade Department had their prices calculated according to the c.i.f. price plus import tariffs, unified industrial and commercial taxes, relevant internal costs, and handling charges for the Foreign Trade Departments. Finished export products had their prices derived from the costs of imported inputs, components and handling charges (Dong Fureng, 1986 : 300).[32]

A second set of criteria involved the cost structure and price ratios. This method was applied to coal, iron, steel, and other industrial prices. After 1979, price increases in the iron and steel industry were based on the cost increases and price ratios between iron and steel and also among different type of steel goods.[33] These criteria were also applied to the adjustment of coal prices in 1979 and 1985,[34] but their 1979 application was jeopardised by institutional conflicts (discussed in the following section).

Another criterion in price adjustment was consideration of peasant income. This criterion was applied to commodities such as chemical fertilisers before reform; it was also applied to certain commodities used by peasants, such as farm machinery and plastics in the 1978–9 reform period. For example, in September 1978, the State decided to cut the price of farm machinery by 13 per cent. This caused 30 per cent of the enterprises in the farm machinery industry to run losses.[35] This policy of reducing prices without considering the production costs of firms affected the output of farm machinery and slowed down the mechanisation of agriculture. However, this policy was revised and a floating price system (10 per cent upward) was introduced in 1980 for agricultural farm machinery.

Yet another criterion concerned the balance between supply and demand. It was applied to cotton and grain between 1978 and 1986. For example, the 9.5 per cent increase in the price of cotton in 1978 was due to the decrease in cotton output from 2.381 million tons in 1975 to 2.055 million tons in 1976, and to 2.049 million tons in 1977 (*Statistical Yearbook of China*, 1985 : 255). The decrease in output directly affected the supply of cotton to the textile industry, and thus threatened daily clothing needs. Under these conditions, the State was forced to follow a short-term strategy, importing nearly 5 million kilograms of cotton in three years and increasing procurement prices between 1978 and 1984.[36]

Consideration of Treasury revenues and accumulation of State funds constituted another criteria of price adjustment. The State used these criteria for adjusting the price of cigarettes and alcoholic beverages. Price hikes for these commodities in 1981 netted several billion yuan in state revenues (interviews with Ye Shangpong, a lecturer in the Division of Price and Cost at the Statistical Department of the People's University of China, 1985). Product quality was also a criterion of price adjustment. Various agricultural goods (tea), commercial goods (alcohol, bicycles and textiles), means of production (steel products, non-ferrous metal products), and services (train and boat transportation) could have their prices raised by 5, 10 or 20 per cent above normal fixed prices if their quality was comparable to that of international markets or was at the peak of the domestic market.[37] It is very difficult to evaluate the implementation of this quality criterion and its effects on consumers; besides, the State-judged standard of 'quality' is unclear.

However, in addition to these economic criteria, administrative price determination and institutional conflicts also affected price setting and adjustment.

3.4 INSTITUTIONAL CONFLICTS AND PROBLEMS

A. Horizontal

In the second stage of price determination institutional conflicts occurred at the horizontal level between institutions within the central and local governments, and between politicians.

One case which involved conflict between a number of institutions in the central government was that of the coal price adjustments of 1979. A request for price adjustments for coal began in 1974, when some coal mines began to make losses, and when low prices seriously impeded the expansion of coal output (Dong Fureng, 1986 : 292). In 1976, the cost of coal was 16.70 yuan per ton and the producer price was 18 yuan per ton; after taxes each ton of coal netted a loss of 0.14 yuan. The ratio of profit to cost was −0.84 per cent (see Table 3.4). In 1977, about 70 per cent of the state-owned coal mines operated at a loss.

In 1979, the Ministry of Coal submitted a proposal to the State Price Bureau and the State Council asking for a price increase from 18 to 30 yuan per ton, based on the average production costs of state-owned coal mines and a small profit margin. This proposal generated controversy and conflicts among institutions.

In February 1979, before the State Council made its decision to adjust the price of coal, a meeting was called by the State Price Bureau to discuss the proposal, which was attended by representatives of 10 institutions. The representatives of the Ministry of Metallurgy, of Commerce, and of Water and Electricity did not resist the idea of a price adjustment for coal; however, they strongly rejected the large increase of 12 yuan per ton. The representative of the Ministry of Metallurgy argued that a hike of 12 yuan per ton was too high, and would reduce the profitability of the iron and steel industry. Their suggestion of a price increase of no more than 10 yuan per ton was accepted by the majority of representatives at the meeting.

The Ministry of Coal was disappointed by this result. In later reports, it insisted that if the price was increased by only 10 yuan per ton, the coal industry would again make losses after only one or two years. However, the State Price Bureau and the State Council, who were concerned that a hike of 12 yuan per ton might affect the national economy, did not approve a reapplication of the Ministry of Coal; and decided on an increase of 10 yuan per ton.

In the third stage, policy implementation, the State Economic Commission (SEC) reported to the State Council that the 10 yuan per ton increase was too high to be implemented. The SEC decided to carry out the policy in two steps (*liangbu zou*).[38] The first increase of 5 yuan was implemented in May 1979; the second 5 yuan increase was delayed and had not been implemented by 1985 (interviews with the State Price Bureau and with economists, 1985).

This case highlights how the pricing system developed from the first stage (where price formation, proposed by the Ministry of Coal, was based on the cost structure) to the second stage (where price determination was a result of compromise among institutions), and finally to the third stage (where the implementation of price policy was ineffectual). This was not an exceptional case: similar situations arose in the cotton sector in the post-reform period.

B. Horizontal and Vertical

Conflicts and tensions also arose between higher and lower institutions, between institutions at the same level, and between institutions and enterprises. One case in point is the controversy over price adjustments for the Beijing Bicycle Factory (BBF) in 1980–1. This case highlights the characteristics of transformation from old to new in the price control system.

Prior to 1979, the traditional pricing system was employed for BBF's output; BBF was forced to sell all its bicycles to the local commercial department. In 1979, the production cost of a no. 03-type bicycle manufactured at BBF was 141 yuan. This was 7 yuan higher than the producer price, and BBF paid no taxes on sale of this type of bicycle. The loss was subsidised by the Beijing no. 1 Commercial Department.

In 1980, production costs of the no. 03 bicycle were reduced from 141 to 122 yuan per set, and the producer price remained unchanged at 134 yuan. Under these circumstances, the Beijing no. 1 Commercial Department proposed to stop the 7-yuan subsidy to BBF, and require BBF to pay tax.

This proposal, however, was rejected by BBF.[39] It refused to sell its output to the Beijing no. 1 Commercial Department and decided to market its bicycles directly to wholesale and retail shops, at BBF asking prices. It sent an application to its higher authority, the Beijing Machinery Department, asking permission to increase its producer price to 147 yuan per set (a total of 122 yuan production cost, 20 yuan tax and 5 yuan profit). The Beijing Machinery Department allowed a price of only 144 yuan. BBF then appealed to the Beijing Price Bureau, and surprisingly the Beijing Price Bureau not only accepted its application but increased the wholesale price to 148 yuan. However, the Beijing Price Bureau prescribed that the 148-yuan price be temporary, and last only one year. To find a long-term solution, the Beijing Economic Commission called a meeting of the three institutions and BBF. No solution was reached in 1981, and the price of 148 yuan per set was in effect from 1980 to 1983.[40]

However, no satisfactory explanation was provided by the institutions as to why the criterion they applied to set the price of the bicycle varied: 134 yuan from Beijing no. 1 Commercial Department; 144 from the Beijing Machinery Department, and 148 from the Beijing Price Bureau.

3.5 SUMMARY

There were problems in each of the three stages of price formation, price determination and price implementation in the administrative price reform in China. In this chapter, we demonstrated that the pricing system became irrational and inefficient, due to not only the lack of a proper formula for calculation but also because of complicated power conflicts in the administrative process of price determination, and a lack of administrative capacity to implement policies.

With regard to price formation, we can say that the producer prices of many important goods were fixed neither according to a scientific method nor a uniform theoretical formula. Price formation for producer and procurement prices between 1950 and 1952 was based on a simple and practical basis. It involved four methods: the model cost method; the deduction method; the individual firm actual cost method; and, finally, historical price data.

In the post-reform period there was also no unique theoretical blueprint applied to the reform of fixed producer and procurement prices. Although some theoretical proposals for resolving the problems of price formation were suggested by Chinese economists, the actual system of determination and adjustment of prices developed in different ways for different commodities. Criteria considered included: international prices; cost structures and price ratios; peasant income; supply and demand; state revenue; improvement of quality; and, finally, political compromise.

The main difference between the pre- and post-reform periods was that the government placed more emphasis on the supply and demand, quality, and price ratio and cost structure criteria for price formation and adjustment in the latter period. These three criteria were taken into account for commodities such as coal, steel, cotton, and bicycles. In Chapters 4 and 5, we shall examine how price changes (adjustment) affected the total output and output composition of these commodities.

4 Price Regulation in Intersectoral Total Output

Chapter 4 examines the effect of administered prices on output in the cotton and coal sectors. Before focusing on the output effects of price adjustment in the post-reform period, we first examine the political and economic devices used by the government to regulate the output of cotton and coal in the pre-reform period.

In order to identify which method – direct or indirect planning – had the greatest effect on output, we study both the relationship between price adjustment and output and the relationship between cost and price. We examine the effects of price changes on cotton output at the national, provincial and district levels. In the coal sector, we consider the relationship between price increases and output, and between price stagnation and output.

4.1 EFFECTS OF DIRECT AND INDIRECT PLANNING ON OUTPUT

Since 1950, the government has tried various ways of regulating the output of industry and agriculture, including price and income policies; planning targets; quota systems; contracting systems; leadership persuasion; and changing from commune to household responsibility systems. These ways can be divided into direct planning methods (using non-price factors such as production targets quantitatively specified) and indirect planning methods (using price incentives). The government decided that indirect planning methods should play a fundamental role in determining cotton output after 1978, and coal output after 1979.[1]

A. Effects of Direct and Indirect Planning on Cotton Output

The alternation and periodicity of direct and indirect planning greatly affected both the growth rate and the composition of aggregate farm output, and the efficiency of resource allocation (Lardy, 1983b).

Lardy defined direct planning as the planning of total farm output in quantity terms. It was characterised by the imposition of detailed sown area and output targets and specific cropping patterns on production units by higher-level authorities. When the State decided to employ this type of planning to regulate output, the central government set targets aimed at increasing output rather than net farm income. Price, thus, had little effect on output.

Indirect planning, again based on Lardy's definition, was characterised by use of price incentives in encouraging agricultural output. It involved:

> more sophisticated manipulation of relative agricultural procurement prices to influence the allocation of land, labour, and other current inputs among alternative crops; greater freedom of agricultural production units to specialise in production based on their comparative advantage; rising rates of marketing based on both state purchases and flourishing rural peasant markets; larger and more efficient rural credit markets; and larger and more secure private plots (Lardy, 1983b : 19).[2]

Indirect planning accelerated the growth of agricultural output. In other words, it affected a broad range of crops including grains, cotton, sugar, and oil-bearing seeds (Lardy, 1983b). This pattern of growth – a simultaneous expansion of both grain and commercial crops – refuted the traditional view which presumed that commercial crop production could expand only with a reduction in grain production (Lardy, 1983b : 93; Leeming, 1985 : 168–9).

Indirect planning also affected the crop mix, steering it towards targets. It encouraged the efficient use of mixture inputs, increasing the productivity of labour and land. It also induced more efficient investment, and the adoption of new, lower-cost, agricultural technology (Brown, 1978 : 84–9; Krishna, 1967 : 503–17).

Other factors such as the exchange of chemical fertilisers for cotton, the guarantee of an adequate supply of cereals for peasants engaged in cotton production [3] and the application of the responsibility system also affected cotton output. However, in this chapter we focus on the affects of the price mechanism.

B. Effects of Direct and Indirect Planning on Output of Coal

The government used direct planning to motivate coal output in the pre-1979 period and price incentives in the post-1979 period.

Prior to 1979, output expansion was stimulated by the use of planning targets and other political and economic policies. During the 1957–79 period, production and costs fluctuated nearly every year, but there were only a few marginal price adjustments (see Table 3.4). Price adjustment on each occasion was stated to be designed for reducing coal mines' financial deficits, not for stimulating output.

Between 1979 and 1982, the price system for coal was based on the adjustment model. It was not designed to affect resource allocation, and had little effect on coal output. Producer prices of coal were increased to compensate for increased production costs and the financial losses accumulated in previous years.

The output of the state coal mines[4] decreased between 1979 and 1981. In order to increase coal output in the short term, prices were adjusted for the output of state coal mines and liberalised for the output of small, local coal mines. Coal output grew significantly after 1982 (increasing by 40 per cent, from 622 million tons in 1981 to 872 million tons in 1985). Whether this rapid growth of the nation's coal output was an outcome of price adjustment for state coal mines, or an outcome of price liberalisation for small coal mines, is discussed in later sections of this chapter.

4.2 CASE STUDY – COTTON

In China, indirect planning was employed to counter serious declines in production due to war, natural disaster and the disturbances of political movements (Perkins, 1966; Lardy, 1983b; Walker, 1984 : 783–812; Leeming, 1985). These factors affected and limited the function and effectiveness of direct planning, and the government thus demanded that direct planning give way to indirect planning (1961, 1965 and 1978–84). Whenever the goal of either restoration or expansion of output was achieved, the government would readopt direct planning (1956, 1958–60 and 1966–77), or a combination of direct planning and indirect planning (1985–7) to regulate output.

Indirect planning in the cotton sector was adopted several times for varying periods.[5] It predominated in the cotton sector in the post-1978 period.

A. Reemergence of Indirect Planning

In 1978, in order to increase the total output of cotton, the State Council urgently announced a revision of the price policy which increased the procurement price for cotton for a three-year period. This change was effected because of the serious decline in cotton output in the pre-reform period.

The *per capita* output of cotton fell by 11 per cent between 1957 and 1978;[6] the State had thus to import cotton.[7] The total output of cotton fell from 2.56 million tons in 1973 to 2.04 million tons in 1977, a decrease of 20 per cent. The decline of cotton output was due both to a shrinkage of sown area and to a decline in unit yield. The sown area for cotton was 1.9 per cent lower in 1977 than in 1973, which in turn was 22.5 per cent lower than in 1956. The average yield of cotton also deteriorated, falling from 69 jin per mu in 1973 to 56 jin per mu in 1977.

The reduction of cotton output between 1966 and 1977 was due to the application of direct planning (Lardy, 1983b). In this period, output targets could be obtained via direct commands to production units. Price incentives aimed at stimulating production or influencing the composition of output were curtailed.[8] The procurement price of cotton stagnated between 1965 and 1977, averaging 102.5 yuan per 100 jin (see Figure 4.1). At the local level, the procurement price was adjusted only once in Hangzhou and Jinhua in Zhejiang province during the thirteen years between 1964 and 1977 (interview, 1985). Stagnation in the procurement price of cotton distorted the cost–price relationship and discouraged the output of cotton. We next examine the cost–price relationship and then study the relationship between price and output.

B. Cost–Price Relationship[9]

Table 4.1 indicates a rising trend in the cost of cotton production – from 62 yuan per 100 jin in 1965 to 108 yuan in 1976, an increase of 73 per cent (Xu Yi, 1982 : 129). The total production cost per mu also increased 43 per cent in the same period (interviews with the State Price Bureau, 1985). The average procurement price increased from 92 yuan per 100 jin in 1965 to 107 yuan in 1976, an increase of 16 per

Figure 4.1

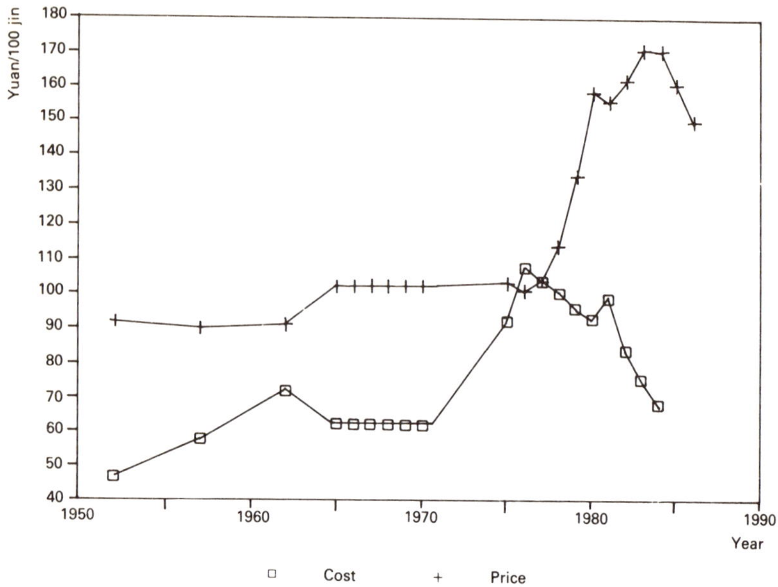

Sources: Production costs (1952–79) from Xu Yi (1982 : 129), (1980–4) from our own survey and interviews, 1984. Procurement prices (1952–85) from our own survey and interview, 1986.

cent (see Table 4.1); this increase was much lower than the increase in production costs in the same period. According to an investigation of 302 production teams carried out by Chinese economists in 1977, production costs plus taxes added up to 109 yuan per 100 jin, when the procurement price was only 106.7 yuan, 2 per cent less than production costs (Jiang Xingwei, 1980 : 75; Lardy, 1983b).

Comparisons of costs and prices (and 'profit' in Table 4.1) must be interpreted with caution, since the production costs include both labour and non-labour costs, and labour costs are based on a notional accounting wage.[10] The notional wage, which has no clear economic meaning, increased during this period. Xu Yi (1982 : 108) suggested, that at the national level, labour costs were kept at a uniform standard of 0.8 yuan per day from 1965 to 1980 and adjusted to 1 yuan in 1981. However, in the Pinghu prefecture, the cost of labour was 0.7 yuan per day in 1973, 1.05 yuan after 1974, and reached a level of 1.32 yuan in 1979 (interview, 1985).

Table 4.1 Cost–price relationship for cotton, 1976–9 (yuan/100 jin)

	1965	*1976*	*1977*	*1978*	*1979*	*1979 over 1965 (%)*
Price[1]	92.37	107.29	107.43	120.42	133.66	44.70
Cost[2]	62.44	108.10	103.95	100.99	95.54	53.01
Tax	5.39	4.41	5.63	9.82	5.19	-3.71
Profit (%)[3]	43.50	-2.78	-1.17	12.83	35.20	-19.08

Notes: 1. The procurement price in Table 4.1 is for standard size no. 3–27 cotton only; it is not the average procurement price of all cotton. 2. See Lardy (1983a) for more detail on the cost structure. 3. Ratio of profit to cost.

Source: Xu Yi (1982 : 79).

It is not possible with available data to separate total cost into labour and non-labour components, nor to decompose the change in labour cost into its constituent parts – that is, changes in the notional wage and changes in labour productivity. Nevertheless, the increase in total cost is largely due to a rise in non-labour cost.[11] This, because of the small increases in procurement prices, reduced the return to labour in cotton production relative to other crops. This appears to have led to a decrease in cotton output, a decline in productivity, an ill-conceived cropping pattern, a decline in *per capita* cotton cloth consumption, and huge imports of cotton from abroad (Lardy, 1983b: 64).

The crisis in cotton production and decrease in productivity prompted the government to restore production incentives by the use of indirect planning and curtailment of direct planning in 1978.

C. Price Adjustment

In 1978, the State Council decided to increase the price of cotton from 104 to 113.9 yuan per 100 jin, an increase of 9.5 per cent.[12] The effect of this price increase on cotton output was marginal in comparison to other crops. Even though output increased slightly (40,000 tons), *per capita* output increased from 4.5 to 4.6 jin, and output per mu also rose from 59 to 65 jin, still, the area sown to cotton declined from 4.86 million hectares to 4.51 million hectares, a shrinkage of 7 per cent (see Table 4.2).

The contraction in the area sown to cotton followed price adjustment as the level of price increase for cotton was less than that of

Table 4.2 Distribution of sown area between grain, cotton and oil seeds, 1977–83 (million hectares)

	1977	*1978*	*1979*	*1980*	*1981*	*1982*	*1983*
Grain	120 400	120 587	119 263	117 234	114 958	113 396	114 047
Cotton	4 845	4 867	4 512	4 920	5 185	5 828	6 077
Oil seeds	5 639	6 222	7 051	7 928	9 165	9 343	8 390

Sources: *China Statistical Yearbook*, (1985); see also Walker (1984 : 809).

other economic crops. The peasants, thus, converted land from cotton to other crops. Chinese economists have pointed out that land freed by the reduction of 0.36 million hectares sown to cotton and of 0.55 million hectares sown to rice in 1979 was diverted mainly to producing oil seed crops. In later years even more area previously sown to grain was converted to oil seed sown since oil seed production was more profitable than cotton or grain (interview with the State Price Bureau, 1985) (see Table 4.2).

The ratio of profit to cost for oil seeds was 13.4 per cent in 1978, and it increased to 44.8 per cent in 1979 (Xu Yi, 1982 : 78–9). These ratios were higher than the corresponding ratios for rice (10.1 per cent in 1978 and 42 per cent in 1979), and cotton (12.8 per cent in 1978 and 35.2 per cent in 1979). As a result, the oil seed sown area expanded from 6.2 million hectares in 1978 to 7.05 million hectares in 1979, an increase of 13.7 per cent (see Table 4.2).

In 1979, in order to rationalise the relative prices of cotton and grain, and cotton and other economic crops, the government decided to raise the procurement price of quota cotton by 15 per cent (the actual increase was 17.6 per cent), and the premium price (*Chuoguo Jiajia*)of above-quota cotton by 30 per cent.[13]

Despite these changes, the price of cotton in 1979 was not yet in line with the preferred previous relative price level (based on the 1950s rate) which exchanged 1 jin of cotton for 8 jin of grain.[14] The government, therefore, decided to increase the procurement price of standard cotton, size no. 3–27, by another 10 per cent in 1980; the average procurement price of all sizes of cotton increased 18 per cent. Provinces in north China received an additional premium of 5 per cent in 1979 and 1980. From 1978 to 1980, cotton prices rose by 39 per cent in central China, and 50 per cent in north China (Lardy, 1983b).

Although the fixed procurement price for standard size no. 3–27 remained stagnant at 153 yuan per 100 jin from 1980 to 1983, the average procurement price of cotton rose in both 1982 and 1983 (see Figure 4.1). This price increase was due to decreases in purchasing quotas and the corresponding increase in above-quota production procured at higher prices and changes in the methods of calculating the procurement price.[15]

According to estimates of economists at the State Price Bureau, at the national level the average procurement price of cotton increased by 50 per cent from 1978 to 1985 (interview, 1985). This price increase had a great impact on efficiency and production. Farmers responded to the price increase not only by increasing cotton output, but also by reducing input use (production costs). Production costs decreased from 103.95 yuan per 100 jin in 1977 to 92.5 yuan in 1980, and to 75 yuan in 1983, a decrease of 38.6 per cent from 1977 to 1983 (see Figure 4.1).[16] This achievement significantly influenced peasant income.[17]

The effects of price changes on production included increases in total output, increases in output *per capita* and output per mu, and the expansion of sown acreage. These effects existed at the national, provincial and district levels.

D. Effects of Price Changes on Output

National Level

At the national level, price incentives, on the one hand, encouraged specialisation and the introduction of new types of cotton such as Lou Mian no. 1 and no. 6.[18] On the other hand, they led to rationalisation of the cropping pattern, both nationally and provincially. According to one World Bank Report (World Bank, 1985c : 11), there was an expansion of the cotton sown area in the areas of north China suited to cotton, and a decline in the less well-suited areas. In 1983 the planted area in Shandong province, the largest producing province, was 40 per cent greater than in 1981, while the area sown to cotton in Sichuan province fell approximately 50 per cent from 1981 levels.

The effects of price incentives on production at the national level include the following. First, output per mu in 1984 rose 86 per cent over 1979 levels. Second, the cotton sown area expanded from 67.68 million mu in 1979 to 103.85 million mu in 1984, an increase of 53.4 per cent. Third, the total output of cotton doubled from 1979 to 1983 and nearly tripled from 1979 to 1984 (see Figure 4.2). China became the biggest cotton producer in the world (see Figure 4.3) and cotton

Figure 4.2

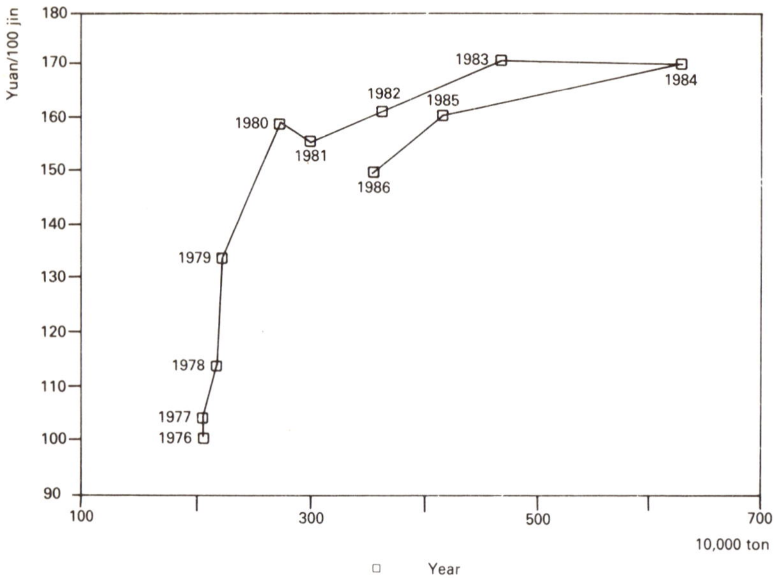

Sources: Output from *China Statistical Yearbook* (1986). Procurement prices from our own survey and interviews, 1985 and 1986.

imports declined. In 1983, the quantity of cotton imported fell to 10 per cent of the imports of the peak years of 1979 and 1980. An excess supply appeared – stocks of cotton reached 1.6 million tons in early 1984 – nearly half a year's consumption. China consequently became a cotton exporter.

Supply continued to grow, and by the end of 1984 the government was storing more than 50 per cent of the world's cotton stocks (Stone, 1988 : 124). In order to decrease cotton output, the government again used the price mechanism and reduced procurement prices (see Figures 4.1 and 4.2). Actually, both the direct planning mechanism (the contract system for cotton procurement, the imposition of a detailed sown area and the decrease of fertiliser allocations), and the indirect planning mechanism (the reduction of procurement prices) were employed by the government to regulate cotton production after 1984. There was an immediate decrease in cotton output between 1985 and 1986 (see Figure 4.2). Cotton farmers reported, in our 1985 interviews, that both direct and indirect planning had an impact on their cotton production decisions. Although most agreed

Figure 4.3

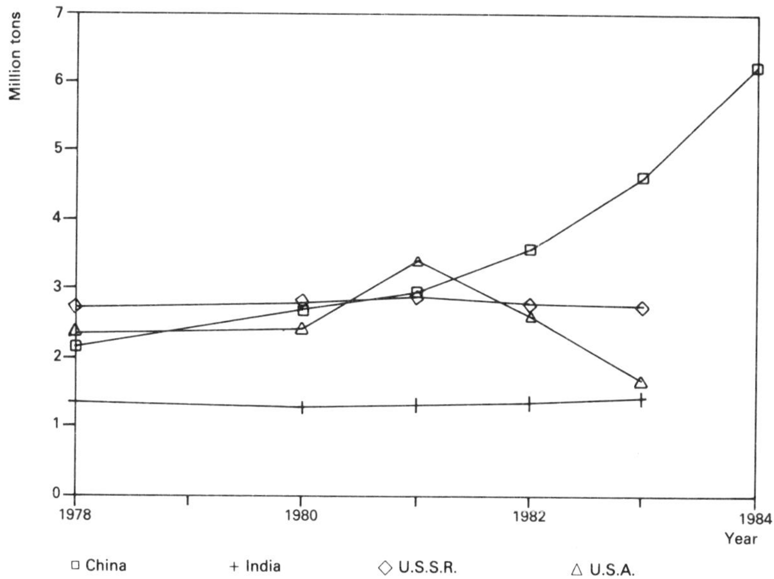

Source: *The Great Achievement of China's Agriculture, 1949–1984*, Beijing, China Statistical Press.

that price reduction was the fundamental factor affecting their decision, the effects of both indirect and direct planning on cotton output in the post-1985 period require further study.[19]

Provincial Level: Shandong Province

At the local level, we consider Shandong province where cotton production has undergone very dynamic changes. Shandong was one of the important cotton producing areas in the 1950s and 1960s, it became a modest cereal exporter in the 1970s, and then turned into the largest cotton producing region in the post-1981 period.

Cotton production in Shandong was concentrated in the prosperous northwestern prefectures in the 1950s.[20] By 1957, Shandong was one of the eight biggest cotton producing provinces. These eight provinces had a share of land sown to cotton which was greater than the national average, and together accounted for 80 per cent of China's cotton sown area and 82 per cent of production (Lardy, 1983b).[21] Cotton exports from Shandong to other parts of China in the 1950s reached a level of 75,000 (metric) tons annually, about 40 per cent of production (Lardy, 1983b). Some countries in the north-western province were renowned for the high income they derived from cotton production.

However, cotton production in Shandong started to decline in 1959 when policy shifted to emphasise grain production (Lardy, 1983b). Agricultural policy in this period (the 1960s and 1970s), was aimed at increasing grain production. Cotton was deprived of good land, water, fertiliser and labour (Leeming, 1985 : 171) and the government was unable to furnish cotton producers with grain (Leeming, 1985; Lardy, 1983b : 177). Nevertheless, this policy of 'taking grain as the key link and ensuring an all-round development' (*yiliang wei-gang*) was adopted. It distorted resource allocation and cropping patterns among agricultural goods.

One consequence of this shift in policy from cotton to grain was that Shandong province ceased to export cotton to other areas, and became a net exporter of food grain. The output of cotton of the four regions in Shandong province fell to 10 per cent of their average levels in the 1950s (Lardy, 1983b : 177). Cotton production fell below the raw material demand of textile plants in the region. According to Lardy (1983b), prior to 1980 provincial cotton output was sufficient to supply only 40 per cent of the raw material required to operate local textile mills. Shandong province thus imported about 68,000 tons of cotton in 1979.

By 1977, the government had become alarmed at the scarcity of cotton and the revenue spent on importing cotton. They consequently decided to adopt a new, indirect planning policy in Shandong. The policy was very successful. The cotton sown area expanded from 9 million mu in 1979 to 25.6 million mu in 1984; output per mu increased fourfold between 1978 and 1984 (interview, 1985).

Cotton production in 1984 jumped to 17 million tons, more than eleven times the level of 1978. This remarkable achievement marked Shandong's reemergence as an important supplier of cotton to other regions. It shipped out 247,500 tons in 1980 (Lardy, 1983b : 179). In 1984, after fulfilment of provincial demand, the state quota, the supply of 3.5 million tons to other regions, and the export of 0.45 million tons, Shandong still stocked 1 million tons of cotton (Xu Honggao *et al.*, 1984 : 17–21).

Figure 4.4

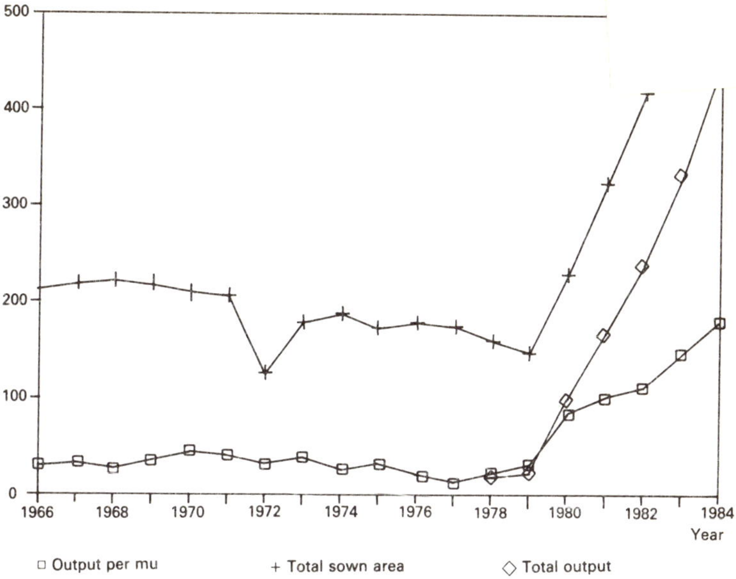

Source: Our own survey and interviews, 1985 and 1986.

E. District Level: Dezhou

Dezhou district, located in northwestern Shandong province, includes 13 prefectures. Over a twenty-year period, 1960–80, the average annual cotton sown area remained at approximately 2 million mu, average cotton output per mu was about 32 jin (see Figure 4.4), and total output oscillated between 0.25 and 0.4 million tons.

After 1979, this district experienced a rapid growth in cotton output and income. Figure 4.4 shows that the cotton sown area tripled, from 1.48 million mu in 1979 to 4.90 million mu in 1984. Yield per mu was 4.7 times higher in 1984 than in 1979. The output of cotton increased steadily from 1979 to 1984: by 322 per cent in 1980, by 69 per cent in 1981, and by 35 per cent in 1984. Dezhou district became the biggest producer and exporter of cotton in Shandong province.

The information and evidence in the above case study thus suggests that the increased procurement price between 1977 and 1984 did have positive effects on the total output of co•ton. In other words, the administrative procurement price did play a resource allocation role in cotton in this period.

4.3 CASE STUDY – COAL

Price reform of the coal industry had endured a more complicated process compared with the case of cotton. According to Lu Nan (1985), Director of the Price Research Institute at the State Price Bureau, the price reform of coal in the Sixth Five-Year Plan was only an initial step. More reform policies will be implemented in the coal industry in the 7th Five-Year Plan (interview, 1985).

The government has been very cautious in its reform of the price of coal since it involves political conflicts among administrative institutions, producers and industrial coal users.[22] If the producer price is to have an effect on output, it probably needs to rise a substantial amount in one stroke, to stimulate the output of coal mines. 'One-stroke reform' (*zuoda bu*) would bring dramatic changes to the financial circumstances of many enterprises and institutions and might cause a cost-push inflationary spiral (Xu Yi, 1982 : 155). Since coal dominates the structure of energy consumption and production, policy has to be simultaneously concerned with controlling the overall price level and increasing the price of coal. To deal with this dilemma, the government adopted multiple reform methods in the coal industry in the post-1979 period.

The first, marginal reform method – price adjustment – was adopted for state coal mines between 1979 and 1981. This method was succeeded by a second method between 1982 and 1987, a combination of adjustment and liberalisation. The third model was one of price liberalisation – relaxing price controls – for the output of small coal mines.

The advantages of applying a number of different methods in reforming the price of coal was, first, that the State could control the price level of coal by determining the price increase for the output of the state mines (interviews with the State Price Bureau, 1985). Second, the State could employ premium prices to encourage more above-quota output from central and local coal mines. Third, the free price system could be used to inspire villages and townships to develop additional small coal mines with little government capital.

The immediate effects of the various reform methods, according to reports in *Renmin Ribao* (1 January 1987) and *China Daily* (24 November 1986), were that coal production had matched consumption, and that the excess demand for coal had eased by the end of 1985. The equilibrium between production and consumption, reflected by price decreases, might have been just a temporary phenomenon.[23] However, it indicated that even in the short term some of the reform methods had positive output effects.

In order to identify which method was most effective and to learn how the government proceeded with its various methods of reform in the coal industry, some aspects of the relationship between price and output should be examined. They include the relationship between production and consumption, the price–cost relationship, and the price effect on output.

A. Production and Consumption

The relationship between the production and consumption of coal can be examined at both the national and local level. At the national level, aggregate supply appeared to equal aggregate demand; however, at the local level, evidence shows that coal shortages existed both before and after 1979.

The relationship between production and consumption at the national level has been studied by Kambara (1984), Pannell and Ma (1983), Nakajima (1985) and a research group in the World Bank (1985b). They reached some common conclusions: first, that coal production was crucial to past and future industrialisation. Coal accounted for approximately 70 per cent of primary energy consumption from 1976 to 1984 (see Table 4.3).

Second, the long-term development of coal production should rely on state coal mines and not on small coal mines. The target annual output of 1200 million tons for the year 2000 should depend mainly on further strengthening of production incentives and a large amount of state capital investment for state coal mines (Kambara, 1984; Nakajima, 1985; World Bank, 1985b).

Third, at the aggregate level, the likelihood of serious coal shortages and supply demand imbalances fell as coal production steadily increased (Nakajima, 1985; Pannell and Ma, 1983). China was self-sufficient in coal; between 1976 and 1984 almost 99 per cent of the coal was consumed domestically and 1 per cent exported (Pannell and Ma, 1983 : 197, World Bank, 1985b) (see Table 4.3).

Table 4.3 Production and consumption of coal, 1974–84 (millions of tons of coal equivalent)

Year	*1976*	*1977*	*1978*	*1979*	*1980*	*1981*	*1982*	*1983*	*1984*
Coal:									
Production	345.4	393.4	441.4	453.9	443.0	444.0	475.7	510.7	551.4
Exports	2.3	2.6	3.1	4.6	6.1	6.3	6.3	6.4	n.a.
Consumption	343.1	390.8	438.2	449.3	436.9	437.7	469.4	504.3	n.a.
Consumption structure									
Coal (%)	69.9	70.2	70.7	71.3	71.8	72.7	73.9	n.a.	n.a.
Oil (%)	23.0	22.6	22.7	21.8	21.1	19.9	18.7	n.a.	n.a.
Gas (%)	2.8	3.1	3.2	3.3	3.1	2.9	2.6	n.a.	n.a.
Hydro-electricity (%)	4.3	4.1	3.4	3.6	4.0	4.5	4.8	n.a.	n.a.

Sources: Ma Hong (1983 : 197); World Bank (1985b : 2); Kambara (1984 : 764).

However, at the local and sectoral levels, the problem of supply and demand imbalances in coal persisted throughout the pre- and post-reform periods (1979–85). For example, in 1979, according to a government investigation of Liaoning province, 1120 of the total 6618 rural and prefecture enterprises (16.9 per cent) suspended manufacturing for the entire year due to the shortage of coal and other sources of energy.

Moreover, between 1979 and 1983, Shanghai (which contributed one-sixth of national revenue) and certain areas of Eastern China faced a shortage of 20 million tons of coal annually.[24] In 1984, according to the state plan, Jiangsu province should have been allocated 24 million tons of coal. They received only 16 million tons – a shortfall of 33 per cent of their total requirements (Yamanouchi, 1986 : 5).

Coal shortage stemmed from both external and internal factors (interviews with Lu Nan and Chen Dezun, 1985; see also Ye Ruixiang, 1983). The external factors included the rising demand for coal from all sectors, especially the rural manufacturing sector after 1979; the inefficiency of power utilisation by coal consumers; and inadequate transportation capacity (World Bank, 1985b : 99–105). The internal factors which affected coal output were the production conditions; the problem of high production costs; and low prices (Ye Ruixiang, 1983; Hu Changnuan, 1982, 1985; Chen Dezun, interview, 1985, Lu Nan, interview, 1985). In the next section we examine the relationship between production costs and producer prices.

B. Price–Cost Relationship

Prior to 1985, the producer price of coal was adjusted four times: in 1958, 1962, 1965 and 1979. It increased from 12.05 to 22 yuan per ton between 1958 and 1984, an increase of 84 per cent (see Table 3.4). In the same period, production costs increased from 9.8 to 22 yuan per ton, an increase of 125 per cent. By 1981, the production cost of coal was equal to the producer price.

Between 1959 and 1979 production costs fluctuated at regular five- to six-year intervals. In 1962, 1967, 1974, and 1979 production costs reached a peak of 17 yuan per ton, and then slipped to between 14 and 16 yuan per ton before once again climbing back to 17 yuan.[26] Each large cost increase was mainly due to raw material and wage bill increases.[27]

Although production costs peaked in 1962, 1967, 1974 and 1979, only in 1962 did production costs exceed producer prices. In the other years, the gap between cost and price was quite narrow, especially between 1964 and 1978, as the producer price was not adjusted for 14 years. Production costs rose as high as producer prices between 1981 and 1983. In 1983, according to Gao Xiang (1986 : 403), 60 per cent of the state coal mines had average production costs 1.5 per cent higher than producer prices. After 1984, national average production costs exceeded producer prices.

Hu Changnuan (1982) argued that the relatively low coal prices negatively affected both the development of the coal industry and the development of the national economy, particularly since it did not encourage coal consumers to economise their consumption of coal.[28]

The relatively low price caused financial deficits in the coal industry in 1962, 1974, 1976, 1977 and 1983. In these years, the ratio of profits to costs per ton of coal was negative (Xu Yi, 1982 : 164; Gao Xiang, 1986). It is believed that 60 per cent (1962), 65 per cent (1977), 35–50 per cent (1979) and 60 per cent (1983) of state coal mines had to rely on government subsidies.[29]

The low price policy, Yamanouchi (1986) argued, prevented coal mines from seeking better mechanisation, advanced equipment and greater welfare of miners.[30] Production was also affected – little effort was made to raise resource-recovery rates. The State set a recovery target of 70 per cent, but state coal mines achieved no more than 50 per cent, and small coal mines, run by farmers, reached only 20 per cent (Yamanouchi, 1986). It has been argued that the low price policy also inhibited non-government investment in the coal industry from enterprises within the coal industry and from other private-sector sources.

The government was aware of the economic problems caused by the low price of coal, and made several attempts to resolve them by means of price adjustment.

C. Price Adjustments: 1958, 1962, 1965 and 1979

In 1957, the State Council stipulated that the average producer price of coal would increase by 2.64 yuan per ton in 1958, a rise of 20 per cent. This decision was made during a period of financial deterioration in the coal industry, with 50 per cent of state coal mines running losses (interview, 1985). The ratio of profit to cost in the coal industry was only 7 per cent, which was very low when compared to the 40 per cent ratio of the industrial sector as a whole (interview, 1985).

After the 1958 price adjustment, the ratio of profit to cost rose by 23 per cent, but this did not last long. Production costs of coal rapidly rose from 9.17 yuan per ton in 1960, to 14.5 yuan in 1961, and to 17.28 yuan in 1962 (Xu Yi, 1982 : 164). By the end of 1962, 60 per cent of state coal mines were making losses and the total financial deficit of the coal industry was approximately 400 million yuan (interview, 1985). The State thus increased the producer price by 2.86 yuan per ton in 1962, an increase of 15 per cent over the previous year. However, this price increase applied only to one particular type of coal – large-sized solid coal. The price adjustment of 1962 had little effect on the financial situation and output of state coal mines. According to an informal estimate by Chinese economists, 50 per cent of the state coal mines were in the red, even after the price adjustment (interview, 1985), and the coal industry fell into financial deficit again between 1962 and 1964.

The State Council decided to increase the producer price by a further 2.06 yuan per ton in 1965 (a rise of 11 per cent over 1964) to deal with these financial difficulties. Coal output jumped from 232 million tons in 1965 to 252 million tons in 1966. It appears that the price increase induced output; unfortunately, output dwindled from 252 million tons to 206 million tons in 1967. Whether or not the output increase in 1966 was due to the price increase of 1965 is a matter that will be examined carefully below.

From 1965 to 1978 the producer price stagnated at 18 yuan per ton. Even so, the coal industry enjoyed a high rate of profit from 1970 to 1973. The ratio of profit to cost in the coal industry was 22.9 per cent in 1970, 21.76 per cent in 1971, 17.61 per cent in 1972 and 14.13 per cent in 1973 (Xu Yi, 1982 : 164).

Since 1973 the financial situation of many coal mines deteriorated seriously due to the price stagnation. After increases in production costs, the profit to cost ratio was −3.38 per cent in 1974, −0.84 per cent in 1976 and −0.3 per cent in 1977 (Xu Yi, 1982). Even when the average profit–cost ratio was a positive 4.4 per cent in 1975, 60 per cent of the state coal mines were in deficit.

In 1977, the government proposed a plan of price adjustment but it was not implemented until 1979, when the government increased the price of coal by 5 yuan per ton for standard coal and by 6.12 yuan per ton for all other types of coal, an increase of 32 per cent over 1978 levels.

From 1958 to 1979, price adjustments were based on several conditions. First, price adjustments were made mainly to offset the financial deficits of state coal mines. They were not aimed at resolving the other economic problems mentioned above which were caused by the low coal prices. Second, the final decision behind each price adjustment was a result of power compromises among political institutions. Every proposal for price increases submitted by the Ministry of Coal Industry was cut or modified by the State Council due to political considerations.[31] This implies the government did not expect the price system to play the role of resource allocation for coal. We can thus assume that the increase in coal output was based on direct target planning and other economic policies, which are dealt with in the next section.

D. Price Effects on Output

We can examine price effects on output by first considering the relationship between price increases and output in 1958, 1962, 1965 and 1979 (see Table 4.4), and then the relationship between price stagnation and output in 1965–78 and 1980–5 (see Table 4.5).

Price Increase and Output

Table 4.4 suggests that output growth in 1959 and 1960 was a response to the price increase of 1958. Production from state coal mines rose by 41.7 per cent in 1959 and again by 12.5 per cent in 1960. However, Xu Yi (1982 : 160) argued that the sudden production increases were a result of the Great Leap Forward. This political

Table 4.4 Output and price changes, 1958, 1962, 1965 and 1979 (per cent)

Price increase	*20 (1958)*		*15 (1962)*		*11.2 (1965)*		*32 (1979)*	
Output from the State coal mines[1]	1959	41.7	1963	–0.6	1966	10.4	1980	–3.7
	1960	12.5	1964	0.6	1967	–23.5	1981	–2.7
	1961	–26.1	1965	6.7	1968	9.5	1982	4.4
Output from all mines[2]	1959	36.6	1963	–1.3	1966	8.6	1980	–2.3
	1960	7.5	1964	–0.9	1967	–18.2	1981	0.3
	1961	–29.9	1965	7.0	1968	6.7	1982	7.0

Sources: 1. For 1958–68 see *Almanac of China's Economy* (1985 : V-58); for 1979–82 see World Bank (1985b). 2. *China Statistical Yearbook* (1983, 1984 and 1986).

campaign was used to raise production, regardless of cost efficiency. When the political movement lost steam, output fell, and unit production costs rose due to deterioration in mine conditions.[32]

The price adjustments in 1962 and 1965 also seemed to affect output. Table 4.4 shows that output increased by 6.7 per cent in 1965 over with 1964, and again by 10.4 per cent in 1966 over 1965. However, some economists at the State Price Bureau believe the increase in coal output in these two years was caused mainly by the policy of 'Readjustment, Consolidation, Filling Out, and Raising Standards'[33] (*tiaozhen, gonggu, chongshi, tigo*), and less so by 1962 and 1965 price adjustments. This policy was interrupted by another political movement, the Cultural Revolution, and output fell, decreasing 23.5 per cent in 1967 from 1966 levels.

The price adjustment in 1979 did not encourage output. Output fell in 1980, decreasing 3.7 per cent, and again in 1981, decreasing 2.7 per cent, even after an increase of 32 per cent in the producer price (see Table 4.4). There is no officially published explanation of why the output of state coal mines failed to grow in these two years; price adjustments appear to have had little effect on coal output in the short term.

Price Stagnation and Output

1. 1965–78 There were two long periods of coal price stagnation: the first stretching from 1965 to 1978 and the second from 1980 to 1985.

Table 4.5 Relationship between price stagnation and output, 1969–78 and 1980–5 (yuan/ton).

	1969–78	*1980–5*
A. Price	18 yuan/ton	22 yuan/ton
B. Increase of output of State coal mines (%)[1]	78.7	20
C. Increase of output of all coal mines (%)[2]	132	40

Sources: 1. For 1958–68 see *Almanac of China's Economy* (1985 : V-58); for 1979–82 see World Bank (1985b). 2. *China Statistical Yearbook* (1983, 1984 and 1986).

Since production was seriously affected by the political campaigns of the 1966–8 period, and because output information was less reliable during this period, our analysis on the first period starts from 1969, when production returned to normal in most state coal mines.

As we can see from Table 4.5, even though prices stagnated from 1969 to 1978, both the national output of coal and the output of state coal mines increased steadily. The high rate of growth of coal production during this period was due not only to the state coal mines, but also to the important contribution of small coal mines, especially after 1970.[34] Output growth in the period of price stagnation was much higher than that of the period of price adjustment (see Tables 4.4 and 4.5). Output increases in this period were clearly independent of price movements.

2. 1980–5 During this period, coal output increased substantially. As Table 4.5 illustrates, output from state coal mines increased from 344 million tons in 1980 to 414 million tons in 1985, an increase of 20 per cent in five years. The output from all mines increased by 40 per cent over the same period. This overall increase masks an initial decline in output between 1979 and 1981, which was subsequently followed by a period of continuous growth. One factor which may have caused the decline of output in the 1979–81 period was that mines had previously neglected development of new seams.

However, the price adjustment of 1979 did not fulfil its goal of helping all state mines rid themselves of financial deficits. About 30 per cent of state coal mines were still making losses in 1979 after the price increases, and the number rose to 65 per cent in 1982 (Ye Ruixiang, 1983 : 611). The growing number of loss-making coal mines implied that the price increase in 1979 was lower that the increase in production costs, thus having little effect on output or efficiency.

New policies were implemented to counteract the serious problems encountered by the coal industry – an output decrease of 2 per cent nationwide, and 6 per cent in state coal mines; a production costs increase of 12 per cent in state coal mines; and increases in the number of loss-making state coal mines. Six new economic policies were implemented.

First, in 1982, the State Council permitted loss-making coal producers to charge additional fees for coal shipped to other provinces (Yamanouchi, 1986 : 5).

Second, in 1982, to increase output, the central government offered incentives to local government, such as lower sales taxes on local coal, and special subsidies for increasing coal shipments to other provinces and for surpassing production quotas (World Bank, 1985b : 94).

Third, in 1983, the central government instituted a system of premium prices for above-quota coal. The government decided to pay 20 per cent to 50 per cent premiums for coal produced by local mines in excess of plan quotas.[35] The premiums were applied to all local coal mines in 1984, and to state coal mines in 1985. The premium prices paid to state coal mines were 50 to 100 per cent higher than fixed quota prices.[36]

Fourth, the government encouraged villages and townships to develop a large number of small coal mines with little investment (Furusawa, 1984 : 4). Actually, small-scale collieries had expanded since the early 1970s;[37] however, it was not until 1983 that the State Council formally approved the report submitted by the Ministry of Coal Industry promoting small-scale coal mines.[38] The effects of the new policy were felt immediately: the number of small coal mines jumped from 16,000 in 1982 to 40,000 by the end of 1983, and then to 50,000 in 1985 (*Economic Daily*, 10 May 1985).

Fifth, in 1984, the State Council implemented another policy, 'The General Contract Responsibility System' (*Zhong Chenbao*), for state coal mines. Under this policy, the Ministry of Coal Industry signed a contract with the State Council to take responsibility for the fulfilment of three requirements: to increase coal output to 40 million tons annually; to reduce financial losses from state coal mines;[39] and to ensure a normal rate of increase of capital construction (*jiben jianshe*) in the coal industry (*Economic Daily*, 13 September 1985).

Table 4.6 Raw coal production by mine type, 1978–85

	1978	*1979*	*1980*	*1981*	*1982*	*1983*	*1984*	*1985*
Shares of output (%)								
A. State mines	55.3	56.4	55.5	53.8	52.5	50.8	49.0	47.5
B. Local mines	28.6	26.9	26.2	25.8	25.6	25.4	25.3	26.5
C. Small mines	16.1	16.7	18.3	20.4	21.9	23.8	25.7	26.0
D. Total	100	100	100	100	100	100	100	100
output (million tons)	618.0	635.5	620.1	621.6	666.3	715.0	789.0	872.0

Sources: 1. For 1979–83 see the World Bank (1985b : 91). 2. For 1978 see *The Great Achievement of China's Agriculture* (1984 : 130); 3. For 1984 and 1985 see *China Statistical Yearbook* (1986 : 215) and *Renmin Ribao* (26 February 1987).

Finally, in 1984, the State formally applied the free price system to stimulate the output of small coal mines.[40] By 1985, two more reform methods had been adopted in addition to adjustment: liberalisation, which applied to small coal mines; and a combination of adjustment and liberalisation for state coal mines.

These policies and methods led to a significant growth in coal output beginning in 1982. At the national level, coal output increased from 622 to 666 million tons from 1981 to 1982, and to 872 million tons by 1985; the average annual rate of increase was 10 per cent between 1982 and 1985 (see Table 4.6).

Table 4.6 reveals that the major contribution to increases in coal output between 1978 and 1985 came from small mines. The output of coal from these small mines increased from 99.79 million tons in 1978 to 227 million tons in 1985, an increase of 127.4 per cent. The percentage increase in output from state coal mines, 18.3 per cent from 1982 to 1985, was much lower than that of the small mines. Liu Xiangyang, Deputy Director of the Energy Bureau at the State Economic Commission, stated that without price liberalisation, the high rate of output increases from small coal mines could not have been achieved (*Economic Daily*, 16 July 1985): in other words, the 40 per cent growth of national output between 1980 and 1985 would have been impossible.

Some Chinese officials believed the increase of 27 million tons of output from state coal mines between 1984 and 1985 was mainly a result of 'The General Contract Responsibility System'.[41] This policy was effective in certain coal mines but less effective than the premium price policy applicable to state coal mines. Both the contract responsibility system and the premium pricing system were based on a reform model which involved a combination of adjustment and liberalisation.

4.4 SUMMARY

In the post-reform period, price adjustment had significant effects on the production of certain commodities, but little effect on others. The reason for the success of price adjustment as a means of regulating cotton, but not coal, output appears to have been, first, that cotton supply was more price-responsive; farmers were more sensitive to financial incentives than state enterprises. Furthermore, farmers could switch from one crop to another, but coal mines did not have this option.

Second, political conflicts concerning administered price changes were probably stronger for coal than for cotton.[42] This was partly because the producer price of coal affected many sectors while the price of cotton affected mainly the textile sector. The conflicts between the textile industry and the cotton sector could be resolved relatively easily by a financial subsidy from the government. Moreover, the textile industry's resistance to a cotton price increase was probably reduced by its expectation that a subsidy would be provided to prevent increases in the retail prices of clothing, a politically sensitive issue. The size of the subsidy required for coal, and the more indirect relationship between coal prices and other retail prices for consumer goods, made such a subsidy unlikely.

The cotton sector, from 1978 to 1986 provides an example of the successful application of administered price adjustment in regulating output. Between 1978 and 1984, increases in procurement prices eliminated a serious shortage, and price reductions between 1985 and 1986 solved the subsequent problem of excess output. It was not easy to judge the correct degree of price adjustment, but a trial and error process was possible.

In the coal sector, the first reform method price adjustment had little affect on output. Producer prices were too low, and adjustments were difficult because of conflicts of interest over price increases. For these reasons, new policies were adopted by the government, which first adopted a combination of adjustment and liberalisation for state coal mines[43] and then price liberalisation for small coal mines.

The latter two methods played significant roles in state coal mines and in small coal mines between 1983 and 1986. The increased coal output from 1982 to 1986, especially the 10 per cent average increase per year between 1983 and 1985, was mainly due to the development of small coal mines.[44] From the short-term point of view, it appears that the liberalisation reform method, as applied to small coal mines was more effective than the method of a combination of adjustment and liberalisation, as applied to state coal mines.

5 Price Regulation in Intrasectoral Output Composition

In Chapter 4, we demonstrated that price adjustment was successfully used to regulate total cotton output, but not the coal output of state mines. In this chapter we examine the role of producer price adjustments in altering the composition of output within particular sectors, with special reference to the problem of the coexistence of shortages and surpluses of certain products. We empirically investigate this problem by using the steel and bicycle industries as case studies. We believe that irrational price ratios are one cause of the coexistence of shortages and surpluses, but the fundamental cause of this problem lies in the system of direct administrative control, and not merely in the prices system *per se*.

5.1 COEXISTENCE OF SHORTAGE AND SURPLUS

A. Symptoms

Substantial output increases in both the steel and bicycle industries in the post-1979 period failed to ease domestic shortages; the government was pressed to import more steel and to ration certain types of bicycles. Simultaneously, large inventories of unsold steel and bicycles existed.

Steel

The coexistence of shortages and surpluses in steel is a long-standing problem. At the end of 1979, the inventory level of steel commodities unused because of their poor quality, inappropriate sizes and shapes, and other reasons, reached 19.6 million tons, nearly half of the level of steel output of that year (Zhang Shuguang, 1981 : 54). At the same time, imports of steel were increasing substantially. They averaged 5 million tons in 1976 and 1977, and increased to 8.64 million tons in

1978, 27 per cent of the total domestic output of that year (Zhang Shuguang, 1981).

In 1980, total output of finished steel products increased to 27.16 million tons;[1] steel inventories increased to 20 million tons; and an additional 5 million tons of steel was purchased from abroad (Yang Hongdao, 1983 : 18; *Statistical Yearbook of China*, 1985 : 337; Furusawa, 1984). By 1985, total output of finished steel had increased substantially, reaching a level of 40.5 million tons, an augmentation of 49 per cent over 1980; however, the problem of the coexistence of shortages and surpluses was not resolved. Inventory levels reached 26 million tons in 1985, an increase of 30 per cent over 1980 (see Table 5.2); steel imports increased to 20 million tons in 1985, an increase of 300 per cent over 1980.

Bicycles

In the bicycle industry, good-quality bicycles, especially the top three brands (Forever, Flying Pigeon, and Dragon-Phoenix) were in excess demand and had to be rationed. In contrast, inferior bicycles (such as Beijing's Swallow and Shamong's Wuyi) were in excess supply, and yet continued to be manufactured.

B. Theoretical Explanations

Two theoretical positions have been taken with regard to the problem of coexistence of shortage and surplus. Those holding the first position believed that 'overproduction of abundant products and underproduction of scarce products' was due to incorrect price ratios.[2]

This position was taken by two groups of people:[3] first, academic economists[4] in universities or research institutions; and, second, applied economists[5] who worked for the central government, especially in the State Price Bureau (the former Price Research Centre of the State Council) and elsewhere.[6] They suggested that a correction of irrational price ratios by the price authorities or other relevant institutions (including enterprises) could resolve the problem.[7] This was not a new remedy: it had been proposed in the debates of the 1950s and 1960s.

This view was accepted by the Chinese government in the Third Plenary Session of the Twelfth Central Committee of the Communist Party of China in 1984. The government admitted that the problem of coexistence of shortages and surpluses in production was due to 'inadequate price differentials for a given product with diverse quality', and 'irrational price ratios between different commodities'. As the vice-premier of the State Council, Tian Jiyun (1985 : 17) explained:

> Fine-quality products cannot have their prices raised and poor-quality goods cannot have their prices reduced. Therefore, the supply of fine-quality products falls short of demand, but production cannot be developed because of low prices. Poor-quality products do not sell well and they get stock-piled, but their production cannot be reduced.

The government thus insisted that a reform of the price system, 'getting the price ratios right', was the key to solving the problem of coexistence and also to reforming the entire economic system (Ma Kai, 1987 : 11; Rosario, 1987 : 75).

The first position was criticised by those holding the second position, who believed that prices had an effect, though only a rather weak one, even in the post-reform period.[8] They argued that it was impossible to eliminate the general problem of shortage and to resolve the problem of coexistence of shortages and surpluses simply by providing a set of 'correct prices'.[9]

The problem of coexistence, according to Kornai (1980; 1985; 1986), is rooted in the resource constraints and the soft-budget constraints generated by the socialist economic system itself. He writes:

> in the resource-constrained system shortage depends not on the supply side but on the demand side . . . Supply can be of any size if demand always tends toward infinity. And this is exactly the situation if the budget constraint of the firm is not hard enough and if no economic force operates to constrain demand. Under such circumstances the firm's demand for both current and capital inputs is almost insatiable. Whatever the relative prices of inputs are, there are and always will be numerous inputs for which demand is unsatisfied (1980 : 349–68).

This statement implies that, at the aggregate level, the fundamental cause of shortage is the constant unsatisfied demand for inputs from enterprises based on 'the soft-budget constraint system' and not the irrational pricing system. A resolution to the problem of coexistence therefore, requires a reform of the entire economic system, not merely a reform of the pricing system. Price reform should shift toward a greater consideration of the problem of 'price responsiveness',[10] instead of merely concentrating on which formula to adopt in order to correct the price ratio. The dominant thought on price reform changed in 1985, following a growth in the belief of the Economics of Shortage theory among the Chinese economists.

In this chapter, we use case studies of the steel and bicycle industries to examine the following hypotheses:

1. At the sectoral level, the problem of coexistence of surpluses and shortages in these two industries sprang mainly from the economic system, and especially from its resource constraints and soft-budget constraints. Irrational price ratios also had an impact on this problem, but it was secondary in nature.
2. In the steel industry, at the sub-sectoral level, in terms of short-term adjustment, some mills were responsive to producer prices for output (but much less responsive on the input side). For some steel commodities, favourable prices encouraged an increase in surplus production while unfavourable prices (low prices) kept steel mills from manufacturing certain products and thus worsened their shortage. However, this was not the fundamental cause of the coexistence problem.
3. In the bicycle industry, at the sub-sectoral level, in terms of short-run adjustment, the response to relative price changes on the output side was rather weak compared with the steel industry (and also weak on the input side). Irrational price signals may have affected the problem of coexistence of surplus and shortage, but their effect was weaker than other economic and political factors.

The above hypotheses are tested by a study of the relationship between the effects of price factors and non-price factors on output in these two sectors.[11] Before we identify whether price factors or non-price factors were the main cause of the problem of the coexistence of shortage and surpluses, we need to look at the relationship between production and consumption in these two sectors.

5.2 PRODUCTION AND CONSUMPTION[12]

Prior to 1979, the steel industry was regarded as the 'key link' to industrial development, and output targets for other industries were calculated to accommodate steel's output target. The clearest example of this was during the period of the Great Leap Forward, 1958–60, when the government launched the 'backyard furnace' movement (Deng Liqun *et al.*, 1984 : 337–40; Wu, 1965 : 118–23). After 1979, steel output was no longer given top priority, and thus steel lost its dominance as the key sector (Findlay and Xin, 1985 : 15–22). The new production policy had little effect on the steel industry. Although the total output of steel did not decrease, steel constantly remained in short supply, and yet steel inventories increased substantially, particularly after 1979 (see Table 5.2).

Prior to 1979, development of the bicycle sector was not encouraged by government policy and this sector was particularly ignored during the Cultural Revolution years of 1966 and 1976. After 1979, the government promoted rapid development despite poor production capacity and backward technology. The post-1979 policy largely resolved the problem of shortage at the sectoral level. However, some brands of bicycles remained in shortage and others came into surplus.

The shortages and surpluses in these two industries during the reform period were not mutually exclusive but closely associated with each other. This unusual situation is further illustrated below.

A. Bicycles: 1952–85

Pre-1979

The development of the bicycle industry can be divided into several periods. During the first period, 1952–7, the bicycle sector was in an initial stage (total output in this period, 2.4 million sets, did not meet the demand of 3.2 million, and 900 thousand sets were imported: interview, 1985). In the second period, 1958–65, the bicycle industry followed a oscillating path: output was determined mainly by political and economic policies, rather than by demand.[13]

During the third period, 1966–76, the bicycle sector developed slowly, but steadily. At the beginning of this period, both central and local governments were reluctant to promote the development of this sector, and thus consumption exceeded production. Annual output increased by an average of 0.4 million sets, a rate far below the rate

Table 5.1 Growth rates of production and consumption in the bicycle industry, 1979–85 (%)

	1979	*1980*	*1981*	*1982*	*1983*	*1984*	*1985*
Production[1]	18	29	34	38	14	4	12.8
Consumption[2]	18	24	34	39	18	9	8

Sources: 1. *China Statistical Yearbook* (1985 and 1986). 2. *China's Trade and Commercial Statistical Data* (1985).

of growth of demand (no detailed information on the demand structure of bicycles in this period was given in our interviews). The government thus initiated a policy of bicycle rationing in 1973 (interviews, 1985).

Post-1979

During the fourth period, 1979–86, and especially between 1979–82, the bicycle sector rapidly developed. Total output of bicycles increased at an annual average of 30 per cent between 1978 and 1982.[14]

During this period, the bicycle sector experienced its highest post-1966 rate of growth in both consumption and production. However, output growth dropped from 38 per cent in 1982 to 4 per cent in 1984, in response to a decline in the growth rate of demand which dropped from 39 per cent to 9 per cent in the same period. In 1985, output growth increased to 12.8 per cent, but the growth rate of demand decreased further to 8 per cent (see Table 5.1). This suggests that the hunger for bicycles was eased by rapid expansion of the bicycle industry in the post-reform period. The substantial drop in output during 1982 and 1985 indicates that the problem of the bicycle sector was no longer one of shortage at the sectoral level, but rather one of the coexistence of excess supply at the sectoral level and shortage, of particular brands, at the sub-sectoral level (survey in 1985 and the beginning of 1986 in Beijing and Shanghai).

The bicycle industry can be characterised by two main features. First, an inefficient expansion at the sectoral level. The rapid expansion of this industry between 1978 and 1982 increased the total number of enterprises engaged in bicycle production from 38 to 140. All but three of China's 29 provinces are now engaged in bicycle production (World Bank, 1985a : 81).[15]

The Chinese bicycle industry appears to have been expanding very inefficiently (World Bank, 1985a). The optimal scale of production requires an enterprise to produce between 300,000 and 500,000 bicycles per year. However, in 1982 average output per enterprise declined (from 225,000 in 1978) to 173,000 sets, and fourteen provinces produced fewer than 500,000 bicycles per year.[16] Not surprisingly, 37 enterprises out of the total 140 were making losses in 1982. Total losses reached 34 million yuan (Shu Rong *et al.*, 1984 : 36). Loss-making intensified in 1985; some bicycle enterprises completely stopped manufacturing and waited for the government to bail them out financially.[17]

Second, expansion was inefficient at the sub-sectoral level. Prior to 1985, overproduction of inferior bicycles seemingly could not be reduced, and underproduction of good-quality bicycles could not be increased.[18] For instance, in 1983, the total output of first-class bicycles[19] was only 7.72 million sets, 28 per cent of total production. Second-class bicycles (nine good local brands),[20] accounted for 6.89 million units, 25 per cent of total production. Third-class bicycles, mainly inferior types, accounted for 12.96 million sets, 47 per cent of total production. One outcome of this inefficient expansion was that first-class bicycles were in serious shortage and had to be rationed.[21] Not only was there a serious shortage of the top three brands, but second-class bicycles such as the Red Flag and the Golden Lion were also difficult to obtain in some places.[22] In contrast, the third-class bicycles, 45–47 per cent of total output, were unpopular and difficult to sell. Inventories of these bicycles increased after 1979. Excess bicycles stocks by the Central Commercial Department (*Shangye Bu*), 1.34 million sets in 1980, increased by 130 per cent to 3.08 million sets in 1982.[23] In 1983, the surplus increased to 3.47 million bicycles, 390 thousand sets more than 1982.[24]

How did this situation occur? What are the main factors causing the problem of coexistence between shortage and surplus? Are they price factors or non-price factors? Which factors were regarded as fundamental by the government? And how did the government try to affect them? What proposals were made? These issues are discussed below after a study of the asymmetric problem in the steel industry.

B. Steel

The coexistence of shortages and surpluses existed at both the sectoral and sub-sectoral levels of the steel industry. At the sectoral level,[25] for each of the 29 years from 1953 to 1981, excluding 1958–60,

Table 5.2 Output, imports, exports and inventory of finished steel, 1977–86 (million tons)

	1977	*1978*	*1979*	*1980*	*1981*	*1982*	*1983*	*1984*	*1985*	*1986*
Production[1]	16.33	22.08	24.97	27.16	26.7	29.02	30.72	33.71	36.93	40.58
Imports[2]	5.25	8.63	8.47	5.00	3.33	4.13	9.62	12.29	20.03	n.a.
Exports[3]	0.22	0.33	0.36	0.39	0.60	0.90	0.53	0.22	0.15	n.a.
Inventory[4]			19.60	20.00	20.00				26.00	30.79

Note: The 30.79 million tons of stockpiles of steel products in 1986 was only up to the end of June of that year; and it was 34 per cent more than the combined stockpiles of the USA and Japan, according to the *China Daily* (11 December 1987).

Sources: 1–3. *China Statistical Yearbook* (1981, 1984 and 1986); also see Findlay and Xin (1985 : 16–17). 4. Zhang Shuguang (1981 : 54); Yang Hongdao (1983 : 18); *Economic Daily* (14 September 1985); *Renmin Ribao* (15 March 1987); Gao Xiang (1986 : 103) Lin Wenyi and Jia Lurang (1981 : 30–37); Zhang Weida (1987 : 23); *China Daily* (11 December 1987); and Koshiro (1981 : 12).

steel inventory levels were approximately 50 per cent of annual output (Deng Liqun et al., 1984 : 351).

After 1979, and especially in 1985 and 1986, the shortage of steel, made up by imports, was almost equal in amount to the steel inventories of users and producers (see Table 5.2). For example, in 1985, the total output of finished steel was 36.93 million tons,[26] while inventory levels reached approximately 26 million tons. One report[27] stated that total steel production plus the inventory for 1985 would be 56.93 million tons, which should meet the demand of 50 million tons without imports. Actually, in 1985, total consumption of steel was 51 million tons[28], which included 31 million tons of domestically produced steel, and 20 million tons of imported steel.[29] Inventory reached 26 million tons.[30] The Stanford Research Institution expected shortages of steel of 20 million tons per year until the year 2000 (information derived from the teaching materials of the Planning and Statistics Department of the People's University of China, Chapter 5, 1985).

To determine which factors caused the problem of the coexistence of shortage and surplus in both the steel and bicycle industries we begin by examining the effects of price factors, and then go on to consider the effects of non-price factors.

5.3 PRICE INFLUENCE

A. Steel

In order to determine whether price factors (price ratios) affected the coexistence problem in the steel industry, we first look at the features of the irrational price ratios. We then examine indirect evidence and official information, which suggest that irrational prices were one of the important factors causing the coexistence problem.

Irrational Price Ratios

Irrational price ratios in the steel industry took several shapes: first, the price disparity between raw material, semi-processed and finished goods; second, the price disparity between different processed goods; and, finally, the price disparity between different finished goods. In this section we consider only the third type of disparity.

Price disparities between finished steel products had several different forms. One form was an irrational price ratio between two different goods of the same kind of steel. One case in point was the price difference between hot and cold rolled steel plates, resulting in varying profit yields. Technologically, there is little difference between the two production processes; however, the profit margin of the former amounted to 8508 yuan per ton, ten times higher than that of the latter.[31]

A second type of irrational price ratio was that between two different categories of steel. For example, 10mm mild steel round bars were priced at 455 yuan per ton and 6.5mm wire rods were priced at 470 yuan per ton prior to 1979. In August 1979, the price of the former was adjusted upward to 585 yuan per ton, 115 yuan higher than that of the latter whose price remained unchanged. This disparity resulted in a serious shortage of 6.5mm wire rods (Xu Yi, 1982 : 148).

A third type of irrational price ratio was that between different sizes of products in the same category of steel – for example, the price disparity between the 18mm and the 19mm mild steel round bars. 18mm mild steel round bars were priced at 495 yuan per ton; 100 yuan higher than the 19mm kind. Not surprisingly, producers preferred to manufacture the 18mm steel rather than the 19mm steel, and a shortage of the latter existed.

The irrational price ratios affected the precise types of steel in shortage – mainly small-size and construction steel, which required more complicated processing procedures and more advanced technology. The steel products in shortage were the same types imported between 1982 and 1985.[32]

Government Acknowledgement

The 'Statistical Report of the Metallurgy Department' (1983), and the State Price Bureau (interviews, 1985) confirmed that the shortage and surplus coexistence problem resulted from irrational price ratios. They discouraged the output of small-size and construction steel and encouraged the output of large-size steel.

Since large-size steel required less complicated processing and was the most profitable to produce, steel producers concentrated on producing it regardless of demand (Xu Wen, 1985). Thus, steel inventories were of large-size steel, including mild boiler plate, ship plate, silicon steel plate and high-quality stainless steel plate (Xu Wen, 1985 : 25). By the end of 1983, the inventory of ship plates and mild boiler plates had increased 23.68 per cent, and silicon steel plates 25.8 per cent over 1982 levels (Xu Wen, 1985). At the second annual steel conference in 1984, there was no demand for certain types of large-size steel. Not surprisingly, the inventory of this type of steel increased again.

Unfortunately, some of the issues relating to inventory problems have been explained neither by the Chinese government nor by economists. There is no explanation of why particular types of steel in short supply were imported while inventory stocks existed.[33] Besides, the government did not analyse the nature of its steel inventories. According to our 1985 survey, there were at least three forms of steel inventory (discussed below). Yet only the overproduction inventory received attention from economists prior to 1984. Moreover, no detailed information is available to break down the 26 million tons of 1985 steel inventory into types. Without such an analysis, it is hard to assess which factors – price or non-price – determined the coexistence problem in the steel industry. Finally, the government also failed to demonstrate that adjusting the price ratios of steel in 1980 and 1984 affected the composition of steel output.

B. Bicycles

Irrational Price Ratio

In the bicycle industry, as in the steel industry, the government and certain economists[34] identified irrational price ratios as the fundamental disease causing the coexistence of surplus and shortage.

Song Jianli (1986 : 30), Zhu Guanxiang (1984 : 49) and Liang Zhongxun (1983 : 44) exposed the fact that producer prices of bicycles were based not on the quality of the goods nor on the law of value, but rather on each enterprise's unit production cost. Such a method of price formation resulted in irrational price ratios, and thus caused the surplus and shortage coexistence problem.

When reform started in 1979, prices based on individual production costs – 'temporary prices' – were adopted by the government (Liang Zhongxun, 1983). This was done to promote the development of the bicycle industry in underdeveloped regions of the country, regardless of antiquated technology and high cost (Furusawa, 1984 : 2–6). In principle, the 'temporary price' was not supposed to last more than one or two years. Nevertheless, in many cases it continued in use and even became a formal administered price for poor-quality bicycles.[35]

The outcome of the 'temporary prices' policy was that unit production costs ranged from 70 yuan in Shanghai to more than 200 yuan in small enterprises in Jilin, Heilongjiang and Nei Menggu.[36] Producer prices also varied parallel with each enterprise's unit production costs. In some cases the producer, wholesale and retail prices of third-class bicycles were higher than those of the first-class bicycles (see Tables 5.3 and 5.5).

Liang Zhongxun (1983 : 44–5), Song Jianli (1986) and Zhu Guanxiang (1984) argued that irrational price ratios created the shortage and surplus coexistence problem in two ways. On the demand side, prices of good-quality bicycles were not high enough to reduce excess demand, and prices of poor-quality bicycles were not low enough to stimulate demand. On the supply side, irrational price ratios discouraged the production of large enterprises and encouraged the production of small firms. It became common for large enterprises to sell their good-quality bicycles at low fixed prices, and for smaller plants to receive high prices for their poor-quality bicycles.

Profitability and Output

To determine whether the above arguments put forward by the Chinese economists are valid requires a further analysis of the relationship between profitability and output, since Chinese economists have not yet tackled this relationship at the sub-sectoral level for firms of differing sizes and bicycles of varying qualities. There is also

Table 5.3 Wholesale prices and retail prices for two types of bicycles in five factories, 1983 (yuan/bicycle)

Location and brand of bicycles	*Types*	*Class*	*Wholesale prices*	*Retail prices*
Shanghai (Forever)	26QE16	1st	136.80	156
Shanghai (Dragon-Phoenix)	26QE65	1st	136.80	156
Shanxi (Yanhe)	26	3rd	142.00	162
Tianjin (Flying Pigeon)	23,24 inch	1st	137.20	156.40
Shanxi (Yanhe)	23,24 inch	3rd	143.00	163.00

Source: Liang Zhongxun (1983 : 43).

Table 5.4 Output, growth and profitability of the bicycle industry (yuan/set)

	Bicycle factories		
	Large 1st class	*Medium 2nd class*	*Small 3rd class*
a. Number of firms (1982)	3	9	128
b. Total output (1983) (million sets)	7.72	6.89	12.96
c. Growth rate of total output (1983) (%)	28	25	47
d. Number of firms in deficit (1982)	none	none	37
e. Total profit and tax handed to State (1982) (million yuan)		1st + 2nd = 550 (71%)	220 (29%)

Sources: Shu Rong *et al.* (1984 : 36); *Jingji Diaocha* no. 1 (1983 : 28); and our survey, 1985.

no explanation as to why the 37–57 loss-making enterprises (out of 140), continued to manufacture bicycles after 1982. One crucial question to be considered is thus – under what conditions could a loss-making bicycle firm continue to manufacture inferior bicycles when its finances were in the red? One other untouched problem is why large bicycle firms failed to increase their output as much as small firms. Finally, the nature of the bicycle industry inventory has not yet been analysed by Chinese economists.

We believe that the coexistence problem in the bicycle sector is derived mainly from the supply side; price factors were only secondary. Evidence shows that the increase in bicycle output was not determined mainly by profitability. At the sectoral level, there were only 12 bicycle firms making profits between 1981 and 1983. These 12 firms manufactured 14.61 million bicycles, 53 per cent of total production, and generated 71 per cent of the profits and taxes, 550 million yuan, in 1983 (see Table 5.4).

In contrast, the remaining 128 small firms, including 37–57 making losses, still produced 47 per cent of the bicycles (12.96 million sets) (see Table 5.4). This implies that the production of the third group of bicycle firms was not affected by price factors.

Sub-sectoral evidence shows that the linkage between price incentives and output was quite weak in both large and small enterprises. Table 5.5 shows that the producer price was 140 yuan per PA12 bicycle produced in Beijing (a third-class bicycle), while the price of the first-class PA12 bicycle produced in Shanghai was 133 yuan. Nevertheless, the latter had a much higher profit rate (33.8 per cent in 1982 and 27.8 per cent in 1983) than the former, which had only 0.7 per cent in 1982, and 2.89 per cent in 1983.

The high rate of profit in the Shanghai firm did not generate a substantial increase in output. There was an increase of only 3 per cent in 1983 over 1982. In contrast, BBF output increased 80 per cent in 1983, despite a profit rate of only 0.7 per cent in 1982.[37] The substantial increase in output of the BBF cannot be interpreted as arising only from price factors; non-price factors also need to be taken into account.

5.4 NON-PRICE FACTORS

Before studying the impact of non-price factors on the problem of coexistence, we need further to define the different characteristics of the problem of coexistence in the steel and bicycle industries.

The type of shortage and surplus coexistence in the bicycle industry can be termed a 'mixed-budget coexistence'. This term arises because consumers, on the demand side, face a hard-budget constraint (fixed income), while producers, on the supply side, face a soft-budget constraint. The type of shortage and surplus coexistence in the steel industry can be termed a 'soft-budget coexistence' since both the consumers and producers face soft-budget constraints.

Table 5.5 Comparison of production costs, producer prices and output for the PA12 bicycle in two factories, 1980–4 (yuan/bicycle)

Factory	*Year*	*Production costs*	*Tax (%)*	*Profit (%)*	*Producer prices*	*Output annual*	*Rate of output (%)*
Beijing	1980	112	15	5	140	114 000	58
	1981	108	15	7.85	140	157 000	37.7
3rd	1982	118	15	0.7	140	100 000	–36
Class	1983	115	15	2.89	140	180 000	80
	1984	120	15	–0.7	140	60 000	–67
Shanghai	1982	68	15	33.8	133	2 570 000	
1st Class	1983	76	15	27.8	133	2 650 000	3

Note: The rate of profit is on sales. Annual output includes all types of bicycles manufactured by these factories.

Source: Survey, 1985.

The 'soft-budget coexistence' of the steel industry caused three types of inventory; overproduction inventory; inferior-quality steel inventory; and hoarding inventory. The units which stocked inventory simultaneously faced a shortage of steel. They included producers, material allocation departments and users, all of whom faced soft-budget constraints. Not surprisingly, they all, especially the users, wanted to hold as much inventory as possible.

According to the *Economic Daily* (14 September 1985) the 26 million tons of steel inventory in 1985 could be broken down into the 20 per cent stocked by producers and material allocation departments and the 80 per cent stocked by users acting as production units. The 20 per cent of inventory steel included overproduction steel arising from the irrational price ratios, and inferior-quality steel caused by poor technology. In other words, irrational price ratios caused only a small part of the coexistence problem, and price factors were therefore secondary. The 80 per cent of inventory stocked by users included a relatively small quantity of unutilised steel of incorrect sizes and inferior quality, and a relatively large share of hoarding inventory. According to the *Renmin Ribao* (15 March 1987), 72 per cent of the increases in inventory in 1986 was due to hoarding by users. It is clear that the coexistence problem in the steel industry came mainly from the demand side, which was influenced by non-price rather than price factors.

The bicycle industry had only one form of inventory, that of inferior-quality bicycles. They were stocked only by producers and commerce departments, which faced soft-budget constraints. Consumers suffered from a shortage of good bicycles, and were unable to bid for good-quality bicycles at high prices in the black market since they faced hard-budget constraints.

A. Bicycles

The problem of coexistence in the bicycle industry mainly arose from the supply side. The overproduction of inferior bicycles was a result of a non-price factor such as an 'expansion drive',[38] based on soft-budget constraints. The underproduction of first-class bicycles was due to resource constraints. The expansion drive developed as a consequence of a change in economic policy which encouraged the development of this sector following the shortages of the Cultural Revolution period.

The financial protection system for firms was one of the fundamental factors in the expansion drive. In the traditional socialist economy firms received detailed output instructions from the government (central or local), and would sell their output to the relevant government departments at fixed prices. If the costs of production exceeded producer prices, then firms would expect a financial subsidy to cover their losses.

This soft-budget constraint system not only financially bailed out firms, but also encouraged them to fulfil their production targets by increasing inputs of labour and raw materials rather than by improving efficiency, productivity and technology.

The expansion drive in the bicycle industry was initiated mainly by local governments. According to our survey in 1985, local governments were very keen to launch the programme of promoting local bicycle industries since they would create jobs for the local population and bring profit revenue to the local government. It contradicted the central government's policy on the development of the bicycle industry. At the end of 1981, the Machine Committee of the State Council decided to expand the total number of bicycle enterprises from 45 to 57 in 1982. However, by the end of 1982, the total number of enterprises reached 140: the extra 83 bicycle firms were set up by local governments (Shu Rong *et al.*, 1984 : 36).

In 1983, the central government planned to reduce the number of bicycle enterprises from 140 to 87 by 1985, but local governments still planned to have 124 in 1985. The sum of the output targets of local governments was 47 million bicycles, 42.5 per cent greater than that of the central government plan (Liang Zhongxun, 1983:43).

B. Steel

The non-price factors causing the coexistence problem in the steel industry were more complicated than those in the bicycle sector. They included, first, the expansion of capital construction, based on the soft-budget constraint system, between 1983 and 1985; second, the inefficient material allocation system; third, the inefficient transportation system; and, finally, the mismanagement of production in enterprises. The first factor, associated with the soft-budget constraint system, was regarded as fundamental by the Director of the Division of the Industry, Transportation and Materials of the State Statistical Bureau.[39] Each of these factors is examined below.

Capital construction, in 1983, expanded mainly in construction, machinery fabrication, shipbuilding and oil development. In 1984 and 1985, capital construction took place mainly in three sectors: construction, machinery fabrication and transportation (the car industry). In order to ease the expansion drive in capital construction, which was identified by the government as the principal cause of the shortage problem, economic policies in 1985 and 1986 gave priority to controlling the scale of capital construction (*Renmin Ribao*, 23 February 1987).

The inefficient and unreliable material allocation system was also regarded as an important factor in the coexistence problem.[40] To cope with the inefficient supply system, enterprises kept supplies of incorrect steel to use as barter to obtain the right types of steel from other enterprises. Thus, users wanted to keep large inventories of steel.

It was reported that the inefficient transportation system, especially rail transport, was unable to meet shipping demand, and thus also contributed to the problem of coexistence. The Anshan Iron and Steel Mill reported:

> Products become stocked up at the rolling mill until there is no place to put them, and sometimes damage was caused by overstocking. This causes major problems for production; users urgently need the products, and Anshan has them, but they can not be shipped.[41]

Economic Information (*Jingji Chankao*, 2 July 1985) also reported that the 770 tons of steel allocated to the city of Fuzhou by the state plan in 1985 were stocked in different places for more than six months because of transportation problems. This, of course, intensified the shortage and was described as 'surplus breeds shortage'.

One case which demonstrates how mismanagement of production led to the problem of coexistence, reported in *Renmin Ribao* (20 June 1987) was that of a small firm, the Linhun Iron and Steel Mill, in Shanxi province. In 1980, the manager of this mill tried to reverse its financial deficit and meet both production and profit targets by shifting production from mild steel plates to strip steel without considering the mill's production capacity and technology. The application was approved by the Shanxi Provincial Division of Metallurgy, the Provincial Planning Committee, and the Provincial Economic Committee without evaluation or appraisal.

In June 1985, the mill stopped manufacturing strip steel after wasting several million yuan in production, and then decided to manufacture its former commodity, mild steel plates, again. Both decreased output and the loss of 9.99 million yuan between 1980 and 1985 were the result of mismanagement.

5.5 EVOLUTION OF NEW POLICY

Prior to the end of 1984, the Chinese government still believed that the shortage and surplus coexistence problem in production was an outcome of irrational price ratios. To deal with this problem, the government applied price adjustment to these two industries between 1979 and 1984.[42]

By 1984 reformers in the Research Institute of the State Reform Committee were aware that the price adjustment policy affected steel output composition only marginally (interviews, 1985). They therefore proposed a programme of price liberalisation to solve the coexistence problem. This proposal was rejected by other institutions, including the State Price Bureau, and thus a compromise combination of adjustment and liberalisation was reached. The compromise proposal was approved by the State Council at the beginning of 1985, and gave rise to the new system of dual pricing.[43]

The State Council, in 1984, planned to increase the producer price of first-class bicycles by 15 per cent to widen price differentials for bicycles of different qualities. They believed that an increase of the producer price for first-class bicycles would encourage big factories to expand their output. Paradoxically, the expansion plan was rejected by the three biggest bicycle factories, mainly because they were already very profitable.[44] Their lack of expansion was not due to price factors but, rather, to non-price factors – resource constraints, particularly the scarcity of land.

In the summer of 1984, the State Council approved a plan, designed by the State Economic Committee, to cut producer prices of third-class bicycles by 5–15 per cent, and to withdraw tax remission autonomy from local governments and to hand it to the Ministry of Finance.[45] The central government also decentralised price-setting power for third-class bicycles to local governments. These policies were aimed at forcing small firms, with an annual output below 100 thousand bicycles and production costs above 125 yuan per bicycle, either to close or to convert to other products. The adjustment policy affected only some small firms such as BBF. The majority of firms were financially protected by local governments since price formation was still in the hands of the local governments, and alternative jobs and types of production could not be immediately created. Without alternatives, local governments had to step in again to bail out these firms financially.

To cut the economic ties between governments (local or central) and small firms, and to harden the budget constraint, in August 1986 the State Price Bureau decreed a new policy of liberalising producer prices of third-class bicycles.[46] One outcome of this policy was (as in the steel industry) the introduction of a dual pricing system in the bicycle industry.

5.6 SUMMARY

The shortage and surplus coexistence problem in the steel and bicycle industries was mainly caused by non-price factors, and only secondarily by price factors. For the bicycle sector, our analysis covers only the supply and not the demand side. It is clear that lower prices and lower profits would not have stopped the output of inferior bicycles, which were in excess supply, nor would higher prices have increased the output of good-quality bicycles, which were in shortage. The output of inferior bicycles was stimulated mainly by the expansion drive of local governments and enterprises. The output of good-quality bicycles was restricted by resource constraints, especially the shortage of land for plant expansion.

In the steel industry, the shortage and surplus coexistence problem was caused mainly by the demand side. In 1985, probably 20 per cent of the steel inventory was caused by price factors. This 20 per cent was stored by producers and consumer departments. The larger portion of the steel inventory (80 per cent) was held by users, probably as a result of a 'security drive' based on the soft-budget constraint system. This also led to a large import of steel during the post-reform period. To solve the coexistence problem, several different policies and reform methods were introduced. The adjustment method was first adopted, and then a combination of adjustment and liberalisation for particular commodities. The combination method had an important impact on the dual pricing system, which is discussed in Chapter 6.

6 Evolution of Dual Pricing

> When reform is executed in an evolutionary mode, it is impossible to avoid having dual systems co-existing for a period of time . . . During the transformation of the economic structure, great shocks could be prevented by applying a pricing policy which combines relaxed control with readjustments and by taking advantage of the gradual increase and decrease of dual pricing to promote the overall reform of the economic system (Liu Guoguang *et al.*, 1985).

In Chapters 4 and 5 we showed the limitations of using price adjustment to regulate sectoral output and sub-sectoral output composition in industry. The government, because of these limitations, decided to adopt a different method, a combination of liberalisation and adjustment, to reform the prices of some important industrial commodities. This resulted in a new pricing system, known as dual pricing.

In this chapter, we are mainly concerned with how the dual pricing system developed and how state control and the market mechanism functioned together in post-reform China. The dual pricing system, which followed the two-tier plan/market economic system,[1] was applied to agricultural goods in 1979 and to industrial goods in 1985. It embraced many goods, but in this chapter we examine only certain producer goods, such as steel, coal, cement, timber and chemical fertilisers. In the following sections we consider, first, the object and purpose of the new pricing system; second, the development of the new system; third, the scope of fixed and free price regulation; fourth, the short-term effects of this system on the economy; fifth, the problem of administrative management; and, finally, the theoretical debates about dual pricing.

6.1 OBJECTS AND PURPOSES

The traditional form of price control changed from 'a high degree of control system' to 'a partial control system', when the government tried to transform the economic system from a 'bureaucratic–hierarchical command economy' to a 'less centralised market economy'.

A high degree of price control implies that fixed prices are applied to all the output of a commodity, and that price control is accompanied by the necessary regulation of production and distribution (Saksena, 1986). Partial control implies that the control system leaves some scope for the play of market forces, and some freedom of action to individual enterprises for determining the price of their products. (Saksena, 1986).

Dual pricing is a type of partial control system where the government directly fixes the price and arranges the distribution of part of a commodity's output, while allowing market forces to affect the remaining portion.[2] Although price control via dual pricing may affect the whole output of the controlled commodity, its direct affect in the market is incomplete (Saksena, 1986).

The dual pricing system arose because of the inefficient administrative resource allocation system, which not only failed to fulfil its supply targets for key sectors, but also failed to supply adequate resources to less important sectors. Dual pricing provided an alternative source of supply to users for some widely-used industrial inputs, such as steel and coal. It also arose because the government wanted to find a new pricing system which, on the one hand, could promote increases in output and changes in output composition by giving enterprises some freedom to set prices and, on the other, allow the State to control a certain portion of the output for its own economic goals. It is very difficult to identify which factor was fundamental in determining the development of dual pricing in China; however, both factors had important impacts on the appearance of the new system.

Regardless of the reasons why dual pricing arose, it was viewed by others as making several contributions to economic development: first, ensuring a smooth transformation from direct administrative control to indirect market control;[3] second, reopening a small free market for the means of production; third, rationalising the producer prices of the means of production (Lu Nan, 1986 : 25) (the reform of producer prices for the means of production is one of the important economic policies in the 7th Five-Year Plan: interviews, 1985); and, finally, as in India, offering an alternative means for the state to achieve the twin objectives of efficiency and balanced growth by allowing the market mechanism to generate efficiency in resource allocation and the planning mechanism to balance economic growth in key sectors.[4]

Another benefit of dual pricing was that politically less powerful units such as county and village enterprises and medium and small

Table 6.1 Three stages of development of the dual pricing producer goods (steel, coal, cement, timber and chemica between 1979 and 1987

Time	*Stages*	*Allocation system*	*(%)*	*Forms of producer prices*
1979		State control	85–90[1]	Fixed price
1983	1st	Black market	10–15	Black market, barter, local temporary and informal negotiated prices
1984	2nd	State control	55[2]	Fixed price
		Nascent market	45	Floating price[3]
1985		State control	40[4]	Fixed price
1987	3rd	Free market	60	Free price

Notes: 1. Interviews, 1985. This estimation by Chinese economists includes all producer goods. 2. For more detailed information see Table 6.2. Another source indicates that 50 per cent of the total output of producer goods circulated in the market in 1984 (Hua Sheng, 1986 : 5). 3. The floating price permitted upward or downward movements within a range of 20 per cent above and below the fixed price. 4. According to Xue Muqiao (1985), the State controlled an average of 44 per cent of coal, steel, timber, and cement in 1985. Yan Tao (*Renmin Ribao*, 12 June 1987), estimates that 40 per cent of the total output of producer goods was priced freely in 1986. However, this figure is based on Table 6.2.

urban enterprises, who often suffered from shortages of supplies and yet were sometimes more efficient than larger state enterprises, could obtain from the market the essential producer goods they required as inputs. At the same time, key sectors could receive sufficient supplies of producer goods at fixed prices (Saksena, 1986).

6.2 DEVELOPMENT OF DUAL PRICING

The dual pricing system developed in three stages, which each followed shifts in economic policy (see Table 6.1): first, pre-1983, a stage of State domination with a small black market, the latter handling between 10 and 15 per cent of producer goods; second, in 1984, a quasi-dual pricing system, where state control coexisted with a nascent market; and third, from 1985 onwards, a formal dual pricing system. We consider each in turn.

A. Administrative Allocation vs 'Back-door Trading': 1979–83

During the first stage, 1979–83, shortages and an inefficient administrative resource allocation system resulted in the emergence of both a black market and hoarding.[5] Scarcity was thus artificially accentuated. This encouraged enterprises and traders to sustain the black market, keep prices high, and barter among themselves.[6] Some enterprises and traders were thus able to increase their profits without corresponding increases in tax remittances to the government. Actually, barter trade and cooperative trade were not isolated cases but a nationwide phenomenon in China after the early 1970s (Hua Sheng *et al.*, 1986 : 5).

B. The Quasi-dual Pricing System: 1984

The quasi-dual pricing system began not in the industrial sector but in the agricultural sector, as early as the 1960s. It was abolished by the government in the 1970s, due to the expansion of the planning mechanism (Gu Shutang, 1986 : 270–83; Dai Yuanchen, 1986 : 43). The quasi-dual pricing system reappeared in agriculture in 1979 when the government introduced higher prices for above-quota purchases (*chaoguo jiajia*) and occasional negotiated prices (*jijia*) for grain and cotton.[7]

However, most grain was traded vertically from the peasants to the government. The horizontal relationships between peasants and traders and among peasants started in 1985, but were less significant than the horizontal relationships in the industrial sectors (survey, 1985). The quasi-dual pricing system in the industrial sector began in May 1984, when the State Council announced the new policy: 'On Further Expansion of Decision Making Power on the Part of State Run Industrial Enterprises' (the Ten Regulations). According to the Ten Regulations:

> there are two components of production, namely, planned economy and non-planned economy; there are two types of material supplies for enterprises, namely, state allocation and free purchase by individual enterprises; the prices of goods produced under the state quota system will be fixed by the State and prices of goods produced outside the state quota system may be manipulated within a range of 20 percent above or below state prices (Wu Jinglian and Zhao Renwei, 1987 : 312; Dong Fureng, 1986 : 298).

The purpose of allowing prices of above-quota output to float was to stimulate both output and changes in output composition. However, the policy was regarded as unsuccessful for two reasons. First, excess demand was so great that in many cases the 20 per cent price increase was insufficient to bring demand and supply into balance. Second, the relaxation of administrative control over the allocation of output allowed a greater proportion of output to be channelled through the black market (Du Lihui, 1986 : 5).

C. Formal Dual Pricing: 1985

In February 1985, the State Price Bureau and the State Material Supply Bureau both agreed to eliminate the 20 per cent floating range limit because of the difficulties of price management and control. They also allowed large steel plants directly to market 2 per cent of within-plan output and all above-plan output at free prices (The Shoudu Steel Mill in Beijing was allowed directly to market 15 per cent of within-plan output: interviews, 1985; see also Byrd, 1987a : 305). There was no control over the price of steel manufactured by small steel plants (Nambu, 1985 : 4). China then made *de facto* dual pricing *de jure* by recognising the real situation and trying to make the best possible use of it.[8]

6.3 RESPECTIVE SCOPES OF FIXED AND FREE PRICE REGULATION

A. Shrinkage of State Control

Three aspects of the government's administrative work are regarded as central to the formulation and implementation of a dual pricing system (Saksena, 1986 : 127). They are: to identify which commodities need to be brought under dual pricing; to determine the levy rate and the proportion of output to be procured; and to determine the levy price.

Compared to India, China took only a short time, 1–2 years, to transform its system of total price control to partial price control for some of its important commodities.[9] The dual pricing system was formally implemented at a time when an effective administrative management system was lacking; consequently, market forces expanded dramatically and weakened the state's position in the economy. The market's challenge to state planning could be seen in the dramatic shrinkage of state control at the central, local, and enterprise levels, and in the large gap between fixed and free prices.

Central Control

The state's control mechanism weakened after 1979 and the number of commodities controlled by the State was reduced, yet the role of state control did not sharply decline until the introduction of dual pricing. At the end of 1986, the number of industrial products subject to mandatory planning was cut from 120 to 60. This caused the share of gross industrial output controlled by the State to decrease from 40 per cent to 20 per cent. The number of goods distributed by the State fell from 256 to 20; the number of commodities managed by the Ministry of Commerce fell from 188 to 23. In 1986, 60 per cent of the total output of producer goods was controlled by the State, and the remaining 40 per cent was traded in the market (Yan Tao, in *Renmin Ribao*, 12 June 1987).

The shrinkage of state control over producer goods can be demonstrated by considering steel, coal, cement, timber and chemical fertilisers. In 1979, the State Council allowed state-owned iron and steel mills to market a small portion of their over-plan output. In the period between 1979 and 1983, a small portion of finished steel (3.6 per cent in 1979, 10.6 per cent in 1980, 19.9 per cent in 1981, and 14.4 per cent in 1982) was sold in the market by producers. In 1983, the percentage marketed was deliberately reduced to 3.5 per cent by the government because of an acute steel shortage. In the coal industry, free market trade increased continuously after 1979 (see Table 6.2).

A sharp change in the ratio of producer goods under state control to those under market determination occurred between 1984 and 1987. Only 25.7 per cent of total coal output was marketed by producers in 1984; this fraction increased to 49.6 per cent in 1985, and 57.7 per cent in 1986. The change for steel products was more dramatic than that for coal. Only 3.5 per cent of steel was outside state control in 1983, but this fraction jumped to 40 per cent in 1984, and reached 50 per cent in 1987 (see Table 6.2).

There is no information on the shifts in ratio of state control to market determination for timber or cement between 1979 and 1983. However, the proportion of total output of these commodities traded outside of state control was much higher than that of steel and coal between 1984 and 1986. 60 per cent of timber was freely traded in the market in 1984, and 70 per cent in 1986. 84 per cent of cement was traded in the market in 1984 and 83.8 per cent in 1986.

Table 6.2 Output shares of the five commodities subject of free pricing, 1979–87 (%)

Years	*Coal*	*Steel*	*Timber*	*Cement*	*Chemical Fertiliser*
1979	16.7	3.6			
1980	18.3	10.6		65	
1981	20.4	19.9			
1982	21.9	14.4			
1983	23.8	3.5			
1984	25.7	40	60	84	17
1985	49.6	43.1	69.3	80.6	
1986	57.7	46.9	70	83.8	
1987		52.9	72.4	84.4	

Sources: 1979–83, for steel, see Deng Liqun *et al.* (1984 : 357); for coal see World Bank (1985b : 91). 1980, for cement see Byrd (1987a : 305). 1984, for cement and chemical fertilisers see Gu Shutang (1986 : 277); for steel and timber, see Ye Bing (1985 : 18). 1985–86, *Renmin Ribao* (21 February 1987). 1987, see Zhang Xiaoming and Song Yaohua (1987 : 24).

Local Control

Information about the ratio of state control to market regulation for producer goods at the local level, and time-series data for 1979 to 1986 are very difficult for outside researchers to obtain. We have information only for Shanghai and Tianjin in 1985, and Nanchong District (Sichuan Province) and Jiangsu Province in 1984.

Table 6.3 shows that more than 50 per cent of the total output of steel, timber and cement was controlled by local government in Shanghai and Tianjin in 1985. These two cities received more than 50 per cent of their total needs for these three commodities from the government, since they were economically important to industrial development and contributed a large share of gross national industrial output.

In contrast, some cities and areas had difficulty in obtaining a supply of producer goods from the government. For example, before the dual pricing system, Jiangsu province and the Nanchong district in Sichuan each received only 30–40 per cent of their requirements of certain producer goods by state allocation (see Tables 6.4 and 6.5). After 1985, state supplies of steel, coal, timber, iron and chemical fertilisers to these areas were further reduced. Since free-market purchases of producer goods accounted for 50–70 per cent of the total, the market mechanism became the principal force in the

Table 6.3 Proportion of market determination of five commodities, Shanghai and Tianjin, 1984–5

Cities	*Years*	*Steel* %	*Timber* %	*Cement* %	*Iron* %	*Coal* %
	1984	28.0			34.0	10.0
Shanghai	1985	39.5	40.0	48.6		
Tianjin	1985	31.0	42.0	60.0		

Sources: Gu Shutang (1986 : 24); Wu Jinglian and Zhao Renwei (1987 : 313).

Table 6.4 Ratio of State supply to market allocation for five commodities in Nanchong District, 1984 (million tons/million cubic metres)

Commodity	*Total use*	*State supply*	*Market allocation*	*Market proportion to total* %
1. Steel	5.0	1.5	3.5	70.0
2. Iron	1.2	0.5	0.7	58.3
3. Timber	8.0	3.0	5.0	62.5
4. Caustic soda	0.4	0.1	0.3	75.0
5. Chemical Fertiliser	45.0	20.0	25.0	55.6

Sources: Gu Shutang (1986 : 24); Wu Jinglian and Zhao Renwei (1987 : 313).

allocation and distribution of producer goods in both small and medium-sized cities, particularly in southern China.

Enterprises

Once again, no comprehensive information on enterprises' market participation in purchasing producer goods as inputs exists. A report by the Technological, Economic and Social Development Research Centre at the State Council (TESDRC), based on research on three cities and one province, indicates that average free-market purchases of producer goods by enterprises has accounted for 30–50 per cent of their total consumption since 1984 (*Price: Theory and Practice*, no. 1,

Table 6.5 Ratio of State supply to market allocation of three commodities, Jiangsu Province, 1984 (%)

	Steel	*Iron*	*Coal*
State supply	35	22	58
Market allocation	65	78	42

Source: Wu Jinglian and Zhao Renwei (1987: 313).

1986 : 9). Another report, from the China Economic System Reform Research Institute (CESRRI) to the State Council in October 1985, based on a study of 429 enterprises in 27 cities, states that:

> as regards the overall situation in the enterprises, in 1984, 51 percent of enterprises of the sample 429 enterprises had already gained varying degrees of autonomy, 77 percent of them found it necessary to adjust their production plans to market demand, and 90 percent relied to some extent on free market purchases for their input (CESRRI, 1986 : 16).

According to the same report, during the first six months of 1985 raw material supplies from the State were sharply reduced. The proportion of major raw materials autonomously acquired by enterprises through adjustment and cooperative arrangements among enterprises in the market abruptly increased, from 26.84 per cent in 1984 to 43.8 per cent in 1985.

The State dominated 50–60 per cent of the total output of producer goods during the 1984–6 period. The rest of the output was marketed. Market forces penetrated small and medium-size cities, less important industrial regions and small and medium-size enterprises. The general shrinkage of state control affected both the price ratios and the movement of free prices for producer goods between 1984 and 1986.

B. Free Price Changes and Price Ratios

Market Price Changes: 1979–86

Price changes in the market in the post-reform period can be divided into two periods; before and after dual pricing.

1. Before Dual Pricing During the 1979–83 period, China's economic planning system suffered because of 'back-door trading' and an inefficient administrative allocation system (see Table 6.1). The black market for producer goods existed before 1979, but flourished in 1982.[10]

In 1983, the prices of market-distributed producer goods, including black market, local temporary, and informal negotiated prices increased. This was a result of demand exceeding supply because of overinvestment in capital construction in 1982 (Hama, 1983 : 7).[11] Many sources indicate rapid price rises for raw materials in 1983. In Shanxi province, for example, prices of rolled steel temporarily rose 20 per cent. The negotiated price of cement was 35 per cent higher than the official price. In Ancheng county of Heilongjiang Province the price of a consignment of rolled steel rose 40 per cent, from 584.5 to 816.4 yuan per ton because of a seven-step selling and reselling chain. In Yinchuan city, the price of rolled steel increased by 34 per cent as a result of nine sales and resales by middlemen (Hama, 1983 : 11).

The unauthorised practice of raising prices of raw materials and producer goods was a widespread phenomenon. Although some enterprises, particularly state-owned enterprises such as the Anshan Steel Corporation, the Shanghai no. 2 Steel Mill and the Xiang Xiang Cement Factory, continued to sell their products at the fixed price, they were in the minority (*Renmin Ribao*, 13, 16, 19 July 1983; Hama, 1983 : 11). The illegal trade and price increases both affected state planning. The government had difficulty allocating and distributing certain producer goods according to its plan.[12]

2. After Dual Pricing Market prices of some producer goods began to rise after the introduction of the nascent free-market policy in May 1984, which permitted floating prices for so-called 'self-disposal' goods. Price rises accelerated in the first six months of 1985 because of the free market. They slowed down when the money supply tightened in the summer of 1985, and certain prices decreased between July and September (see Table 6.6 for the market price increases of certain producer goods).

Price Ratio of Quota to Above-Quota Production

In 1984, enterprises were permitted to price their above-quota output in the range of 20 per cent above or below fixed prices. Prices of

Table 6.6 Market price index of producer goods, August 1984–September 1985

Commodity	*August 1984* %	*January 1985* %	*December 1984* %	*July 1985* %	*July 1985* %	*September 1985* %
a. Wire rod	100	115	100	126[1]	100	99.8
b. Steel round thread bar	100	120	100	127	100	96.1
c. Mild steel round bar	100	125	100	129[1]	100	95.2
d. Foundry pig	100	118	100	130	100	104.1
e. Cement	100	100	100	123[1]	100	101.7

Source: Survey, 1985.

many producer goods actually floated above this limit. For example, the fixed price of quota wire rod was 585 yuan per ton, the floating price for above-quota output should not have exceeded 702 yuan per ton, yet the market price reached 1350–1370 yuan per ton, 130 per cent higher than the fixed price. This was not the only case.[13]

In 1985, when dual pricing was formally approved by the government, fixed producer prices of certain producer goods remained very close to 1984 levels. However, free-market prices increased sharply and the gap between free and fixed prices widened. For instance, the free – fixed price ratio of wire rod rose from 2.3 in 1984 to 3.67 in 1985, an increase of 60 per cent. The free price of cast iron was 117 per cent higher than the fixed price, the free – fixed price ratio rose from 1.67 in 1984 to 2.18 in 1985, an increase of 31 per cent. The free – fixed price ratio of steel round thread bar rose from 2.19 in 1984 to 3.13 in 1985, an increase of 43 per cent. The ratio between the free and fixed price of coal also increased, rising from 3.41 in 1984 to 4.08 in 1985, an increase of 20 per cent (see Table 6.7).

Having studied the purpose and development of dual pricing, and the price ratios of fixed to free prices, we now go on to consider the impact of dual pricing on the economy.

6.4 SHORT-TERM EFFECTS

Is the dual pricing system, in the short run, a better alternative in terms of improving efficiency, equity and economic stability than the

Table 6.7 Price ratios between fixed and market prices for seven producer goods in major cities, 1984–6 (yuan/ton)

	1984[a]		*1985*[b]		*1986*	
Commodity	*Fixed price*	*Market price*	*Fixed price*	*Free*[1] *price*	*Fixed price*	*Free*[2] *price*
1. Car CA-15[3]			18,700[4]	47,000		
2. Wire rod[5]	585[6]	1350	585[7]	2,150		
3. Cast iron	270[8]	450	308[9]	670		
4. Coal	22[10]	75	25[11]	102		
5. Cement[12]			56	140	90	167
6. Steel round thread bars	630[13]	1377	640	2,000		
7. Chemical fertiliser			410[14]	570[15]		

Notes: 1., 2. Prices quoted were the highest in the market. 3. Liberation car. 4. Survey in Shanghai, 1985. 5. 6.5mm wire rod. 6. The wholesale price was 650 yuan/ton. 7. The average wholesale price in Shanghai and Nanjing was 719 yuan/ton in March 1985. 8. This price applied to iron in general. 9. This price applied only to the foundry pig. 10. The wholesale price of coal in 1984 was about 50–60 yuan per ton, according to our survey in Beijing, 1985. 11. See Chapter 4 for more detailed information. 12. No. 500#. 13., 14., 15. Data from *Jingji Chankao* (10 October 1985).

Sources: *a* Our survey, 1985. *b* Gu Shutang (1986 : 23).

total price control system? Can the dual pricing system eliminate the difficulties of a total price control system?

That short-term effects of dual pricing on the economy are both positive and negative is widely acknowledged by Chinese economists,[14] regardless of their ideological and theoretical stand with respect to the new system. We consider both the positive and the negative effects in terms of efficiency, income distribution, economic stability, and economic calculation and evaluation.

A. Efficiency

Positive Aspects

One positive aspect of the dual pricing system was that it stimulated production and alleviated excess demand. Cases which support this view are coal and cement.

According to Li Kaixin,[15] Director of the State Material Allocation

Bureau, and Wu Jinglian and Zhao Renwei (1987 : 313), the market-supply response was most evident in coal production, which had an annual increase in total output of 8.35 per cent in 1984 and 1985. This was due to the contribution of small coal mines and the establishment of a free coal market (see Chapter 4). At the local level, the Hubei province plan target was set at 5.5 million tons for 1984, but actual output reached 7.43 million tons, an increase of 19 per cent over 1983. Because of the rapid increase in output, the free market price of coal fell from 150 to 200 yuan per ton (1984) to 80 to 120 (1985) in places such as Jiangsu (Wu Jinglian and Zhao Renwei, 1987 : 313).

There is evidence which suggests, at the national level, that cement output was stimulated by the price increases. After a 29 per cent increase in the average price level (average of free and fixed prices, where the latter increased by 60 per cent alone) cement output increased 16.36 per cent between January and September 1986 over the same period for 1985 (Liao Yingmin and Dai Guoqing, 1987 : 18–20).

At the local level, the Ning Bo Cement Factory in Zhejiang, a small firm with an annual capacity of 60,000 tons, increased its output in response to increases in the fixed price level of 60 per cent. The total output of this firm reached 80,000 tons, 33 per cent above the plan target. It thus had 20,000 tons of cement for disposal at market prices (survey, 1985).

A second positive aspect of dual pricing was its effect of forcing economy in materials and energy. Wu Jinglian and Zhao Renwei (1987 : 313–14) argued that both energy conservation and management quality improved when the price level of producer goods sharply rose. They suggested that the 18 per cent reduction in steel consumption per 10,000 yuan of output value in 300 steel-consuming enterprises in 1985 was a result of the higher price level.

A third beneficial aspect of dual pricing was that it provided an incentive for producers and institutions to invest, improve technology, and expand production capacity and produce more of the goods in shortage. The medium-sized Xiang Tan Steel Mill of Hunan Province, which had an annual production capacity of 0.39 million tons of rolled steel, was able to collect more than 37 million yuan for its Technical Betterment Fund (*Jishu gaizao*). The 37 million yuan was raised from several sources.[16] This money made technical improvement feasible and the mill's annual output capacity increased from 0.39 million tons to 0.56 million tons within three years (TESDRC report, *Price: Theory and Practice*, no. 1, 1986 : 9–14).

Other industrial sectors and institutions also invested in the manufacture of producer goods and raw materials. For example, to ensure a sufficient future supply of steel, the Allocation Company of Guangzhou City signed a 9.8 million investment contract with Maanshan Steel Mill, and the Allocation Company of Guangdong invested 100 million yuan in the Handan Steel Mill in 1985 (survey, 1985).

A fourth benefit of dual pricing was that it stimulated the development of county and village enterprises (Chen Huijun, 1986 : 52). The county and village enterprises who were vulnerable to short supplies of essential goods in the pre-reform period were able to obtain their minimum requirements of producer goods under dual pricing by paying higher but affordable prices.

Dual pricing also encouraged enterprises to market their surplus stocks of producer goods and raw materials. This helped ease the inventory problem to some extent (Chen Huijun, 1986 : 52; Yao Lin, 1985 : 21; Liu Fushan, 1987 : 41). This occurred for commodities such as coal, which faced buyer's markets. Dual pricing did not ease the steel inventory problem. Steel inventories again increased by 0.072 per cent in the six months between January and June 1987. Lacking better alternatives, the State Council used administrative orders to cut steel inventories in the summer of 1987 (*Economic Daily*, 1 September 1987).

Negative Effects

Implementation of dual pricing also generated a number of negative efficiency effects. It stimulated enterprises' hypocritical behaviour and undermined the planning mechanism and the fulfilment of plan targets.

Since the implementation of dual pricing, many enterprises have, on the one hand, tried to hide their real production capacity from the government, so as to obtain lower production quotas and, on the other, striven to claim as large an allocation of material at fixed prices as possible.[17] They could thus keep their input costs low and sell more output in the market at higher profits. The problem of unfulfilled quotas has intensified since 1984, despite increases in total output.

Table 6.8 shows that the fulfilment rate of quota steel delivered to the state was 97.8 per cent in 1983. It decreased to 97.1 per cent in 1984, despite the 9.7 per cent increase in total output and 6.6 per cent increase in total sales (*Jingji Chankao*, 13 March 1985). In 1985, the fulfilment rate of quota steel delivered to the state dropped by 8.6 per

Table 6.8 Percentage of fulfilment of quotas for four commodities from State-owned enterprises to the State, 1983–5 (%)

Year	*Steel*	*Coal*	*Cement*[1]	*Iron*	*Total*
1983	97.8	98.1	99.2	n.a.	98.4
1984	97.1	97.6	97.9	97.1	97.6
1985[2]	88.5	96.9	93.0	89.5	92.0

Notes: 1. Cement data is based on 57 big and medium-sized firms. 2. According to Wu Jinglian and Zhao Renwei (1987: 315), in the first half of 1985 unfulfilled quotas of steel and iron totalled 510,000 tons; coal 2.98 million tons; and cement 470,000 tons.

Sources: 1983 and 1985 from our own survey. 1984 from *Jingji Chankao* (13 March 1985).

cent, from 97.1 per cent to 88.5 per cent, a large fall from the previous year. Coal output increased by 4.2 per cent in 1984 over 1983, total sales increased by 4.9 per cent, but the rate of quota fulfilment decreased by 0.5 per cent in 1984 and a further 0.7 per cent in 1985. The situation in the iron and cement sectors was worse than that in the coal sector.

Dual pricing caused an irrational utilisation of resources and investment, and also created economic inefficiency. High prices and profits encouraged the development of small and relatively inefficient firms, especially in the iron and steel industry. After dual pricing was implemented, investment flowed into these sectors and gave rise to a number of inefficient 'backyard furnaces'. In Shanxi, more than 1000 'backyard-size blast furnaces' emerged between 1984 and 1985 (CESRRI, 1986 : 31). In Hebei, in 1983, there were only 5 small-scale, simple furnaces. This figure increased to 17 in 1985 and to 44 in 1986. Small-scale rolled steel mills increased in number from 30 in 1984 to 120 in 1986 (Qi Xiangdong, 1985 : 10–11; 1986 : 35).

There is no doubt that the large number of small-scale furnaces, iron factories and rolled steel mills served some economic purposes, such as increasing production (even though quality was poor), creating jobs for the rural population, and supplementing the output of State-run enterprises (Qi Xiangdong, 1985, 1986; Wu Jinglian and Zhao Renwei, 1987 : 315). However, small-scale enterprises also competed with large state-owned enterprises for raw materials and energy.

B. Income Distribution

The dual pricing system changed the established pattern of income distribution among individuals, enterprises and the government.[18] Certain people and social groups benefited from it while others did not. Firms who could sell their goods at higher prices, and those who were previously denied access to producer goods and could now buy them, even at high prices, were gainers. Firms, who now had to pay more for their inputs, while their output faced a buyers' market, were losers.

Gainers

Individuals, enterprises and institutions involved in the market were in a better position to gain profit than those whose economic activity continued to mainly rely on state control. In general, small enterprises, small cities, local government, and the producer goods' and energy sectors benefited from dual pricing. Ordinary people involved in trade and manufacturing also benefited (Chu Minwei *et al.*, 1987 : 21–5). Workers and peasants who worked in firms or institutions which made producer goods and raw materials that could be self-marketed also benefited by dual pricing, since their income increased. For example, in 1985 the income of each peasant who worked in the forest of Rongshui County in Guangxi increased by 70 yuan. This increase was made possible by a 200–230 per cent increase in timber prices (Jing Xiaodao and Zhu Jinfan, 1985 : 32).

Losers

The central government, large enterprises, and the processing industrial sector were disadvantaged by dual pricing. For example, the industrial sectors in Shanghai lost an estimated 733 million yuan in profit because of fixed and free price increases in five major commodities in 1985 (see Table 6.9).[19] The total loss of profit in the Shanghai industrial sector (including price increases of other goods) amounted to approximately 1 billion yuan. This represented 6.6 per cent of Shanghai's total government revenue and 50 per cent of the local government expenditure in 1983, 5.53 per cent of the total local government revenue and 21.7 per cent of the local government spending in 1985 (Hu Changnuan, 1986 : 30–3).

At the enterprise level, especially in the processing industrial sector, costs were affected by the dual pricing system.[20] Roughly

Table 6.9 Total price increase of five commodities, Shanghai, 1985 (total requirement 10,000 tons/cubic metre: price increase per unit ton/yuan, cubic metre/yuan)

	Steel	*Non-ferrous*	*Iron*	*Timber*	*Coal*	*Total*
Total						
requirement Total	140	21	320	121	1158	
State supply	110	19	313	106	1058	
Market supply	30	2	7	15	100	
Price increase per unit						
Fixed prices	118	406	44	43	7	
Free prices[a]	500	1500	277	200	40	
Cost increase (requirement × price increase) (million yuan)	279.8	107.14	157.11	75.58	114.06	733.69

Note: *a* The increase of free prices for these four commodities had been modified downward, see Table 6.7 for a comparison. According to Professor Hu Changnuan, the total cost increase, 733 million yuan, includes 464 million yuan due to price increases of fixed prices, and 269 million yuan due to market price increases.

Source: Hu Changnuan (1986 : 30).

speaking, if an enterprise received a ton of steel at the fixed price, it was equivalent to receiving a subsidy of 1000 yuan (Wu Jinglian and Zhao Renwei, 1987 : 315). In other words, enterprises without access to state steel had to pay 2 to 3 times as much for a ton of steel in the market. Their production costs were thus affected.

C. Economic Stability

Positive Effects

The dual pricing system moderated the risks of economic reform, especially the reform of producer prices of the means of production, by causing several small tremors rather than a big economic shock. This concept won support not only from Chinese economists but also from East European economists such as Brus. They believed that dual pricing could be a bridge, making the transfer from direct control to indirect control as smooth as possible.

Negative Effects

Dual pricing caused inflation.[21] The inflation problem was more serious than the reformers expected. Prices of the means of production increased by only 30 per cent in 1985 over 1984. This calculation was based on the assumption that 30 per cent of the total output of producer goods was traded in the market, and that the free prices were 1 to 2 times higher than fixed prices.[22] The 30 per cent increase in producer prices of the means of production resulted in a 21 per cent increase in total production costs of the processing industrial sector in 1985 (Zhang Baohua and Dai Guanlai, 1986 : 17). This was the largest price increase in producer goods since liberation. It was much higher than the 10 per cent which could be accepted by the processing industrial sector without leading to inflation (Lu Nan, 1986 : 24).

D. Economic Calculation and Evaluation

Unfortunately, dual pricing did not provide a better system for evaluation of enterprise performance. Since most enterprises tried to take advantage of the dual pricing system, the government found its calculation methods too complicated to produce an objective standard for assessment of enterprise performance.

Under the dual pricing system, a well-managed enterprise which received a large production quota from the State was less able to produce extra output for its own profit via the free market, while a less efficient factory was in a better position to gain profit in this way (Wu Jinglian and Zhao Renwei, 1987 : 315). Enterprises could make large profits by eliciting high input quotas, and reducing output quotas to the State, without trying to improve techniques and management (Wu Jinglian and Zhao Renwei, 1987). In this sense, enterprises lost a common criterion for economic evaluation and competition.

Finally, the dual pricing system induced smuggling in distribution. It was reported that a smuggler could become a 'ten thousand yuan household' by means of illegal trading with only one 4.5 ton truck (Wu Jinglian and Zhao Renwei, 1987). The Chinese government admitted that smuggling was one of the main obstacles in the reform of producer prices, especially in the steel industry, and in the implementation of the dual pricing system (interview, 1985). A study of the problems of administrative management in dual pricing is therefore required.

6.5 PROBLEMS OF ADMINISTRATIVE MANAGEMENT

The core problems related to administrative management in dual pricing (particularly in the steel industry between 1984 and 1986) were, first, the collection of the levy (delivered quota). In principle, this could be easily carried out since China was accustomed to a direct administrative system. In reality, it was not easily done, since there was a sharp shrinkage in State control over producer goods, and an increasing proportion of non-delivered quotas. Second, it also proved difficult to build up buffer stocks for regulating market price fluctuations. With shortages, especially in steel goods, buffers could not be built without increasing imports. As explained in Chapter 5, steel imports reached 20 million tons in 1985, more than half of total production, and there was both a trade deficit and a shortage of foreign currency in 1985 and 1986 (interview, 1986). One other problem of the system was that China lacked an efficient administrative management system which could both prevent leakages and monitor the effects of the dual system on the economy.[23]

Moreover, the ratio of free prices to fixed prices became so great that large-scale leakage seemed unavoidable. Some dealers diverted sizeable quantities of producer goods and raw materials intended for public distribution, to sell at 2 or 3 times fixed prices in the market. Therefore, for some commodities, the dual pricing system did not eliminate the problem of the black market but, rather, intensified it.

Between 1985 and 1987, Chinese newspapers such as *Renmin Ribao*, the *Economic Daily*, and *Jingji Chankao* repeatedly reported problems of surreptitious flows of quota production into the market by traders, producers, and institutions.

A. By Traders

Economic Daily (9 and 15 March 1985) reported that in 1984 the Huaping Trading Company illegally traded 511 tons of steel, swelling their profits by more than 33,000 yuan. *Jingji Chankao* (3 September 1985) reported that 20 tons of steel priced at 787 yuan/ton went through an illegal reselling chain between Liaoning and Heilongjiang. The price per ton increased by 70.15 per cent as a result of the reselling, conducted by so-called 'companies' or 'trade centres'.[24]

The number of these 'companies' and 'trade centres', and the total quantity of producer goods and raw materials directly involved in illegal trade nationwide, is not available. Nevertheless, it has been suggested that in the 1984–5 period, some 200,000 companies without resources and equipment emerged to specialise in this field (Wu Jinglian and Zhao Renwei, 1987 : 315). It is also believed that at least 20 per cent of the total output of steel was illegally traded in the market in 1985.[25]

B. By Producers

The *Economic Daily* (29 July 1985) reported that the Inner Mongolia Material Company illegally traded 910 tons of steel and received 80,000 yuan in extra profit between 1984 and 1985. A report in *Renmin Ribao* (4 September 1987) shows that the Dongfang Steel and Iron Mill leaked 5000 tons of iron from State control to the market, thereby swelling profits by 1 million yuan. The same source stated that 70,000 tons of cement were leaked by three cement factories, allowing them to gain an illegal profit of 3 million yuan.

C. By Institutions at the Local Level

According to *Renmin Ribao* (4 September 1987), some local governments and institutions were directly or indirectly involved in the leakage problem. For example, the Price Bureau of Hebei Province ignored central government policy and illicitly exercised their power to allow State quota steel, manufactured by their local steel mills, to be sold at higher prices in other provinces.

To minimise the problem of leakage, the government simultaneously undertook several measures in 1985. First, the government introduced a temporary price ceiling for above-quota output. However, this was only occasionally implemented by local governments for certain commodities which affected large numbers of people (for example, in some places in Jiangsu and Zhejiang Provinces, local governments set price ceilings for chemical fertilisers in 1985 : survey, 1985). It was not enforced nationwide until 1988 (*Price: Theory & Practice*, no. 3 1988 : 50).

Second, the State Council and the Secretariat of the Communist Party decided to monitor prices once a year (price monitoring was often used in the post-1979 period: interviews, 1985). A specific price monitoring of the means of production took place in April 1987 (*Renmin Ribao*, 31 August 1987).[26] A preliminary report claimed that there were 33,797 cases of illicit trading of the means of production from 1986 to May 1987, amounting to 332 million yuan in value (*Renmin Ribao*, 31 August 1987).[27] The government then stipulated new regulations for preventing leakages (*Gongren Ribao*, 21 September 1987).

Third, the government established a nationwide means of production market (MPM) (*shengchan ziliao shichang*).[28] The MPM set up a network of 'Material Trading Centres' (MTCs) which were managed either by the State Material Supply Bureau, or by a local material supply bureau, or by both.[29] Prices of the means of production in the MTC were free, and the role of the MTC was to provide information and to strengthen the exchange network.

The MTC played a significant role in trade. The Shenyang MTC handled over 235 million yuan of trade within its first six days of operation (*Jingji Chankao*, 18 May 1985). There were more than 140 MTCs nationwide in 1985 (*Jingji Chankao*, 18 May 1985), and the number had increased to 644 by the beginning of 1986 (*Renmin Ribao*, 22 February 1986). In 1986, transactions in the MTC reached 15.8 billion yuan, an increase of 47.7 per cent over 1985 (*Renmin Ribao*, 21 February 1987).

The purpose of setting up the MTC was to prevent leakages. The most well-known and successful model of a MTC was the one in Shijiazhang city in Hebei. In the Shijiazhang MTC, both within-plan and outside-plan producer goods sold at the market prices. Holders of State plan input allocations were later subsidised to offset the difference between state and market prices for their plan allocation (*Renmin Ribao*, 29 September 1985; *Jingji Chankao*, 20 January 1986; Byrd, 1987a : 305). However, starting in 1986, the subsidy was handed to financial institutions instead of to buyers, following a State Price Bureau order.

The Shijiazhang model gradually eliminated the problem of leakages of producer goods. Steel leakage decreased from 276 tons in 1984 to 60 tons in 1985 and to nil in 1986 (*Renmin Ribao*, 11 June 1987). Nevertheless, it did not solve the problem of barter trade, as the MTC had to hand the subsidies to financial institutions after 1986. Since neither producers nor users gained profit under the new regulation, barter trade increased among them.[30]

6.6 THEORETICAL DEBATES AND NEW POLICY

As soon as the positive and negative effects of the dual pricing on the economy were realised, a serious theoretical debate among Chinese economists began. Economists generally agreed that dual pricing was only an interim measure (Wang Zhenzhi *et al.*, 1986 : 24). However, the Centralisers argued that the producer prices for the means of production should return to a single fixed price system, and that the government should abolish dual pricing as soon as possible.

Members of the other two schools of thought believed that the dual pricing system should be transferred into a single pricing system, but they disagreed on the goals and techniques of transition. Economists in CESRRI, Market Reformers such as Diao Xinshen ahd Zhang Shaojie, argued that dual pricing should be changed to a single free price system via price liberalisation as soon as possible (Diao Xinshen, 1986 : 43–8). Economists in the State Price Bureau and TESDRC, Administrative Decentralisers such as Lu Nan and Chen Dezun, believed that the dual pricing should and could be changed into a new single price system (fixed or free is unclear), by a combination of gradually increasing fixed prices and reduced state control in terms of quotas.

Up to the present time, there has been no indication that the Chinese government has the intention or the means to abolish dual pricing immediately.[31] Recent information indicates that the government considers that dual pricing might continue through the reform period and even beyond. Therefore, in 1987, new policies were adopted by the government to enforce an efficient distribution arrangement by the Material Supply Bureau, to improve the MTC[32] and to ensure that above-quota output of producer goods is traded at government-run shops.[33]

6.7 SUMMARY

The simultaneous combination of a bureaucratic management system with a market mechanism for price determination and function was the outcome of certain political and economic conditions. Since the development period of dual pricing was too short for the government to form an effective administrative management system, dual pricing inevitably had both positive and negative effects on the economy.

The main problems of the dual pricing system were that, first, it was no easier to administer than the total price control system. Second, although pressure on resource allocations to less important sectors was reduced, illegal trade increased. Third, it did not function according to theoretical expectations and, to some extent, it failed to protect deserving sections of the community, the vital public-sector units and priority sectors from high prices. Finally, it did not achieve a balance of demand and supply, even though excess demand could find an outlet in the open market.

Dual pricing will remain in place in China for some time, since the State cannot go back to the old system, nor does it have the capacity immediately and entirely to abolish all control. Thus, it is in China's interest to improve and make the best possible use of the system. Two things are urgently needed: first, a more effective administrative management system. China can learn some lessons from India's experiences.[34] Second, an understanding of the impact of dual pricing on a firm's behaviour is required. It is very important to know how this new system affects firms, and how firms respond to the new system. Further reform decisions on the pricing system should take the firm's response into account. So far, we see only discussions in the newspapers and journals on how the system has affected firms. Nevertheless, we deal with the problem of price-responsiveness in Chapter 7.

7 Price-responsiveness of State Enterprises

> All the party were placed along the course, here and there. There was no one, two, three, and away; but they began running when they liked and left off when they liked, so that it was not easy to know when the race was over. The Dodo suddenly called out 'The race is over' and they all crowded round it, panting, and asking 'But who has won?' That question the Dodo could not answer without great deal of thought and it stood for long time with one finger pressing upon its forehead while the rest waited in silence. At last the Dodo said 'Everybody has won, and all must have prizes'.[1]

In Chapter 6, we studied the development of dual pricing and its effects on the economy. In this chapter, we study how firms responded to the change in price system. On the input side, key issues concern whether the firms responded strongly or weakly to price signals and whether price-responsiveness became stronger after reform. On the output side, issues concern production responses to exogenous price changes and deliberate manipulations of production aimed at influencing market prices and benefiting firms. Price-responsiveness in the pre-reform period is discussed, but the focus of this chapter is firm-responsiveness to dual pricing in the post-reform period.

The problem of price-responsiveness is regarded as the primary issue in socialist price reform by economists such as Kornai (1985 : 15). Unfortunately, our data are sufficient only for a study of the short-term aspects of the problem. Long-term firm's behaviour is therefore excluded.

We first summarise and criticise Kornai's model of price-responsiveness. The second section is an empirical study of firms' price-responsiveness in the pre-reform period, while the third studies how changes in the macro-economic system created dual dependence in state-owned firms, and how this affected firms' response to price changes. The fourth section develops two different theoretical models of price-responsiveness of firms in the post-reform period.

The fifth section is an empirical study of price-responsiveness of firms in the mixed market of the post-reform period, and the sixth an empirical study of price-responsiveness of firms in a sellers' market in the post-reform period.

7.1 THEORY

A. Kornai's Model

The short-term 'price-responsiveness' of state-owned firms – the reaction of firms to input and output price changes – becomes stronger in a post-reform period (Kornai, 1980; Zhou Shulian, 1986 : 29). However, it is still weak. Profitability is not a life and death matter for firms; price therefore is not a decisive criterion for a firm's management under soft-budget constraints. Kornai's model includes price-responsiveness of inputs, price-responsiveness of outputs, and the asymmetry between input and output price-responsiveness.

Input Adjustment

According to Kornai, the price-responsiveness of inputs in a traditional firm is weak. This weakness stems not only from an irrational pricing system, but also from the economic planning system as whole. The factors which cause weakness in the price-responsiveness of inputs are economic shortage, and 'soft-budget constraints' (Kornai, 1980, Ch. 13).

In a chaotic shortage economy, Kornai argues, the firm has a strong incentive to obtain as many inputs as possible, and to do so as quickly as possible. Firms will purchase available inputs regardless of price; high prices which cannot be absorbed by the firm's budget are passed on to buyers or to the government. Firms lack financial discipline.

Weak input price-responsiveness is reflected by a substitution weakness, by a weakness in reducing production costs, and by a weakness in improving management.[2] Kornai concludes that improvement in input price-responsiveness is insignificant in the post-reform period because the impact of price changes is still dampened by soft-budget constraints.

Output Adjustment

In a pre-reform period, when a firm's output is plan-determined and based on a rather loose measure of total output, firms respond only partially to price signals by changing the composition of their output, and not by changing total output. Firms respond to price changes in this way since they can more easily fulfil short-term targets in physical and value terms by manufacturing more expensive and less technically sophisticated goods (Kornai, 1980 : 365).[3]

In a post-reform period, the degree of price-responsiveness on the output side increases if a firm receives more autonomy without short-term targets. The price-responsiveness of output composition remains stronger than that of total output. The firm no longer seeks an easy fulfilment of plan targets but, rather, an increase in profit.[4] Although profit incentives affect firms, they are not life-and-death matters as long as firms face soft-budget constraints.

Asymmetry in Input and Output Price-responsiveness

Kornai emphasises the asymmetry of input and output price-responsiveness: the firm is in a weak position as a buyer, and is in a strong position as a seller. As a buyer, the firm selects inputs on the basis of availability, rather than relative price. The idea that costs do not matter spreads among managers, and is largely responsible for the demand-pull pressures in a pre-reform period, and their intensification in a post-reform period.[5]

As a seller, the firm is strongly guided by relative prices in output composition. It chooses what it will produce according to relative prices since there is little resistance from buyers in shortage conditions. Cost-push pressures are therefore inevitable in both pre- and post-reform periods. Demand-pull and cost-push pressures spring from the same roots – 'shortage' and 'soft-budget constraints'. These two factors intensify in a post-reform period, when serious shortages bring price rises, but price increases fail to eliminate excess demand.[6]

B. Limitations of Kornai's Model

Kornai's model, based on the Hungarian experience of a sellers' market for both inputs and output, is limited in application. It cannot be employed to analyse a firm's behaviour in a buyers' market or in a mixed market where a firm simultaneously faces a buyers' market for output and a sellers' market for inputs, or vice-versa, as often occurred in China in the post-reform period.

If a firm, in a mixed market, faces a buyers' market for inputs and a sellers' market for output, then it is in a strong position as both a buyer and a seller. The firm will have no desire to hold excess stocks of inputs, since they are plentiful. It also does not need to worry about selling its output since it is in shortage. The price-responsiveness of inputs and output in this type of firm is much weaker than in Kornai's model.

If a firm faces a sellers' market for inputs and a buyers' market for output, then the firm is in a weak position, not only as a buyer, but also as a seller. Under such conditions, the firm wants to stockpile inputs because of shortages and the soft-budget constraint. However, its desire to hold stocks is weaker than that of the firm in Kornai's model, since input cost increases are not compensated because of the buyers' market for output. The firm is thus forced either to improve the quality of its output or to reduce its prices to compete in the market. The price-responsiveness of a firm in this type of mixed market is stronger than either the firm in the above mixed market, or the one in Kornai's model.

In this chapter, we apply two theoretical models. The first, Kornai's model of price-responsiveness of firms, is applied to the Chinese firms which faced sellers' market before and after reform. The second model, price-responsiveness of firms in mixed markets, is applied to firms which face a mixed market in the post-reform period only. We first look at the price-responsiveness of Chinese firms in the pre-reform period.

7.2 PRE-REFORM REALITY

To investigate firm input and output price-responsiveness in state-owned firms in pre-reform China, four elements should be considered: first, the relationship between the planning mechanism and firm's behaviour; second, firms' input and output situations; third, demand-pull and cost-push tendencies; and, fourth, firms' budget constraints. We study a sample of firms.

The empirical data for eight firms were collected in 1985 and 1986, and supplemented by reports of the World Bank and various Chinese research institutions (see Table 7.1). Some of the sample firms fitted Kornai's model of a pre-reform period; some clearly did not.

A. Similarity of Sample Firms to Kornai's Model

Most of the sample firms,[8] as with the firms' behaviour in Kornai's model, regarded fulfilment of short-term output targets as their fundamental goal, although they had multiple targets numbering

Table 7.1 Sample firms

Name	*Location*	*Scale*[7]
1. Beijing Bicycle Factory (BBF)	Beijing	Medium
2. Tianjin Bicycle Factory (TBF)	Tianjing	Big
3. Wujin Chemical Fertiliser Factory (WCFF)	Jiangsu	Medium
4. Changzhou Chemical Fertiliser Factory (CZCFF)	Hebei	Big
5. Changzhou Small Chemical Fertiliser Factory (CZSCFF)	Hebei	Small
6. Shoudu Iron and Steel Mill (SISM)	Beijing	Big
7. Anshan Iron and Steel Mill (AISM)	Liaoning	Big
8. Suzhou Iron and Steel Mill (SZISM)	Jiangsu	Small
9. Datong Coal Mine (DCM)	Shanxi	Big
10. Beijing Coal Mine (BCM)	Beijing	Big

Sources: 1., 3., 4., 5., 6., 8., 9., 10., our field work, 1985. 7., World Bank (1983). 2. Report by a Chinese research institution.

between four and eight[9] at various times[10] (Kornai, 1987 : 317; Dong Fureng, 1987 : 44–59). This was a result of the fact that administrative authorities, because of the difficulty of checking an enterprise's plan implementation, concentrated on total output value targets.

To meet output value targets easily, some of the sample firms responded to price changes by altering their output composition and making products with high output values. They were unwilling to produce new products or to substitute cheaper inputs. Firms like AISM, which produced 330 types of steel and 8200 products (World Bank, 1983 : 14), and TBF, which manufactured more than 50 different kinds, sizes, and qualities of bicycles, responded to price changes with changes in output composition (the sample firms, listed in Table 7.1, will hereafter be referred to by their initials).

Firms such as DCM, BCM, CZCFF, and CZSCFF which produced so-called 'standard mass-produced goods' with a low degree of processing, did not display price-responsiveness in output composition. To fulfil their output value targets easily, they tried either to conceal their production capacity from the State, or to underreport it, and overdemand input materials.

The weak responsiveness of firms to price changes in inputs and outputs was rooted in the soft-budget constraint system. As in Hungary, soft-budget constraints in China had a 'levelling' effect, which depressed the profitability of successful firms, and helped out the losers (Kornai, 1987 : 325). The government, on one hand, acted as a greedy father, taking most of the profits of the financially successful firms; on the other hand, it acted as a weak father, helping out the unsuccessful firms. The government was a weak father to BBF, CZSCFF, and BCM. It was a greedy father to CZCFF, SISM, AISM, and DCM.

'Weak Father' Activities

In 1978 and 1979, BBF's financial losses were bailed out by the local government. In 1978, for example, the production cost of a no. 11 bicycle was 129 yuan, 14 yuan higher than the producer price. The loss was subsidised by the Beijing Commercial Bureau. The no. 03 bicycle was also subsidised by 19 yuan per bicycle in the same year (interview, 1985).

CZSCFF also suffered financial losses from 1972 to 1980 because of inept operation (see Table 7.6). This loss was jointly bailed out by the State Commercial Ministry and the Provincial Financial Bureau, in accord with the policy of 'More Subsidy for More Loss, Less Subsidy for Less Loss, and No Subsidy for Profit Makers' (a policy implemented in the mid-1970s and applied only to the chemical fertiliser industry: interview, 1985). It is believed that in 1979, more than half of the 1450 small chemical fertiliser factories made losses. The government subsidy to these firms amounted to 900 million yuan in 1976 but reduced to 400 million yuan in 1979.

'Greedy Father' Activities

The government acted as greedy father to the profitable firms for two main reasons: to ensure annual State revenue, and to produce an egalitarian situation among firms.

Table 7.2 demonstrates that the ratio of profit retention of the 11 most profitable state-owned iron and steel mills was low in 1979 (8.84 per cent for AISM and 20.37 per cent for SISM – the annual total output of these 11 mills exceeded 1 million tons). With the exception of the Tianjin, Shanghai, Maanshan and Benshi Steel Mills, profit retention in 1979 was 10 to 27 percentage points lower than in 1984 (see Table 7.2).

A World Bank Report (Tidrick and Chen, 1987, Table 2–6 : 17) also indicates a lower rate of retained profits for 20 out of 22 sample

Table 7.2 Profit retention rates for eleven State-owned iron and steel mills, 1979 and 1984

Firms	*Ratio of profit retention (%)*	
	1979	*1984*
Anshan	8.84	18.15
Wuhan	24.07	37.64
Baoto	37.65	64.14
Taiyuan	20.32	35.60
Shodu	20.37	39.14
Maanshan	12.66	14.34
Benshi	15.17	20.11
Panzihua	51.07	72.11
Shanghai	9.81	13.46
Tianjin	13.79	13.54
Tanshan	11.86	32.36

Note: 'Profit retention rate' is the ratio of retained profit to total profit.

Source: *China's Industrial Economics Journal*, no. 1, vol. 6 (1986 : 116).

firms in 1978 in comparison to 1982. The state was thus greedier with respect to profitable state-owned firms in the pre-reform than in the post-reform period.

Representatives of CZCFF, SISM and DCM complained, in our 1985 interviews, about the low rate of profit retention. SISM, for example, could not complete its construction of a gas pressure station until 1979, 21 years after the project began, because it lacked retained profits. The project was completed only 11 months after the adoption of a new profit retention system (Wang Jiye and Zhu Yuanzhen, 1987 : 937).

B. Differences Between the Sample Firms and Kornai's Model

There were a number of differences in the price-responsiveness of Chinese firms and Kornai's model. Kornai's model of demand-pull and cost-push tendencies in state-owned firms was too narrow; it did not universally apply to China.

In China, these two tendencies were strong in some firms and weak in others. In some cases, demand-pull and cost-push were not necessarily symmetrical. Firms like SISM, TBF and AISM preferred to concentrate on producing goods with high profit margins. They did not have a strong incentive to access more inputs by bidding up their price (demand-pull), since they could obtain what they wanted by barter trade. Both DCM and BCM claimed that they did not bid up input prices nor increase output prices in the pre-reform period.

Demand-pull and cost-push tendencies in the pre-reform period were less significant in China than in Kornai's model. In China these two tendencies were stronger in small and medium-sized firms and weaker in large state-owned firms, the reverse of the Hungarian situation. Large firms like SISM, BCM, TBF, DCM and AISM normally received all their inputs from the State. If they received insufficient or incorrect inputs, they could obtain supplies by bartering their own output with other firms. For example, to ensure a sufficient supply of good-quality coal for input, SISM would barter its steel for coal with the BCM; this was a benefit to BCM, since they were short of steel (survey, 1985). The barter trade prices were normally at the same level or lower than fixed prices.

Small or medium-sized firms like SZISM, CZSCFF, WCFF and BBF had strong demand-pull and cost-push tendencies since they had no high-quality commodities to barter in return for inputs; they had to pay high prices for black market inputs. The losses due to high input prices were normally subsidised by the government rather than being compensated by output price increase in the pre-reform period.

In summary, the pre-reform price-responsiveness of sample firms was weak, since the State was responsible for issuing production tasks, distributing products, allocating equipment, supplying materials, assigning personnel, collecting profits, and assuming losses. Although some firms responded to price changes with short-term changes in output composition, there was little impact on total output. The price-responsiveness of firms became more complicated after 1979 when dual dependence firms appeared.

7.3 DEVELOPMENT OF DUAL DEPENDENCE FIRMS AFTER 1979

A. Differences in Chinese and Hungarian Experience

The new economic system, with firms relying on both the State and the market (dual dependence), differed in China and Hungary. The difference created special features of the price-responsiveness of Chinese firms in the post-reform period.

Table 7.3 Different characteristics of the dual dependence of the firm, China and Hungary

Country	*Horizontal*	*Vertical*
Hungary	All buying and selling dependent on the market with single monitoring price	Financial tie Administrative tie
China	Buying and selling partly dependent on the market with free pricing system	Financial tie Administrative tie Inputs, output partially depend on the government, fixed price

Sources: Survey, 1985.

In Hungary, after the mandatory planning system had been abolished in one stroke in 1968, state-owned firms had a dual dependence. Firms depended entirely on the market for inputs and output. Buyers and sellers had equal legal status in the horizontal relationship (see Table 7.3). The quantity and quality of inputs and outputs traded were decided by enterprises themselves, and were subject to a single monitoring system, the competitive pricing system.[11]

In terms of vertical relationship, state-owned firms depended on the government for financing and investment (see Table 7.3). Government agencies had the right to issue binding resolutions to state-owned firms. The financial relationship between the State and enterprises was similar in China and Hungary.

In China, the dual dependence firm depended on both the government and the market for buying and selling.[12] The fixed pricing system applied between the government and firms. Free prices were applied to enterprises in the market. Thus, in China, 'price-responsiveness' coexisted with 'quota-responsiveness' – the reaction of firms to changes in input and output quotas. Firms on the one hand asked for more inputs from the government to maintain low production costs, and on the other demanded lower delivered quotas to sell more above-quota output at free prices.

B. Development of Dual Dependence in China

In China, highly centralised enterprises, free enterprises, and dual dependence enterprises coexisted after the dual allocation system

Table 7.4 Types of enterprises in China after 1979

Firm type	*Input*		*Output*	*Relationship with market and State*
State domination	*A*.State		State	Total control
	B.State		Market	Non-existent
	C.State		State and Market	Dual dependence
Market domination	*D*.Market		State	Non-existent
	E.Market		Market	Free
	F.Market		Market and State	Dual dependence
Dual economic domination	*G*.State	Market	Market	Non-existent
	H.State	Market	State	Total control
	I.State	Market	State and Market	Dual dependence

Source: Survey, 1985.

(plan and market) made its debut (see Table 7.4). Highly centralised enterprises, such as types *A* and *H* in Table 7.4, relied mainly on the government for inputs and outputs. Such enterprises were in the minority in the post-reform period; they cared little about price changes.

Highly decentralised firms, such as type *E* in Table 7.4, had their inputs and output determined by the market. They were very sensitive to prices and tended to be mainly village and township enterprises (*xiangzhen qiye*). The number of such enterprises increased, but they were still less significant, in economic terms, than large state-owned firms.

Dual dependence firms, such as types *C*, *F* and *I* in Table 7.4, faced three types of dual dependence. In the first case, the government played the main role in determining the firms' inputs and outputs (type *C* firms). Such firms included large state-owned firms and medium-sized firms. In the second case, market forces determined firms' inputs and outputs (type *F* firms). Such firms included medium-sized firms, small state-owned firms and collective enterprises. In the final case, the government and the market played nearly equal roles in firms' inputs and outputs (type *I* firms). This case applied to a wide range of enterprises including large, medium and small state-owned firms.

The degree of price-responsiveness of these firms can be symbolised as $A, H < C, F, I, < E$. State-owned, dual dependence firms, like C, F and I, are in the majority in present-day China (CESRRI, 1986).[13] The sample firms in our field work, highly centralised before 1979, became dual dependence firms in the post-reform period when allowed to market part of their output. SISM, AISM, and DCM became dual dependence firms in 1984–5; BCM in 1981–2; CZCFF in 1983; BBF in 1980; and WCFF and CZSCFF in 1982.

Although each sample firm was a dual dependence firm, their market conditions differed. Some of the sample firms, such as CZCFF, WCFF, SISM, AISM, BCM, DCM and TBF, faced sellers' markets for both inputs and output. Other firms, such as BBF and CZSCFF, faced a sellers' market for inputs and a buyers' market for output. The price-responsiveness of firms should be analysed with either a sellers' market model or a mixed market model, depending on the market conditions.

7.4 THEORETICAL POST-REFORM MODELS

A. A Sellers' Market Model

The main features of responsiveness of firms to price changes in a sellers' market model are the coexistence of price-responsiveness and quota-responsiveness, and the combination of output response and composition response. These characteristics differ from those in Kornai's model. In China, the manipulation of input and output quotas and prices must be considered together.

The gap between fixed and free prices and the problem of underallocation of producer goods led to the existence of price- and quota-responsiveness. Firms tried to respond to this situation by selling more output in the market (manipulation of average output price). To do so, they refused to fulfil some of their output quota (manipulation of quota). On the input side, firms demanded greater input supplies from the State to keep their production costs low. If they failed to obtain more inputs, they asked the government to cut their output targets and to allow them to sell more output in the market at higher prices.

Another main feature of firms' responsiveness in a sellers' market was that firms responded to price changes not only with changes in output composition, but also with changes in total output. Firms increased their profits by concentrating on the manufacture of commodities with high profit margins, and by increasing the total output so as to sell more above-quota output at high prices. The sellers' market model is applicable to the energy and heavy industrial sectors such as coal and steel.

B. A Mixed Market Model[14]

The responsiveness of the firm in the mixed market model is to some extent similar to that in the sellers' market model. The main difference between the two models is that the firm, in the mixed market model, is in a weak bargaining position with suppliers and consumers for inputs and output. Its position in the input and output markets is symmetrical, not as asymmetrical as in the sellers' market model. The firm, as a buyer, faces a sellers' market and has to compete with its counterparts for raw materials by bidding up prices. As a seller, it faces a buyers' market, and has to improve the quality of its products or lower its production costs to compete. Under such circumstances firms can survive with profits; cease operations; or make financial losses and face the possibility of closure if it is unable to improve its efficiency.

Unlike the firm in a sellers' market, where both demand-pull and cost-push tendencies exist, the firm in a mixed market model faces only a 'demand-pull' tendency. The cost-push tendency of the firm in the mixed market model is greatly limited by the buyers' market for its output. Price becomes a decisive criterion for the profitability and growth of a firm in a mixed market model. The price-responsiveness of firms in this model is much stronger than for firms in the sellers' market model. We use this model for light industrial sectors.

7.5 THE MIXED MARKET MODEL: APPLIED TO BBF AND CZSCFF

Both BBF and CZSCFF passed through several development stages after 1980. First, their financial relationship with the government changed and they became self-marketing firms. Second, their financial situation improved, and they moved from deficits to profitability. Finally, they went bankrupt and closed down.

As mentioned earlier, BBF and CZSCFF were accustomed to making losses and relying on government subsidies. In 1980 the financial relationship between BBF and the Beijing no. 1 Commercial

Department changed.[15] At that time, the Beijing Commercial Department proposed cancelling subsidies and stopping tax exemptions for BBF, since the production costs of its no. 03 bicycle had decreased from 142 to 122 yuan (before tax) per set. This proposal was rejected by BBF as its after-tax production costs of 142 yuan per bicycle was higher than the producer price of 134 yuan; BBF, therefore, proposed to market its own output. After obtaining the permission of the Beijing Economic Committee and the Beijing Price Bureau, BBF began to sell its own bicycles.[16]

The fate of CZSCFF was not very different. In 1980, a new financial policy known as the 'Contract System on Revenue and Expenditure' (*caizheng shouzi baogan*) was introduced by the central government to the industrial sectors to help improve their financial situation.[17] In 1981 the local government suspended its financial subsidy to CZSCFF; CZSCFF was asked by the local Means of Production Company (*shengchan ziliao gongsi*) to market its own products according to prevailing retail prices.

The new type of relationship with the government and the new self-marketing system made price an important criterion for survival and growth in both BBF and CZSCFF. The price-responsiveness of these two firms increased, and both firms temporarily became profit-makers.

A. Output-responsiveness in BBF and CZSCFF

BBF and CZSCFF responded to the self-marketing system by increasing total output and by producing new products (see Tables 7.5 and 7.6). The financial departments of both firms stated that the experience had taught them that increasing total output could lower production costs and increase profits; they thus increased total output rapidly after 1978.

The total output of BBF bicycles increased from 50,000 sets in 1978 to 180,000 sets in 1983. They also introduced three new types of bicycle in this period. Their financial situation improved, and BBF became a profit-maker in 1981. Total before tax profit was 1,798,000 yuan in 1981, 260,000 yuan in 1982, and 1,277,000 yuan in 1983 (see Table 7.5).

CZSCFF followed a similar pattern in 1982. By increasing its output of chemical fertilisers, CZSCFF increased its total profit from 86,000 yuan in 1982 to 856,000 yuan in 1984 (our interviewees did not specify whether this was before or after taxes). It was the first time

Table 7.5 Cost, price, total output and total profit, BBF, 1979–84

	No. 03	*PA12*	*ZA01*	*no. 26*	*Total output*	*Total profit*	*Stocks*
	(Yuan/unit)				*(thousand yuan/thousand units)*		
1979					72	n.a.	n.a.
1. Cost	142						
2. Producer price	134						
3. Subsidy	8						
1980					114	n.a.	n.a.
1. Cost	122	112					
2. Self-marketing price	165	158					
3. Producer price	148	140					
1981					157	1798	6
1. Cost	121	107					
2. Self-marketing price	165	158					
3. Producer price	148	140					
1982					100	260	15
1. Cost	117	118					
2. Self-marketing price	165	158					
3. Producer price	148	140					
1983					180	1277	80
1. Cost	115	115	112	121			
2. Self-marketing price	165	158	156	157			
3. Producer price	148	140	138	139			
1984					60	–2475	n.a.
1. Cost	133	120	127	146			
2. Self-marketing price	165	158	156	157			
3. Producer price	144	140	136	139			
1985 Stop manufacturing							
1986 close down							

Sources: Interviews with BBF, 1985.

Table 7.6 Cost, producer price, retail price, profit and total output, CZSCFF, 1972–86 (yuan/ton)

Year	*Cost*	*Producer price*	*Retail price*	*Total output*	*Profit*
1972	212	150	170	6 622	deficit
1973	218	150	170	6 837	deficit
1974	193	150	170	7 974	deficit
1975	185	150	170	9 969	deficit
1976	268	150	170	5 672	deficit
1977	233	150	170	9 007	deficit
1978	214	150	170	12 649	deficit
1979	183	150	170	17 042	deficit
1980	164	150	170	21 422	deficit
1981	151		182	19 585	n.a.
1982	145		182	22 162	86 000
1983	148		190	28 822	500 000
1984	143		195	31 149	856 000
1985	190–200		165–175	n.a.	deficit
1986	Stop manufacturing				

Sources: Interviews with CZSCFF (22 August 1985).

since 1969 that CZSCFF made profit. In 1984, both total output and total profit reached a peak. However, the profitable periods for BBF and CZSCFF did not last long, since market conditions changed for output (see Table 7.6).

Due to lack of market information and inexperience in marketing, both BBF and CZSCFF failed to realise the change from a sellers' to a buyers' market for their output in the post-reform period; they continued to increase their total output. In 1982, bicycle demand slumped. BBF output decreased 57 per cent in 1982 (see Table 7.5); BBF believed that the decrease in demand was because its bicycles were too old-fashioned, and in 1983 they launched two new types of bicycles for suburban peasants and the urban population. Without the benefit of market research, 180,000 of these bicycles were manufactured, an increase of 80 per cent over 1982. The firm managed to sell only 100,000 of them in 1983; the other 80,000 remained in the firm's inventory (see Table 7.5).

Not until July 1983 did BBF learn that they faced a buyers' market. They then proposed to cut the price of one type of bicycle in September, 1983.[18] However, the price reduction was not approved by the Beijing Price Bureau until 1984. According to BBF's financial department, the main factors contributing to their deficit of 2,475,000 yuan in 1984 were the overproduction of 1983, an incorrect production policy in 1984 (another 60,000 bicycles were produced), and the delay in price reduction.

The rather small CZSCFF also suffered similar problems. It made its output decisions without knowing the output plan of its competitor, the large chemical fertiliser firm, CZCFF, located only a few miles away.[19] In 1983, the output of the larger firm decreased by 34.3 per cent; there was a consequent shortage of chemical fertilisers in Hebei.[20] Under these circumstances, CZSCFF (the small firm) correctly adopted an expansion strategy. However, in 1984 the total output of CZCFF (the large firm) increased from 267,000 to 314,000 tons, and the small CZSCFF also augmented its total output by 8 per cent. Unfortunately, the national demand for chemical fertilisers fell by 7.2 per cent in 1985 and there was a large quantity of imported chemical fertilisers available (18.35 million tons). A buyers' market for chemical fertilisers thus appeared in Hebei in 1985.[21] This forced CZSCFF to stockpile its fertilisers. Retail prices decreased from 195 to 165–175 yuan per ton in 1985, and CZSCFF plunged into a financial deficit (see Table 7.6).

The output problems constitute only half the story. Some questions remain unanswered. For example, why could BBF only cut 2 yuan from the producer price of a new type of bicycle? Why did CZSCFF fail to survive when its retail prices were still 165–175 yuan per ton? And why was it unable to keep production costs at an average of 145 yuan per ton between 1982 and 1984? We attempt to answer these questions by looking at the price-responsiveness of inputs.

B. Input-responsiveness in BBF and CZSCFF

High production costs undermined the competitiveness of these two firms. Tables 7.5 and 7.6 show that the production costs of bicycles and chemical fertilisers increased rapidly in 1984 (BBF), and in 1985 (CZSCFF). The BBF's production costs increased between 4 per cent and 21 per cent for different bicycles. High costs also made it difficult to compete in a buyers' market (the cost of production of a PA12 bicycle was 120 yuan per set (before tax) at BBF, 50–52 yuan (71 per cent–76 per cent) higher than the cost of production in the Shanghai no. 3 Bicycle Factory in 1984: interviews with BBF, 1985).

CZSCFF production costs increased from 143 yuan per ton in 1984 to 190–200 yuan per ton in 1985, an increase of 33 per cent–40 per cent in one year (see Table 7.6). Production costs in 1985 were 15 per cent higher than retail prices. BBF and CZSCFF both lost ground in the market because of their high costs of production.

These two firms failed to reduce production costs to a level which would enable them to compete in the market for several reasons. They faced a sellers' market for inputs and had to pay high prices for raw materials; they had no incentive to reduce production costs and improve the quality of their goods because of the soft-budget constraint; and they had a strong incentive to increase the profit shares of workers rather than undertake technological innovation.

Since BBF and CZSCFF both faced a sellers' market for inputs it was difficult for them to reduce production costs to a great extent. For example, the most appropriate input steel for BBF was tubular or steel plate (*dai gang*). Because these types of steel commanded low prices producers were unwilling to supply them. BBF, therefore, often had to purchase round plate steel (*jiangang*) from producers and process it first into steel plate and then into tubular form. Such processing raised the cost approximately 200 yuan per ton.

BBF also had to purchase input steel from the market at high prices, since they received little steel from the Beijing Allocation Bureau after 1980. This also contributed to the relatively high costs of raw materials at BBF compared to the Shanghai no. 3 Bicycle Factory which received a large quantity of input steel from the government at fixed prices. In 1984 the cost of raw material (mainly steel) per bicycle at BBF was 67 per cent higher than that at the Shanghai no. 3 Bicycle Factory (interviews with BBF, 1985).

CZSCFF also faced a sellers' market for inputs. In 1984, it received only 50 per cent of its required input of anthracite, and 20 per cent of its required input of lignite from the local government. The rest of the coal had to be purchased from the market at higher prices. Production costs, therefore, increased 30–39 per cent in 1985.

When BBF and CZSCFF began making profit in 1980 and 1981, they had little incentive to improve the quality of their products. The quality of the PA12 bicycle improved to 9.2 in 1983, far behind the 9.9 or 10 of a first-class bicycle.[22] The quality of the chemical fertilisers at CZSCFF also did not improve after 1981. Poor quality was one of the reasons for the decrease in retail prices in 1985 (interview, 1985).

Quality improvements were very minor because retained profits were distributed as bonuses and welfare benefits for workers rather than being invested in product innovation and technological improve-

Table 7.7 Distribution of retained profits, BBF and CZSCFF, 1983 and 1984

		BBF (1983)	*CZSCFF (1984)*
A	Total profit	1 277 000	865 000
B	Profit to the State (%)	55	55
C	Profit retention by the firm (%)	45	45
1.	Employee welfare fund (%)	25	10
2.	Employee incentive fund (%)	55	35
3.	Reserve fund (%)	5	15
4.	Production development fund (%)	12	40
5.	New product trial run fund (%)	3	none

Sources: Interviews, 1985.

ments. In 1983, the last year before BBF went into the red, it made profits of 1,227,000 yuan. It handed 55 per cent of its total profit to the local government and retained the remaining 45 per cent. The firm spent 25 per cent of its retained profits on the Employee Welfare Fund, 55 per cent on the Employee Incentive Fund, 5 per cent on the Reserve Fund, 12 per cent on the Production Development Fund, and the final 3 per cent on the New Product Trial Run Fund (see Table 7.7).

The retained profits spent on improving production capacity and efficiency were lower than that spent on the welfare and incentive funds in both firms, particularly in BBF. They totalled only 15 per cent (including the new product trial run fund) for BBF, and 40 per cent for CZSCFF. The bulk of profits were spent on welfare and bonuses.[23] Consequently, such firms faced the prospect of closing down[24] and it was reported that 36,000 firms closed down between 1985 and 1986 (*Ming Bao Yuekan* vol. 22, no. 11, November 1987 : 40).[25] Perhaps many of them, like BBF and CZSCFF, faced a mixed market for inputs and output.

The survivors in a mixed market were required to improve quality, widen variety, reduce prices, and speed delivery. Price became an important survival and growth criterion, and price-responsiveness had to be stronger than that of firms in a sellers' market. In the following section, we look at the price-responsiveness of the firms in sellers' markets.

7.6 THE SELLERS' MARKET MODEL: APPLIED TO CZCFF, WCFF, AISM, SZISM, BCM, DCM, TBF AND SISM

In this section we consider both the input- and output-responsiveness of certain sample firms: CZCFF; WCFF; AISM; BCM; DCM; TBF; and the SISM.

A. Input-responsiveness in Sample Firms

One important characteristic of input-responsiveness in the sample firms in the post-reform period was a quota-responsiveness. The quota-responsiveness of firms was strong because the system of state monopoly in the distribution of producer goods was weakened while output targets remained unchanged. For example, the total supply of natural gas from the Dagang Oil Field to CZCFF dropped by 50 per cent in 1983. CZCFF thus did not fulfil its output target, and its output of fertilisers decreased from 407,000 tons in 1982 to 267,000 tons in 1983, a decrease of 34 per cent (interviews with CZCFF, 1985).

The sudden decrease in the supply of natural gas also affected production costs and total profits. CZCFF demanded that the government restore its supply of natural gas to former levels. A meeting was held between the Oil and Chemical Ministry, the Agricultural Ministry, and the State Economic Commission to discuss their request; no solution was reached. CZCFF then demanded compensation for its lost profits by asking the government to increase the share of its output which could be sold at free prices.

Underallocation of input materials was also a problem for other sample firms such as WCFF and AISM.[26] Moreover, because of the existence of a large gap between fixed price and free prices and the continuation of planned targets, the problem of raw material underallocation prompted most sample firms to demand larger allocations of raw materials from the government.

The sample firms can be divided into two groups, according to the causes of production cost increases. The increase of production costs for the first group of firms mainly came from the underallocation problem. This group included CZCFF and WCFF. The increased

Table 7.8 Cost structure of coal in the DCM and BCM, 1983–4 (%)

	DCM		*BCM*	
	1983	*1984*	*1983*	*1984*
1. Raw materials	31.9	30.9	23.6	19.4
2. Wages	23.6	26.1	34.8	41.0
3. Electricity	6.3	5.7	8.1	7.3
4. Welfare fund	2	2	2.7	3
5. Overhaul fund	10.7	11.3	7	6.8
6. Maintenance	16.4	15	11.2	10.4
7. Other expenses	9	9	12.5	12.1
8. Total	99.9	100	99.9	100

Sources: Interviews, 1985.

production costs failed to cause CZCFF and WCFF to reduce their use of raw materials (coal and natural gas) and improve efficiency; rather, they demanded more coal and natural gas from the government, or purchased them in the market regardless of price. They managed to make a profit by manipulating the dual pricing system.

The second group of firms, which included BCM, DCM, SISM, AISM and TBF, found their production costs affected by a number of factors, underallocation being only one. They thus had weaker quota-responsiveness incentives.

Table 7.8 shows that factors which affected the production cost increases in the DCM and the BCM between 1983 and 1984 included wages increases, bonuses, foodstuff subsidies and others. The increase in wages was the key factor. Because increased production costs were not mainly caused by material underallocation, and because these firms could barter their output for raw materials, the quota-responsiveness of these firms was weaker than in firms of the first group. (In interviews with these two firms, both pointed out that the reduction of the wage bill was their main concern.)

The price-responsiveness to inputs was weak in both groups of firms because of the dual pricing system. The quota-responsiveness on the input side was stronger for firms in the first than in the second group.

B. Output-responsiveness in Sample Firms

Firms in sellers' markets were quota-responsive and price-responsive in terms of both total output and output composition.

Firms which tried to bargain with the government for lower production targets so as to sell more above-quota output in the market at higher prices included CZCFF, AISM, BCM and DCM. In 1984 CZCFF agreed to purchase half of its natural gas at market prices from the Dagang oil field, on condition that the government lower their production target and allow them to sell more above-quota output in the market. The government permitted CZCFF to divide its output into two parts. The part which used government natural gas inputs was handed over to the government; the remaining output, made with natural gas purchased in the market, was sold in the market.

BCM also successfully bargained for lower production targets in 1984. It began to bargain for lower production targets in 1981, when coal output started to decrease and cause financial losses.[27] In 1985, BCM received permission to reduce its production target from 6.2 million tons to 5.9 million tons.[28]

The strongest demand to reduce production targets and increase above-quota output came from large state-owned firms in the iron and steel industry. In 1983 SISM was permitted to self-market 15 per cent of its annual planned output of rolled steel. Other large iron and steel mills including AISM were permitted to self-market only 2 per cent of their output. This difference created a controversy between SISM and other large mills, and between the other large mills and the Ministry of Finance and the Ministry of Metallurgy. Whether SISM could keep its high rate of self-marketing was decided by Deng Xiaoping and Zhao Ziyang in the Autumn of 1987, when SISM renewed its profit contract (*Renmin Ribao*, 20 October 1987). This case highlighted the seriousness of quota-responsiveness in the steel industry between 1983 and 1987.

The responsiveness of firms to price changes in terms of changes in output and changes in output composition differs in degree. We first look at the price-responsiveness of total output in the firms with weak responses, such as DCM and TBF, and then in those with strong responses, such as WCFF, CZCFF, BCM and SISM.

'Weak response' implies that price changes give little incentive to firms to adjust their total output – that is, price changes have little impact on the profitability and growth of these firms. These firms paid attention to price only if their net profits from sales were affected by input prices. But they continued to make profits without increasing output prices. For example, neither TBF nor DCM had strong incentives to respond to price changes in either inputs or outputs. Net profits at DCM increased from 297 to 347 million yuan between 1979 and 1984; at TBF net profits increased by 30 per cent between 1982 and 1984 (interview, 1985). Whether total output could be increased was limited by production scale in TBF, and by transportation constraints in DCM, not by price factors.

Although price was not a life-and-death matter to these firms, they were aware of how easily they could take advantage of the new pricing system. TBF, for example, rejected government proposals to increase the producer price of its first-class bicycle in 1984, when its production costs remained the same level as in 1983. It asked the government to increase the producer price in 1986, after production costs had increased an average of 3.3 yuan per set for six types of bicycles in 1985.[29] The increased production costs of 1985 slightly affected the profit of TBF, but did not affect its growth. Nevertheless, it wanted to pass the increased production costs on to its customers via legal means.

One of the most profitable coal mines, DCM, adopted a different way to protect its profit. It imposed a hidden price increase to its customers. In the 1985 survey, some coal users complained that although DCM did not raise the price of coal, it did ask users to pay several years' payments in advance to ensure coal delivery each year (a situation denied by DCM: interviews, 1985).

'Strong response' in total output means that price factors affect the growth and profitability of firms to a certain extent, yet without threatening their survival. Nevertheless, they responded to price changes in inputs and outputs to avoid running into financial deficits. The strong response firms, WCFF, CZCFF, BCM and SISM, had price-responsiveness stronger than TBF and DCM, but weaker than firms in mixed markets.

CZCFF and WCFF admitted that they tried to increase total output as much as possible so as to have extra above-quota output to sell in the market. It is believed that half of the 1984 output of 314,000 tons of urea produced at CZCFF was sold in the market at 600 yuan per ton, and the remainder sold to the government at 410 yuan per ton. The outcome was an 89 per cent increase in net profits of CZCFF in 1984, mainly derived from output sold in the market.

BCM responded to price changes not by increasing its own output, but by purchasing coal at low prices from small local pits and reselling it in the market at higher prices. Beginning in 1980 or 1981, BCM bought 200,000–300,000 tons of coal annually from these small pits. In return, BCM supplied the small pits with machines, engineers, transportation and some capital funds. Prior to 1985, part of the coal bought from these pits was handed over to the government as quota output, the remaining portion being sold in the market at prices 2 to 3 times the fixed prices. From 1985 onwards, all this coal was sold in the market at free prices.

In the iron and steel industry (according to the research study by the CESRRI in 1985 concerning 12 medium-sized steel mills) if 10 per cent of steel output were self-marketed by a firm, then prices would affect its total output.[30] This principle also applied to the large steel mills in our sample. The proportion of self-marketed steel at SISM was 15 per cent after 1983: the output of its rolled steel increased from 1 million tons in 1981 to 1.98 million tons in 1984, an increase of 98 per cent. This does not imply that the increase was totally due to the 15 per cent self-marketing policy, but rather suggests that the 15 per cent self-marketing policy had a positive impact on total output.[31]

The effect of prices on output composition can be demonstrated by AISM and SISM. The marketing department of AISM admitted that their output composition was affected by price ratios. In 1983, AISM learned there was a serious shortage of strip steel and welded steel, but was unwilling to increase its output of these products since the company would make a loss by producing them.[32] AISM was not worried about overproducing the types of steel which commanded higher prices since it faced a sellers' market for its output.[33]

Prices also had an impact on the output composition in SISM. It preferred to produce the 18mm mild steel bars for 495 yuan per ton, rather than the 19mm type priced at 375 yuan per ton. SISM reported that its incentive to respond to price changes by changing total output and the output composition increased after the institutionalisation of dual pricing in 1985 (interview, 1985).

7.7 SUMMARY

The price-responsiveness of inputs and outputs of firms was stronger in the post-reform than in the pre-reform period. In the pre-reform period, to meet output value targets more easily, firms responded to price changes by changing output composition rather than total output. The main difference between the situation in China and Kornai's model was that the demand-pull and cost-push tendency in China were not symmetrical in the pre-reform period. These tendencies were stronger in the small and medium-sized firms than in the large state-owned firms in China, another difference from the Hungarian situation.

In the post-reform period, in both sellers' and mixed markets, price-responsiveness coexisted with quota-responsiveness, and both total output and output composition were affected. These responses did not occur in the pre-reform period in China or in Kornai's model.

In sellers' markets, the price-responsiveness of input decisions in most of the sample firms in the post-reform period was still weak because of the dual pricing system. However, quota-responsiveness on the input side was strong for some firms and weak for others. On the output side, quota-responsiveness asking for a reduction in output quotas and an increase in input supplies from the government was strong for most of the sample firms.

The responsiveness of total output and output composition to price changes varied in sellers' markets. Some sample firms' responsiveness was strong, others was not. In sellers' markets, firms had both demand-pull and cost-push tendencies in the post-reform period; however, they preferred to pass cost increases on to customers. It was easier to manipulate the dual pricing system to preserve profits than to ask a subsidy from the government.

In mixed markets, firms (both as sellers and buyers) were in a weak position, and had strong incentives to meet customers' needs by improving efficiency. Although there was a tendency towards demand-pull because of shortage, it was not as strong as in firms in sellers' markets. The cost-push tendency was almost eliminated as these firms faced buyers' markets for output. Since firms could not pass cost increases on to their customers, they had to improve the quality of their products or reduce production costs. Price, therefore, became an important factor affecting the profitability and growth of firms.

The price-responsiveness of firms was much stronger in mixed markets than in sellers' markets. Improving the price-responsiveness of firms in sellers' markets requires more reform of the pricing system and the economic system, especially dual pricing and the financial relationships between the government and enterprises. It also requires a transformation of sellers' markets to buyers' or mixed markets.

8 Summary and Conclusions

This study set out to investigate the characteristics, achievements and difficulties involved in the process of reforming the producer and procurement pricing system in China. Although our study dealt with only five specific commodities, its findings are significant since the goods were important, and studying them sheds light on the reform of the pricing system as a whole. The findings of our research are summarised here in terms of the characteristics of Chinese price reform, its achievements and its problems. We also consider the future development of, and obstacles to, price reform.

From 1979 to 1986 China tried to transform its pricing system from a high degree of price control in a bureaucratic–hierarchical command economy to a system of partial price control in a less centralised socialist economy. It sought to place less emphasis on the accounting and income distribution roles of prices and more emphasis on resource allocation. These objectives were to some degree achieved. The pricing system developed from a single fixed price system to a mixed price one. The new price system stimulated output, and contributed to the balancing of supply and demand for certain commodities.

The current situation in China is complex and controversial, since dual pricing, which now predominates, is a source of conflict in both allocation and distribution. The plan and the market, like two cogs in a mechanism, have meshed. Each competes to control the direction of the other. These incompatible and mutually exclusive economic mechanisms now confront each other in important economic spheres such as the industrial sector. This situation has affected enterprise behaviour and the relationship between enterprises and the government in both positive and negative ways. It has also caused the Chinese price reform experience to differ from the East European experiences.

8.1 CHARACTERISTICS OF CHINESE PRICE REFORM

Chinese price reform began in 1979. In the beginning, many Chinese economists believed that the traditional price system was too centralised, and that price-setting was not based on the law of value and therefore failed to reflect both costs and the relationship between supply and demand. Suggested remedies included administratively decentralising the system and applying a new formula to 'get the prices right'.

This view was criticised and gradually replaced by a new theoretical and political position in the mid-1980s, which claimed that the inefficient and distorted price system did not stem simply from problems of price-setting and administrative implementation. It was also a result of the nature of the whole socialist political and economic system, which determined the characteristics of price formation and the role of prices. Price problems could not therefore be solved by simply improving the price system, a wider reform of the political and economic system was also needed.

In the history of socialist pricing systems, three patterns of development can be identified: pricing in a revolutionary economy; pricing and price reform in a bureaucratic–hierarchical command economy; and pricing and price reform in less centralised market socialism.

Price reform in socialist countries appears to have followed two paths. One involved reform within the existing price and economic systems, for example the 1968 reform in the Soviet Union; the other involved government attempts to transform not only the old price system but also the entire economic system, as was the case in Hungary and Yugoslavia. Price reform in China, between 1979 and 1986, belongs to the latter category.

Three methods of reform were employed by the Chinese government to transform the pricing system from a high degree of price control in a bureaucratic–hierarchical command economy to one of partial price control in a less centralised market economy. They were adjustment, liberalisation, and a combination of adjustment and liberalisation. These three reform methods reflected conflicts between various political and economic groups in the government.

Price reform in China has been an outcome of conflicts and compromises among the Centralisers, the Administrative Decentralisers, and the Market Reformers. Each group put forward different proposals, which included the methods of reform, the principle of price formation, and the time frame of reform. These divergent proposals shaped the policy and process of price reform, and determined the three stages of price reform between 1979 and 1986.

8.2 ACHIEVEMENTS AND PROBLEMS

A. Price Formation

In socialist countries, there have always been some economists who argued that administered price formation should be based on a particular theoretical principle or formula. Controversies have therefore arisen over which principle should be adopted to replace old formulas of price setting.

In practice, there appears to have been no uniform principle for setting either producer or procurement prices in the pre-reform period. Cost-plus pricing, which was proclaimed as a basis for price-setting, was not widely or strictly applied. Actual price-setting was determined by political, economic and historical factors.

In the post-reform period, price adjustment again did not follow any one blueprint. Price adjustments were variously based on international prices; cost structure and desired price ratios; income considerations, especially for peasants; balances between supply and demand; implications for state revenues; and quality improvements. The various adjustments resulted in both successes and failures. One successful case of price adjustment was that of cotton, where price adjustment improved the balance between supply and demand. In contrast, it proved impossible to implement price adjustments based on a quality principle for bicycles in 1984.

Problems in price adjustment were deeply rooted not only in the principles of price formation, but also in power conflicts in the administrative process of price determination, and in the lack of administrative capacity for implementation. This was demonstrated in the case of price adjustment for coal in 1979, and in the case of the Beijing Bicycle Factory (BBF) in 1980–1. To have an efficient fixed price system, it is important for the government not only to try to find the right price formula, but also to improve the efficiency of price determination and implementation capacity.

B. Price Functions

It is often stated that administered prices have limited potential for stimulating output and for shifting output composition than free prices. The fixed price system was blamed both for causing shortages in total output and for the problem of the coexistence of shortages and surpluses in output composition.

An investigation into these issues indicates that price was an important, but not the key, factor in affecting total output, output composition and the coexistence problem. Our study on the use of prices to regulate the total output of coal and cotton during the post-reform period found that the output of cotton increased and decreased significantly in response to price changes, yet the output of coal did not. Apparently, farmers were more sensitive to price changes than state enterprises, and political conflicts over cotton price increases were weaker than those over coal.

Coal output, especially in state coal mines, was governed mainly by plan targets but was also affected by production conditions, technology, and investment. Price changes affected the profits of coal mines, and coal output was price-sensitive (though less so in large state-owned coal mines than in small, collective mines). However, political conflicts prevented a large enough price adjustment and thus, in the post-reform period, output from big state-owned coal mines was not stimulated significantly by price adjustments. A combination of liberalisation and adjustment (for large coal mines) and liberalisation alone (for small coal mines) was used to raise prices while getting around political conflicts. Free prices, especially, had important impacts on the output of small, village and collective coal mines, which were the main contributors to increased aggregate coal output.

Concerning the use of prices to regulate the output composition of steel and bicycles, we also found that irrational price ratios were not the key factor causing the problem of coexistence of shortages and surpluses. In the bicycle industry, the coexistence problem stemmed from the supply side. The limited increase of good-quality bicycles was mainly the result of a non-price factor – a resource constraint, particularly the shortage of land for enterprise expansion. The fundamental, non-price factor that encouraged increased manufacturing of inferior bicycles was the expansion drive (investment hunger) of both enterprises and local governments. However, price influences became important in certain sectors when a buyers' market and a dual pricing system appeared. These factors strongly conditioned and affected economic performance and, to some extent, hardened the budget constraints of some firms.

In the steel industry, the coexistence of shortages and inventory mainly stemmed from the demand side. 80 per cent of steel inventory was held by users in 1985, a result of a security drive under the shortage and soft-budget constraint syndrome. This type of inventory bred shortages, and vice versa, giving rise to a vicious circle.

Although the transformation of the price system was incomplete, prices played a varied role – accounting, income distribution and resource allocation – depending on the nature of the commodity and government policy for that commodity. The procurement prices of cotton, for example, regulated resource allocation between 1979 and 1985. Free prices regulated the output of small steel mills, village and collective coal mines and small chemical fertiliser factories, and also affected income distribution. Nevertheless, administered producer prices were still important in accounting and income distribution for quota-output of state-owned steel mills, coal mines, chemical fertiliser plants, and bicycle enterprises.

Between 1979 and 1984 price adjustment dominated category one commodities and affected the output of certain other important commodities such as cotton; it was not very effective for other commodities, particularly industrial goods. The goal of using price reform to emphasise the role of prices in resource allocation for important commodities could therefore not be achieved by relying simply on price adjustment. Neither could this goal be achieved by relaxing price control 'at one stroke', since immediate liberalisation would cause a great shock to the economy. Under these conditions, the dual pricing system – a system of bureaucratic and market coordination in price determination – was adopted for certain important commodities in 1985. It was an important step in the reform of producer prices of important commodities such as industrial capital and intermediate goods. It was designed to serve as a relay-station for transforming the price system from an administratively-oriented to a market-oriented one.

C. Dual Pricing and Price-responsiveness

The dual pricing system had both positive and negative effects on the macro-economy in terms of efficiency, income distribution, economic stability and economic calculation and evaluation.[1] Dual pricing also had a great impact on enterprises at the micro-level. Price effects on enterprises and enterprise response to price changes are important criteria for the evaluation of correctness of price policy and the rationality of price functions: 'getting prices right' in socialist countries is not only a matter of how prices are set, but also a matter of whether or not enterprises respond to them.

According to Kornai's model, the price-responsiveness of the inputs and outputs of a firm is weak in a sellers' market and under soft-budget constraints. We find the price-responsiveness of the pre-reform period in China to be close to Kornai's model, with some differences. However, enterprise response to price changes in the post-reform period was too complex to be explained by Kornai's sellers' market model. This model, based on the Hungarian experience, did not consider certain factors which developed in post-1979 China.

One such factor was the impact of the simultaneous dual pricing and administrative allocation systems on enterprises. In Hungary, after the abolition of the mandatory planning system, state-owned firms depended entirely on the market for inputs and output, and depended on the government for financial subsidies, capital supply and investment. In China's post-reform period firms depended on the government for both inputs and output, and for financing. Firms also relied on the market for inputs and output. This resulted in a complicated pattern of incentives and behaviour. Firms responded both to price changes and to alterations in quotas (for input supply and output). Firms also had an interest in manipulating both prices and quotas to their own advantage, through action in the market and through administrative negotiations. This situation had no parallel in the Hungarian case.

A second factor was that a buyers' market on the output side for some commodities developed in post-reform China. Firms thus typically faced either a sellers' market for both inputs and output, or a mixed market – a sellers' market for inputs and a buyers' market for output. Mixed markets were not dealt with in Kornai's model. Nevertheless, the model of price-responsiveness in mixed markets provides great insights into why 36,000 firms folded between 1985 and 1986 (*Ming Bao Yuekan*, vol. 22, no. 11, November 1987 : 40).

In short, the price-responsiveness of inputs and output in firms was stronger in the post-reform than in the pre-reform period in China. In the post-reform period, the price-responsiveness and quota-responsiveness of firms which faced mixed markets was stronger than that of firms which faced only sellers' markets.

For firms which faced mixed markets – mainly medium-sized and small firms such as BBF and the Changzhou Small Chemical Fertiliser Factory (CZSCFF), dual pricing became an important factor influencing profitability and growth. Dual pricing was less important than quota-responsiveness in firms such as the Datong Coal Mine (DCM) and the Anshan Iron and Steel Mill (AISM) which faced sellers' markets. Changes in input supply quotas and output delivered quotas affected the profit and growth more than price changes for such firms.

The dual pricing system had both positive and negative effects on the economy and on enterprises, but it was not able to identify which – the positive or the negative – predominated in the period between 1985 and 1986. Since China cannot abolish dual pricing immediately, nor easily replace it with a single fixed or free pricing system, it is in China's interest to improve the administrative management system of dual pricing, by drawing lessons from India, which seems to conduct its system quite well.

Government reports and Chinese newspapers in 1988 indicate that dual pricing is now perceived as having had more negative than positive effects, and has become an obstacle to the future of price reform.[2] The main drawback of the present dual pricing system is that it makes the circulation of commodities more complicated and more difficult to administer than the total pricing control system. The traditional circulation system collapsed and a new circulation system which comprises both planning and market distribution has not yet been effectively constructed. Many goods such as steel and iron are illegally traded many times in the circulation chain before hitting the production process. Moreover, after 1985, large price hikes for certain important commodities appear to have made little or no contribution to solving the problem of shortage.

Since free prices were 2 to 3 times higher than fixed prices, the market mechanism challenged and threatened state planning. There has, so far, been no effective measure to ensure that the output quota of enterprises is fulfilled according to plan. One report in the *Economic Daily* (2 August 1988) indicates that the contracts for the output of 14 important commodities, all of which are subject to the State Plan, were seriously underfulfilled in the first four months of 1988.

Dual pricing did not generate a balance between demand and supply of important goods, even though excess demand could find an outlet in the market. Dual pricing may even have intensified the problem of coexistence of shortages and surpluses. For example, steel inventory increased from 26 million tons in 1985 to 30.79 million tons in 1986, an increase of 18.4 per cent.[3]

Dual pricing also had positive features. It helped to channel resources to the less administratively influential but economically potentially important sectors such as rural enterprises and medium and small urban firms. This undesirably affected key State projects (*Economy Daily*, 2 August 1988). Since key projects did not receive sufficient requirements of producer goods at fixed prices, and had to purchase raw materials from the market at much higher prices, their total costs increased. This increase in construction costs sometimes prolonged the completion of projects, due to government financial constraints.

Under such circumstances, there were controversies, between politicians such as Zhao Ziyang who was reported (*Financial Times*, 28 October 1988) to favour dual pricing, and some influential figures who favoured a move back towards administrative pricing. Nevertheless, a new reform of producer prices of important goods such as steel, coal and iron, was officially announced by Prime Minister Li Peng (*Renmin Ribao*, 7 July 1988).[4] The new reform moved the system towards free pricing.[5]

8.3 FUTURE DEVELOPMENT AND OBSTACLES

The direction of producer price reform is clear. Can the goal of transforming dual pricing into a free price system be achieved in five years, as suggested by the Chinese government?[6] This will depend to what extent, and how quickly, the government can remove or minimise the obstacles to price reform. The fundamental obstacle to future price reform is political. As in the 1979–86 period, politics and price reform intertwine and interact.[7] Since short-term political factors determine the shape of the price reform programme and condition its development, future price reform success depends on the balance of power among the three political and ideological groups (the Centralisers, the Administrative Decentralisers and the Market Reformers).

Future price reform also requires an improvement in the efficiency of the administrative system and the establishment of effective institutions for policy enforcement. Prior to 1985, there was only one institution, the State Price Bureau (SPB), which implemented price policies. The main task of the SPB was to increase or to decrease prices; there was no link or network between the SPB and other institutions such as the Finance Ministry, the Ministry of Materials Allocation,[8] the Central State Planning Commission, and the Central State Economic Commission, to monitor price reform at the microeconomic level. An effective institution and network, therefore, is necessary to prevent the leakage of important goods from plan control to the market. Other institutional changes and enterprise reform will be needed to prevent price relaxation leading to inflation. Inflation in 1985 and 1986 was due partly to the late 1984 and early 1985 decentralisation of the banking system and the new credit system. Price reform, thus, requires a compatible monetary policy. This requires close cooperative work between the SPC, the Central Bank, the Finance Ministry and other institutions.

More fundamentally, price reform cannot succeed without compatible reform in other areas of the economy, such as the resource allocation system and the enterprise wage system. Will enterprises respond appropriately to a new pricing system if they are still state-owned and under soft-budget constraints? This research supports the view that all types of pricing systems will be less effective under soft-budget constraints. The form of the price (free or fixed) is not very significant if enterprise response to price changes is weak; successful price reform cannot therefore be achieved without changing the soft-budget constraint system. Such a change would involve a reform of the ownership system, which would imply a whole reform of the socialist economic system. If China wants to achieve both correct prices and strong price-responsiveness, then more than five years may be needed.

Notes and References

1 Historical and International Context

1. Moore and White (1987) argue that liberalisation is a long-term process involving a basic change in relations between government and society: 'Almost all countries, rich and poor, capitalist and socialist, large and small, have moved away from state control of the economy to favour the private sector and the competitive markets . . . In the socialist countries liberalization represents a response to the perceived inadequacies of centralized planning and administration of the economy. In the Third World it is seen as a way out of economic stagnation and is frequently embodied in structural adjustment programmes advocated and supported by the international institutions'.
2. Kornai (1985 : 15) calls the positive approach explanatory theory. See also Leftwich and Eckert, 1985 : 9; Kornai, 1980 : 5–6; Meier, 1983 : 54.
3. These economists differ in their approaches to socialism but agree on fundamental price issues.
4. Hayek (1935) argued that 'it was not the possibility of planning as such which has been questioned, but the possibility of successful planning'.
5. Sweezy's criticises Lange's model in that the central planning board, is not a planning agency at all but, rather, a price-fixing organ, and production decisions are left to independent units, just as they are under capitalism (Sweezy, 1949 : 233).
6. In traditional Marxist thought, land and capital are not viewed as contributing to costs.
7. Such prices caused differences in the level and/or rate of profits (or losses) which were unrelated to the performance of firms or their contribution to the economy.
8. Lu Nan (1985), Director of the Price Research Institute at the State Price Bureau. Information here is derived from one of his unpublished articles, 'An Introduction of the Price Reform in the Soviet Union and East European Countries', which was based on his participation in the Price Conference of the CMEA countries held in Poland in June 1985.
9. 'There are still large proportions of prices which deviate from factor cost to reflect the opportunity cost of the utilization of land, capital and labour' (Wilczynski, 1973 : 105).
10. Different types of buyers and sellers faced different plan prices for the same product (Wilczynski, 1973 : 105).
11. For more details see Wilczynski (1973 : 107).
12. Wilczynski (1973) argued that even if the State tried to raise prices to reflect new costs, there was no guarantee that producers would respond accordingly. In the post-reform period, Hungarian managers failed to react to price changes as high as 10 per cent. The problem of weak price responsiveness was highlighted by Kornai in his theory of economic shortage (Kornai, 1980).

13. According to Chinese economists, if inflation were inevitable then a rate between 3 per cent and 6 per cent would be best for China (based on an informal talk with Huang Da, Vice-President of the People's University of China, 1985). This was also the rate that Hungary aimed for in the 1985–9 period.
14. For more detail on the issue of price formation see Chapter 3.
15. This was aimed at: first, the separation of producer and retail prices to enable the State to control or influence the market situation while constructing the planning system (Perkins, 1966 : 10–20); second, allowing the State to increase output of certain goods, rationalise redistribution of income between different social organs, and maintain price stability (the State could increase producer prices and reduce retail prices of the same product at the same time to encourage both producers and users); and, third, enabling the State to raise revenue from producers rather than consumers.
16. From December 1949 to March 1950, the retail price index rose 122 per cent, grain 152 per cent, foodstuffs 196 per cent, energy 81 per cent, and cotton cloth 113 per cent. After March 1950, inflation came under control (interview with Zhu Chengping, 1985). This change was due not only to monetary and fiscal controls, but also to other methods. According to Zhu Chengping, the recovery of production was a fundamental factor in the control of inflation. 1950 gross output value of agriculture and industry was 23.3 per cent above 1949 levels. The gross output value of industry itself increased by 36.4 per cent while the gross output value of agriculture increased by 17.7 per cent (in 1950 constant prices) (Perkins, 1966).
17. The market price of grain in many areas was 20–30 per cent above official prices in 1953 (Perkins, 1966).
18. The contract system introduced in 1952 a springtime agreement on the price and quantity of goods to be delivered to the State in the fall. Farmers were then given an advance, in effect, an interest-free loan ('rich peasants' had to pay a low rate of interest). The advantages of this system were thus, first, it protected the farmers from adverse price fluctuations due to market forces; and, second, it provided farmers with funds when they needed them most.
19. The system of planned purchase was introduced for different goods at different times: for grains in 1953, and for cotton in 1954. This involved a system of compulsory purchase quotas.
20. In China, commodities were classified into three categories for the purpose of controlling allocation. Category one goods were allocated by the State planning commission and category two goods by the various industrial ministries, while category three items were regulated by the local governments and could be freely exchanged. The first two categories included all goods vital to the economy such as iron and steel, coal, cement, petroleum, electricity, lumber, major machinery, construction materials, grain, edible oils, cotton and other important raw materials and fuels. The list varied from time to time according to national priorities, politics, and – most importantly – whether an item was in short supply or not. The first two categories encompassed 70 per

cent to 80 per cent of the value of production (Koziara and Yan, 1983.
21. This involved a new policy of planning decentralisation. See Lin (1981) and Perkins (1966) for detailed descriptions of the policy.
22. 'Regulations on Further Economy in Making Revolution, Restricting the Purchasing Power of Collectives, and Strengthening Control over Funds, Supplies and Prices.'
23. By 1976, the average production cost of 21 goods in the metallurgy industry had increased 30 per cent over 1965 levels.
24. This refers to the inequitable price parities in the exchange of agricultural and industrial products.
25. State subsidies for farm prices amounted to 7.8 billion yuan in 1978, 14.6 billion in 1979, 20.8 billion in 1980, and 32.0 billion in 1981 (Wang Zhenzhi *et al.*, 1982 : 229).
26. See Chapter 3 for more detail.
27. These irrational prices ratios, causing a coexistence of shortage and surplus in industry, are examined in detail in Chapter 5.
28. Wider profit margins were found in industries such as watchmaking, 61 per cent; rubber processing, 45 per cent; bicycles, 40 per cent; dyestuff, 38 per cent; daily utensils, 30 per cent; pharmaceuticals, 33 per cent; and cotton textiles, 32 per cent. The narrower profit margins were found in industries like chemical fertilisers, 1.4 per cent; iron mining, 1.6 per cent; coal mining, 2.1 per cent; ship building, 2.8 per cent; chemical mining, 3.2 per cent; farm tools, 3.1 per cent; cement, 4.4 per cent; and farm machinery, 5.1 per cent (Wang Zhenzhi *et al.*, 1982 : 229; Ishihara, 1983).
29. Certain kinds of minerals, raw materials and processed materials were produced either in quantities below state targets or in poor quality.
30. These industries produced goods in quantities exceeding state quotas.
31. The problem of 'price-responsiveness' is very important, and is discussed further in Chapter 7.

2 From Adjustment Towards Liberalisation

1. In journals such as *Jingji Yanjiu*; *Jiage Lilun Yu Shijian*; *Zhongguo Shehui Kexue*; *Jingji Guanli*; *Renmin Ribao* (for translation of journal titles, see pp. xiv–xv) and books such as: Hu Changnuan (1982) and Jia Xiuyan (1984).
2. Liu Guoguang (1986); Li Yining (1986); Xu Yi (1982 : 34); Zhang Weiying (1985 : 338–66); Wu Jinglian in *Renmin Ribao* (1 May 1985); Hu Changnuan, (1982 : 27); Tian Yuan (1986); Zhang Zhuoyuan 1983; Dai Guanlai (1985).
3. Zhang Zhuoyuan (1983); Wu Jinglian (1985); Zhou Shulian *et al.* (1979); and Zhang Weiying (1985).
4. Hu Changnuan (1982 : 30); Tian Yuan (1986); Jia Xiuyan (1984 : 34).
5. Jia Xiuyan (1984 : 32); Hu Changnuan (1982 : 28); Yuan Jia in *Renmin Ribao* (17 January 1986).

6. According to Huang Da (1981), the policy of 'absolute price stability' adopted in China after the successful cessation of inflation in 1950 proved unscientific; thus, the policy was changed to aim at 'basic stability'.
7. After liberation, China tried to pursue a policy of exchanging agricultural products for industrial products at equal or approximately equal values. This policy was termed a reduction of the 'price scissors'.
8. Tian Jiyun 1985; *Guowu Yuan Gongbao*, 1984 : 899–916; *The 7th Five-Year Plan of the P.R.C. for Economic and Social Development*, Chapter 45, Section 2.
9. See Xue Muqiao (1981); Liao Jili and He Jianzhang (1982) in Wang (1982); Ishikawa in Maxwell and MacFarlane (1984); Perkins in Barnett and Clough (1986); White in Gray and White (1982); Zhang Zhuoyuan and Zhou Sholian in Lin and Chao (1982); and World Bank (1985a).
10. In industry, the production pattern was increasingly decided by direct bargaining among enterprises. In agriculture, production patterns were determined by the new responsibility system and the system of contracts between the State and the peasants.
11. The programme of profit retention underwent a number of metamorphoses, from the Sichuan experiment in 1978–9, to the profit contract system in 1981–2, to tax-for-profit schemes 1983 (Perry and Wang, 1985).
12. This policy of wage reform was halted in 1986 for fear of causing irrational inter-enterprise differentials in workers' incomes.
13. The names of these three groups are adopted from one of White's articles (1985).
14. This principle was set forth by Chen Yun when he summed up the experience of the first Five-Year Plan.
15. This method is discussed in more detail in Chapter 3.
16. This is discussed in more detail in Chapter 3.
17. Farm products of category one were key commodities, such as grain, edible oil and cotton, which were under State monopoly for purchase and marketing, and which had a great bearing on the national economy and the people's livelihood. Farm products of category two were commodities fairly important to the national economy and the people's livelihood, those not produced in some regions, those in short supply, and those produced for export. This category included pigs, eggs and jute (*Beijing Review*, vol. 28, no. 4, 1985 : 19).
18. Li Yining (1986); Liu Guoguang (1986); Zhang Weiying (1985); Wang Xiaoqiang *et al.* (1985); Yang Zhongwei and Li Bo (1985); Hua Sheng *et al.* (1985).
19. This issue is further discussed in Chapter 3.
20. The Centralisers argued that profitability margins varied between different products because of political and social decisions. They, therefore, rejected the idea of an average rate of profit (*pingjun lirun lu*) based on the 'price of production' (*shenchan jiage*) proposed by the Administrative Decentralisers to resolve problems of income distribution between the State and enterprises. They considered that the best way to overcome this problem was to use financial policies and the tax system (Xu Yi, 1982).

21. Zhang Weiying (1985); Yang Zhongwei and Li Bo (1986); Liu Guoguang (1986); Li Yining (1986).
22. There were disagreements within this group as to which formula should be applied for price setting. See Lu Nan (1983); Tian Yuan *et al.* (1986); and Zhou Xiachuan and Lou Jiwei (1984).
23. The advantages of the floating price were summarised by Wang Yongzhi in his paper for the International Symposium on Economy and Management (1985) as follows: (1) It helps to improve the management of China's macro-economy and revitalise its micro-economy. (2) It helps to maintain a basically stable price level and is conducive to timely readjusting of irrational prices. (3) It promotes price competition, stimulating the advanced enterprises to work better while encouraging the backward factories to shape up. (4) It facilitates direct contact between producers and users, helps to strengthen their links and promotes production of fine-quality goods and food in high demand. (5) It is conducive gradually to readjusting the existing irrational price system and to relaxing the contradictions resulting from unreasonable prices. (See also Tian Yuan (1986); Zhang Weida (1986); Dai Yuanchen (1986).)
24. Total inflation includes open inflation and suppressed inflation. According to Chen Nai-Rueun and Hou Chi-Ming (1986 : 820), 'the degree of inflation cannot be measured by the price indexes compiled by China, since they, at best, indicate the degree of "open inflation" and do not reflect concealed inflationary pressures'.
25. Yuan Jia, *People's Daily* (17 January 1986).
26. According to Dong Fureng (1986 : 297) 'since September 1982, prices of 100 minor commodities had been set by firms'.
27. Some principles, for instance, nos 14, 19 and 20 of the 'Provisional Regulations', stipulated respectively, that the prices (producer prices) of commodities of the light and textile industries could be negotiated among enterprises; that the range of floating prices for industrial commodities was to be decided by either the price authorities or the responsible industrial ministries; and that retail prices of some commodities (in the light and textile industries) in category three could be fixed by small retailers.
28. See Chen Nai-Rhenn and Hou Chi-Ming's article (1986) for more detail on the inflation problem of 1983.
29. The purpose of this 1985 policy was, first, to crack down on illegal trade and, second, to use price as an incentive mechanism to stimulate output. This policy created the dual price system. This new system brought strong pressure for a secular increase in the share of total output allocated by the market and a corresponding reduction in the share subject to plan control. It did not ease the problems of shortage and illegal trade. Byrd (1987a : 201) argued that 'it enhanced the flexibility of supply, but at high cost'.
30. Based on our 1985 survey carried out in Shangdong and Zhejiang.
31. In the 1979 the price of rolled steel (small) increased 20 per cent, welded steel pipe and zinc-plated steel increased by 21 per cent and wire roll increased by 17 per cent.

32. In some places, the price of steel manufactured by small enterprises was still supervised by local price bureau.
33. According to an informal interview with Wu Mingyu, Deputy Director General, Research Centre for Economic, Technological and Social Development, in the conference organised by 'The Royal Institute of International Affairs, The 48 Group of British Traders with China, The Euro-Asia Centre and INSEAD' in London (23–24 June 1988).

3 Administrative Price Reform in Theory and Practice

1. See Bornstein (1964); Ronimons (1950); Dobb (1961); Bornstein (1970); Csikos-Nagy (1975) for debates on socialist price formation in the Soviet Union and East European countries.
2. Chen Nai-Ruenn (1966); Rieman (1967); Lin (1981); Hu Changnuan (interviews, 1985) and Wang Zhenzhi (interviews, 1985).
3. The average producer prices of heavy industrial goods in the 1950s were five times higher than the 1936 level, while those of agricultural products were only twice as high (Chen Nai-Ruenn, 1966).
4. Some Chinese economists alleged that the policy of a relatively high price for heavy industrial goods would enable the government to accumulate capital for industrialisation. Opponents, such as Luo Gengmo (1957), argued that it would widen the already existing price differentials between industrial and agricultural products, and hence would destroy peasant incentives.
5. This irrational method of pricing new products was criticised by Chinese economists. The criticism led the State Statistical Bureau, at the beginning of 1958, to change the basis of pricing new products to actual production cost during the first month or quarter of production. But the pricing of new products in this way still led to high prices. The problem was not solved by the 1958 policy.
6. The prices of certain petroleum products were 1.45 times higher in Northeast than in Northwest China (Chen Nai-Ruenn, 1966).
7. One proposal suggested that regional differences in prices should be abolished, and that uniform prices throughout the whole country should be adopted. This proposal was rejected by a majority of economists on the grounds that 'the adoption of nationally uniform prices would discourage commercial agencies from selling commodities in areas distant from sources of supply and, thus, would hamper economic development in these areas' (Chen Nai-Ruenn, 1966). Nevertheless, there was no agreement on the principles that should be applied to the problem of irrational regional prices.
8. A small cut of the producer prices of some heavy industrial goods in 1957 was an outcome of compromises between institutions (Wang, 1980 : 92; Rieman, 1967 : 68–71).
9. Lin (1981) and Chen Nai-Ruenn (1966).
10. This theoretical debate on price formation in the second period has been

detailed by economists such as Chen Nai-Ruenn (1966); Perkins (1966); Rieman (1967); Lin (1981) and Cheng (1982).

11. Chen Nai-Ruenn (1966).
12. Cheng (1982 : 239).
13. Lin (1981 : 26).
14. Vol. 3 of *Capital*.
15. This was quoted by Chen Nai-Ruenn (1966), from Min Xuan, 'Discussing the Basis of Prices under Conditions of Socialism', *Guangming Ribao* (21 July 1964).
16. Rieman (1967) argued that the production price school was not interested in using production prices to balance supply and demand, to reflect social labour, nor to distribute wealth between various social strata. The intention of this school was that the system of production price should become a basis for rational investment decisions at the central planning and factory management levels.
17. The profit and taxes component of price was considered as surplus value (Hu Changnuan, 1982 : 97). In principle, 'the surplus value of an individual product was calculated by distributing the total surplus value of the economy among individual products in proportion to their prime costs of production' (Chai, 1986 : 3–4; Hu Changnuan, 1982 : 112; Cheng, 1982 : 239).
18. Quoted from Sun Yefang (1982 : 39).
19. The wholesale price per ton of coal in 1962 was 15.60 yuan in Jilin Province, 15.70 in Heilongjiang Province, 17.30 in Liaoning Province, 33 in Guangdong Province, 39 in Zhejiang Province, and 44.10 in Shanghai.
20. At this time, most private enterprises had ceased to operate in China.
21. The problems of cost structure in small and semi-modern furnaces is dealt with by Wu Xuejun (1965 : 120–7). The average cost of a ton of steel manufactured in small furnaces was 290 yuan, 160 yuan higher than the same product produced by large-sized steel mills. The average production cost of pig iron was 550 yuan per ton for small furnaces, and 95 yuan in large state-owned mills. It was impossible for the State to enforce the prevailing fixed price of pig iron at 150 yuan per ton in 1958. Therefore, local, temporary pricing was required; these prices varied from 240 to 340 yuan per ton for pig iron. This system of management by the local government was enforced until 1985.
22. The criteria applied to define the size of a firm are discussed in Chapter 7.
23. Liu (1971) argued that 'The fertilizer industry had been able to sustain profitable operation because of the high profit margins fixed by the government . . . Also, high profit margins of fertilizer production means that small plants can operate profitably despite higher costs than large-scale plants'.
24. According to our 1985 survey in Hebei and Zhejiang Province an average 30 per cent of medium-size and 45 per cent of small-size chemical fertiliser firms were financially in the red between 1965 and 1982.
25. Economists such as Ji Long, Wang Zhenzhi and Wang Yangzhi supported this proposal.
26. Economists such as Ma Kai and Zhu Chengping, supported this proposal.

27. Economists such as Lou Jiwei, Zhou Xiaochuan and Tian Yuan were in favour of this proposal.
28. This formula was first proposed informally by Xue Muqiao in 1982.
29. For details on this formula see Hu Changnuan, (1982 : 103).
30. There is only one textile enterprise in Shanghai experimenting with two-channel pricing: interviews with the Price Research Institute at the State Price Bureau, 1985.
31. Information on the exchange rate used to convert international prices to yuan is not available.
32. Taking oil as an example, in 1983 partly imported crude oil sold in the domestic market at international prices. Prices increased five times, from 122 to 590 yuan per ton (Hua Sheng, *et al.*, 1985 : 27–32).
33. For example, in 1979, the average cost of production of a ton of iron ore was 40.2 yuan and its producer price was 45.4 yuan. The rate of profit on capital in this industry was only 2.3 per cent, while the average rate for the iron and steel industry was 9.2 per cent, and for certain steel products was as high as 60–70 per cent (Dong Fureng, 1986). Under such circumstances, the Chinese government decided to increase the producer price of iron ore and steel products in 1980, 1981 and 1984.
34. For more details on coal price increases, see Chapter 4.
35. A typical case was the double-sided plough, manufactured by the Heilongjiang Agricultural Machinery Factory, whose price was cut from 1600 yuan per set to 1350 yuan, a price lower than production costs.
36. See Chapter 4.
37. See *Price: Theory and Practice*, no. 2, 1986 : 44–45, and no. 3, 1986 : 57.
38. The State would increase the producer price of coal in 5 yuan per ton increments.
39. They argued that if producer prices remained unchanged with the loss of the subsidy their factory would lose 7 to 8 yuan per set; this was because the tax of 15 per cent (20 yuan) per set caused total costs to reach 142 yuan a set.
40. BBF decided to reduce its price from 148 yuan to 144 yuan in 1984, when it realised that its inventory of this type of bicycle had increased.

4 Price Regulation in Intersectoral Total Output

1. *Document Collection of the State Purchasing and Selling Policies on Grains, Cotton, Oil-bearing Crops, 1951–1979*, People's University of China (1979) pp. 164–8.
2. The use of price to influence the allocation of resources did not imply the non-existence of a national plan in explicit quantity terms. However, the form of the national planning, especially after 1979, has been transferred from 'mandatory targets' to 'advisory targets'. See also Walker (1984).
3. This factor was regarded as the most important in increasing production of sugarcane in Fujian province and Hsienyu county (Lardy, 1983b : 179). See also Leeming (1985).

4. Central coal mines, hereafter referred to as state coal mines, were administered directly by the central government. Small coal mines were operated by villages, townships and private households.
5. Both Perkins (1966), and Lardy (1983b) have written detailed studies on the oscillating relationship between direct and indirect planning and its effects on production output between 1950 and 1979.
6. *Per capita* cotton production decreased from 5.9 jin in 1965 to 5.6 jin in 1970 and to 5.2 jin in 1975, 4.4 jin in 1976 and 4.3 jin in 1977. It increased slightly to 4.5 jin in 1978 (see *Statistical Yearbook of China*, 1985 : 273). Also see Balassa (1986a).
7. The quantity of imports increased substantially between 1952 and 1980 in 1952–62, the average annual import was 50,000 tons; in 1965–77, it was 170,000 tons, three times higher than the previous period. From 1978 to 1980, the average annual import was 650,000 tons, an increase of almost four times that of 1965–77 period. According to the United States Department of Agriculture, the average annual import in 1978–80 was 770,000 tons (Lardy, 1983b : 64).
8. Evidence indicates that the procurement price of most agricultural goods remained stagnant for 12 years after 1966 (Hu Changnuan, 1982). The index of prices of all farm products procured by the State rose from 162 in 1966 to 169 in 1977 (1952–100) an increase of only 4 per cent, less than four-tenths of 1 per cent per year (Lardy, 1983b : 47, 108).
9. According to Lardy (1983a : 13), evaluating price–cost relationships for specific agricultural products in China is problematic, due to the lack of an appropriate wage rate for valuing labour, and the lack of a proper valuation of capital's contribution to output.
10. Non-labour costs include three main parts: production costs such as seeds, chemical fertilisers, insecticides, costs of irrigation and mechanised ploughing, repair of farm implements, purchases of some hand tools; management fees; and other expenditures. They exclude depreciation (Lardy, 1983a : 13).
11. At the national level non-labour costs as a percentage of gross farm output increased from 26.5 per cent in 1957 to a peak of 35.7 per cent in 1977 (Lardy, 1983b : 87). In cotton production, at the local level, in the Pinghu prefecture of Zhejiang province non-labour costs increased from an average 24 yuan per mu in 1973–5 to an average 27 yuan in 1976–8, a hike of 12.5 per cent.
12. The procurement price mentioned here is an average of all sizes of cotton, and thus is lower than the price for standard size no. 3–27 as shown in Table 4.1.
13. The premium price was that the price paid for deliveries beyond the basic quota.
14. This relative price level, 1 jin of cotton exchanged for 8 jin of grain, was derived from the historical record, and was regarded by the government as the best ratio for these products (Xu Yi, 1982 : 114).
15. The price calculation system for cotton had changed from the quota purchasing system (*jisu jia*), the fixed quota price and the above-quota premium prices (50 per cent higher than the fixed prices), to the ratio price (*bili jia*). The latter system divided the output of cotton from each

peasant into two parts. To the northern peasant, the government paid the unified standard price for 20 per cent of cotton, and the premium price for the other 80 per cent. To the southern peasant, 60 per cent of cotton output was paid at the unified standard price, and the balance of 40 per cent was paid according to the premium price. The ratio of the purchasing quantity based on the unified standard price and the premium price was revised again for the northern peasants in 1985.

16. The effect of the production responsibility system on productivity would also apply to other crops. This rise in labour productivity may also have been due to the adoption of the production responsibility system.
17. This is an important issue, but it is outside the scope of this research. We discuss it briefly in Chapter 6.
18. A new type of cotton with better quality (see Yao Xihong *et al.*, 1984 : 29–32). All information from *Nongye Jishu Jingji* was contributed by Dr Joseph Dahms, who kindly let me to use his collections.
19. Stone (1988 : 127) argued that the refusal by the government to guarantee purchase above contracted amounts had a major impact on output after 1985.
20. According to Lardy (1983b : 77), 'they allocated, on average, 530,000 to 600,000 hectares to its production, over 20 per cent of their total cultivated area and 70 to 80 per cent of the province's cotton acreage'.
21. The other seven major cotton producers were: Hopei, Hupei, Hunan, Shansi, Shensi, Kingsu and Sinkiang.
22. See chapter 3 for more detailed study.
23. See *China Daily* (24 November 1986); *Price: Theory and Practice*, no. 2 (1985 : 44).
24. See *China Reconstructs*, vol. XXXII, no. 10 (October 1983 : 25).
25. The cost structure includes four main elements: raw materials; wages; electricity; and others. 'Others' include mainly management expenses related to the production process.
26. The decreases in production costs were probably due to rising productivity derived from investment.
27. In 1962, when production costs increased by 20 per cent over 1961 levels, the cost of raw materials and the wage bill increased by 12 per cent. In 1967, when production costs increased 12.5 per cent over 1966, the wage bill alone rose by 10.5 per cent. In 1974 and 1979, production costs rose 12 per cent and 10 per cent respectively over 1975 and 1978 levels. Again, in these two years, the wage bill increased more than other expenses. Wages increased by an average of 4 per cent while raw material expenses increased by 3 per cent in 1974 and 2.5 per cent in 1979.
28. There is no information available on the total amount of coal wasted by industrial users every year in China. But compared with other developed countries, the fuel efficiency rate for China by the early 1980s was under 28 per cent, compared to 57 per cent for Japan, 51 per cent for the USA, and 40 per cent for the EC countries (Yamanouchi, 1986 : 4). One other important effect of the low coal price was that it acted as an indirect subsidy to the establishment of inefficient enterprises. It also distorted the criterion for evaluating enterprise performance in other sectors, since

a large part of their profit was derived from the low cost of input (coal), and the higher price of output (Chen Dezun, interview, 1985).

29. The total amount of state subsidy to the coal industry is not yet available.
30. According to Pannell and Ma (1983 : 199), the level of mechanisation in the Chinese central coal mines remains low. In China, less than 50 per cent of the coal is mechanically extracted, loaded, and conveyed. By contrast, in the USA and the Soviet Union, each operation is almost 100 per cent mechanised.
31. The original proposal of price adjustment in 1958 was an increase of 32 per cent, but the final decision announced by the State Council was an increase of 20 per cent, the outcome of institutional compromise. This situation occurred again in 1979; see Chapter 3.
32. Coal output fell rapidly in 1961, decreasing 26.1 per cent from 1960.
33. This was a policy adopted by the Central Committee of the Chinese Communist Party in 1961 to correct the ultra-left mistakes committed during the 'Great Leap Forward' (interview, 1985).
34. The contribution to output by the small coal mines increased from 31 million tons to 95 million tons (some reports say 99 million tons) between 1970 and 1978. See *Almanac of China's Economy* (1985): V-58.
35. For local mines under the management of 22 coal administrative bureau in the east China region (*Almanac of China's Economy*, 1984 : 22).
36. This policy of premium price created a dual pricing system, which is discussed in Chapter 6.
37. For example, in 1980, there were 20,000 small-scale coal mines: output from them accounted for one-third of the nation's total. See *Beijing Review*, vol. 23, no. 26 (1980 : 4–5) and Pannell and Ma (1983 : 197).
38. The Ministry of Coal Industry proposed that 'the government should grant permits for such establishments more liberally, and give them generous support, while supervising them closely' (*Almanac of China's Economy*, 1984 : 22).
39. The contraction of the financial loss will become profit to the Ministry of Coal Industry, and the greater the contraction in the financial loss the more profit to the Ministry of Coal Industry.
40. It is believed that this policy was informally adopted in some areas of southern China as early as 1982.
41. The Minister of Coal Industry, Yu Hongen, supported this view (*Renmin Ribao*, 26 February 1987).
42. See Chapter 3 for institutional conflicts relating to price changes.
43. Price liberalisation was designed to stimulate the above-quota output of state coal mines.
44. *China Statistical Yearbook* (1986 : 206); *Renmin Ribao* (21 February 1987).

5 Price Regulation in Intra-sectoral Output Composition

1. Unfinished steel output was 37.1 million tons in 1980.
2. According to the Chinese definition, the 'price ratio' (*bijia*) means the

ratio between prices of two different but substitutable products which are sold in the market at the same time, which reflects their differences in value (see Furusawa, 1984 : 2). The two products could be different in type, kind, size or category, but substitutable for each other in production or use.

3. Mainly the Centralisers and the Administrative Decentralisers.
4. Yang Hongdao (1983); Song Jianli (1986); Hu Changnuan (1982); Dong Fureng (1986); Bai Qinchai (1985); Xue Muqiao (1982); and Gao Xiang (1986)
5. Such as Tian Yuan, Chen Dezun and Yang Lu (1988) and Xu Yi *et al.* (1982). For more detail, see their report 'A study of Theoretical Prices and their Application', in *Zhongguo Shehui Kexue*, no. 4 (1986 : 15–26).
6. It is important to point out that the school of Centralisers and the school of Administrative Decentralisers (for more detail of these two schools see Chapter 2) had no controversy on this issue of price effect on production.
7. Xue Muqiao (1982 : 67–71) argued that 'prices for abundant products should be allowed to fall, and prices for scare products should be allowed to rise. To do this, we should allow enterprises to negotiate buying and selling prices; and actively adjust our plan prices with reference to these prices so as to reduce overstocked inventory and encourage production of scarce products'.
8. Kornai (1980); Ma Kai (1987); and some young economists in the Economic Research Centre at the State Reform Committee who are Market Reformers.
9. For more detail see Kornai (1980) Chs 13, 14.
10. Responsiveness means the closeness of the linkage between price signals and reactions of firms. Responsiveness depends partly on the behavioural characteristics of the firm, and partly on technology and on the state of the market (see Kornai, 1980 : 336). This issue will be tackled in Chapter 7.
11. Non-price factors include, first, the problem of an ambitious planning system; second, the problem of mismanagement by institutions or managers in enterprises; third, the problem of the inefficient transportation system; fourth, the problem of resource constraints; and, finally, the system of soft-budget constraints.
12. The demand side will be considered later. There is a fundamental difference in the demand side of these two industries. Bicycle demand comes from households, who face hard-budget constraints. Steel demand comes from enterprises, who face soft-budget constraints.
13. During the first half of this period, the output of bicycles increased from 1.17 million in 1958 to 1.76 million in 1960. Total supply met total demand during this period. However, the production of bicycles collapsed in 1961 due to the 'Great Leap Forward', and output fell from 1.76 to 0.74 million. It took three years for production to return to the 1960 level; in only 1965 did total output of 1.83 million match total consumption of 1.76 million.
14. Consumption patterns also changed. Rural consumption (4.05 million in 1978, 4.86 million in 1979) increased to the same level as the urban sector

(4.04 million in 1978, 4.68 million in 1979). However, from 1982 onwards, the demand for bicycles from the rural sector was double that of the urban sector. Total consumption in the rural sector reached 17.37 million sets in 1983, an increase of 426 per cent over 1977. Since that time, the rural sector has continued to be the main market for bicycles.

15. The three provinces which do not have bicycle enterprises are Qinghai, Tibet, and Guizhou.
16. According to a report by the Economic Research Institute of the State Economic Committee (in *Jingji Diaocha*, no. 1, 1983 : 30), there were only 8 enterprises with output greater than 500,000 sets. Among them, the output of the four biggest enterprises – Forever, Fly Pigeon, Dragon-Phoenix and Red Flag, exceeded 1 million sets. See also World Bank (1985a : 81).
17. See Chapter 7 for a case study.
18. The causes of this phenomenon are discussed below.
19. For more detail of the definition of these three classes bicycles see Zhu Guanxiang (1984 : 49–50).
20. Red Flag (*Tianjin*), Golden Deer (*Qingdao*), Five Sheep (*Guang Zhou*), Long March (*Wuxi*), Golden Lion (*Chang Zhou*), Fly Flowers (*Shaoxing*), Fly Eagle (*Anyang*), Plum Blossom (*Anshan*), Fly Forward (*Yulin*).
21. In principle, each household in large cities, such as Beijing, was entitled to receive a coupon from the local authorities allowing them to buy one first-class bicycle. According to law, the coupon was valueless and not tradeable; however, it was being traded for between 50 and 70 yuan in Beijing in 1985.
22. Song Jianli (1986) reported that in Henan Province, besides the fixed price set by the State, consumers, also had to pay bribes of 50 jin rice, 5 jin cooking oil and other foodstuff to obtain a Red Flag bicycle.
23. *Price: Theory and Practice*, no. 4 (1984 : 49).
24. *Jingji Guanli*, no. 9 (1984 : 36).
25. There is some data available on the structure of steel production but little on the structure of steel consumption. The available information is in Yuan-Li Wu (1965) for the period 1950–1963; Wang (1977) for 1972–5; Findlay and Xin (1985) and Deng Liqun *Ma Hong et al.* (1984), for the 1980s.
26. Ranking 4th in the world (Findlay and Xin, 1985).
27. *Jingji Chankao* (3 July 1985 : 4).
28. *Jingji Chankao* (3 July 1985 : 4).
29. In 1985 the government spent 6 billion US dollars to import steel (*Jingji Xue Zhoubao*, 4 May 1986).
30. One-fifth of the steel in inventory, 5.6 million tons, could construct another Anshan Steel Mill, which is the biggest steel mill in China (*Renmin Ribao*, 15 March 1987).
31. Xu Yi (1982 : 148); *The Economist* (27 October, 1984); Balassa (1986a : 23–4); Furusawa (1984 : 2–6).
32. They included the wire rods, the seamless steel pipe, the mild steel plates, the thin steel plates, and the light sections. See *Statistics of World Trade in Steel, 1981–1985*, Economic Commission for Europe, Geneva, United Nations; *Jingji Chankao* (1985); *Jingji Ribao* (1985); *Changzhou Ribao* (1985).

33. For example, in the first six months of 1984, there was an increase in the inventory of mild steel plates (27.6 per cent over 1983), of thin steel plate (27.7 per cent over 1983), and of steel tubes (10 per cent over 1983). At the same time, there was a substantial import of steel plates (1.68 million tons), an increase of 10 per cent compared over 1983, and a 31 per cent increase in the import of steel tubes in 1984 over 1983 (Xu Wen, 1985 : 26).
34. Dong Fureng (1986 : 293–4) argued that irrationality in relative prices has produced irrationality in resource allocation. For example, since the price and profitability of some manufactured goods is too high, output expanded blindly, causing overstocking of many products such as bicycles and sewing machines.
35. Liang Zhongxun (1983) argued that preferential treatment was sometimes necessary for fostering industrial development in remote or relatively backward districts of the country. However, extending protection by maintaining high prices, and thereby ensuring high producer profits, could discourage efforts to cut costs and improve efficiency. For example, the Yanhe bicycle, manufactured in Shanxi province, kept its price at the initial level for 13 years.
36. See the World Bank (1985a : 81).
37. The increase of output of 80 per cent in 1983 was not due to an increase in demand. See Chapter 7 for more detail.
38. An 'expansion drive' (Kornai, 1986 : 23), could come from all levels of institutions – the central government, and medium- and low-level economic management authorities. Every firm, without exception, wanted to grow, and superior authorities also wished sectors in their charge to grow. Investment hunger was therefore widespread.
39. *Economic Daily* (29 July 1985).
40. Wang Guiwu, Vice-Chairman of the China Society for Research on Material Distribution, held this view. See *China Daily* (11 December 1987).
41. World Bank (1983 : 84).
42. Under the policy of price adjustment, the irrational price ratios of some steel products were revised in 1980 and again in 1984.
43. The purpose of adopting this new system was that on the one hand, it could stimulate output (on the supply side), and on the other create a small free market for the means of production where enterprises traded steel from inventory or from overproduction (on the demand side).
44. Their average ratio of profit – cost in 1982 was 47 per cent.
45. This meant that all small firms making losses and asking tax remission needed permission from the Ministry of Finance.
46. Compiled extracts from documents on price, in *Price: Theory and Practice*, no. 2 (1987 : 42).

6 Evolution of Dual Pricing

1. The two-tier plan/market economic system of resource allocation, which involved simultaneous allocation of the same industrial goods by both

mandatory planning and (rudimentary) market forces emerged in China in the late 1970s (Byrd, 1987a : 295–308).

2. See Saksena (1986) for dual pricing in the industrial sector in India. See Sender and Smith (1987) and Harvey (ed.) (1988) for dual pricing in agriculture in some African countries.
3. When the pricing system of producer goods needs reform but a 'package mode' – relaxing price control at one stroke – is unacceptable due to financial constraints, or to this need to prevent great shocks in the economy, then the dual pricing system will be a better alternative. See Liu Guoguang *et al.* (1985 : 3–19); Zhao Renwei (1986 : 12); Hua Sheng, *et al.* (1986 : 3–11).
4. See Saksena (1986) for India.
5. Koziara and Yan (1983 : 697) argued that the administrative allocation system in China, which functions passively, manages to divert resources to its priority industries and projects, but is far from achieving its economic potential. Moreover, it also destroys initiative, breeds inefficiency and encourages the production of sub-standard and unmarketable items.
6. The total coal requirement in Wuxi city in 1983 was 850,000 tons. The government was able to supply only 350,000 tons (40 per cent) at the wholesale price of 49 yuan/ton, of which 320,000 tons were assigned for residential consumption and the remaining 30,000 tons allocated to the construction sector. The industrial sector had no coal supply from the government and thus had to get access to coal through other channels. The most popular ways were to use the black market and barter or use cooperative trade with local coal mines and small pits (Hu Changnuan and Liu Fengqian, 1984 : 66–78).
7. For instance, in 1984, there were 40 million tons of grain purchased by the government according to fixed quota prices (*tongguo jiage*), 40 million tons based on higher fixed prices for above-quota output (*chaoguo jiajia*), and another 45 million tons sold at negotiated prices (*jijia*) (Zhao Renwei, 1986 : 13). See also Dai Yuanchen - (1986 : 43–8); Hua Sheng *et al.* (1986 : 3–11); Gu Shutang (1986 : 270–83).
8. As in India, allowing a certain portion of output to be sold in the open market at whatever price it could command eliminated one of the causes of the black market, as excess demand was not allowed to exert an upward pressure on price. Excess demand at controlled prices, when part of the output is sold under a system of dual pricing, finds an outlet in the market (Saksena, 1986 : 125–6).
9. India spent about 10 years (1963–73) transforming its total statutory price control to a dual pricing system, and was quite successful in its formulation and implementation.
10. Hama, 1983 : 11; 'State Council Emergency Notice', *Price: Theory and Practice*, no. 5 (1983 : 3).
11. According to Hama (1983), capital construction amounted to a record 55.5 billion yuan, up 25.4 per cent, or 11.2 billion yuan, over the previous year, while production of rolled steel increased only 8.6 per cent, cement only 13.5 per cent, and timber output fell 11.7 per cent.
12. For instance, in 1982, the central government failed to achieve its plan to

procure and distribute 2.87 million tons of cement, 2.25 million tons of rolled steel and 11.82 million tons of coal. The central government had to import one-third of the rolled steel required for government allocation (132 per cent more than in 1982) and to purchase 23 million tons of coal and 4 million tons of cement from local governments at a cost of 600 million yuan (Li Kaixin, *Hongqi*, no. 17, 1983; Hama, 1983 : 12).

13. The market price of iron was 67 per cent higher than the fixed price; the market price of coal was 240 per cent higher; and the market price of steel round thread bars was 119 per cent higher than the fixed price (see Table 6.7).
14. See Liu Guoguang (1986 : 18); Diao Xinshen (1986 : 45–57); Liu Fushan (1987 : 38–41): Zhang Zhibin (1986 : 25–31); Wu Jinglian and Zhao Renwei (1987 : 313–16); Jing Xiaodao and Zhu Jinfan (1985 : 32–4); Yao Lin (1985 : 17–21); and Dai Guanlai *et al.* (1986 : 16–23).
15. In *Jingji Chankao* (18 May 1985).
16. According to a TESDRC report: 20 million yuan came from part of the 'self-sales' of 30,000 tons of steel; 5 million yuan was collected from joint ventures or joint business operation; and the remaining 12 million yuan came from tax remission obtained by selling 30,000 tons of steel to the provincial government at a price (1350 yuan/ton) lower than the market price but higher than the fixed price.
17. See Chapter 7 for more detail on enterprise dual dependence.
18. The complicated patterns of income distribution influenced by dual pricing varied enormously. Unfortunately, there is little data available for a study of this phenomenon.
19. The fixed price of steel increased 118 yuan per ton, and the free price increased 500 yuan per ton in 1985. This led to an increase in total costs of steel inputs of 279.8 million yuan for the Shanghai industrial sector (see Table 6.9).
20. White and Bowles (1987 : 19, 51) reported that the decrease in sales profit of some enterprises in the textile industry was caused by dual pricing.
21. Despite the government-announced Consumer Price Index (CPI), a lack of data makes the inflation rate caused by price increases of producer goods difficult to estimate. The problem of the price level effects of the dual pricing of producer goods will therefore be left for future study.
22. See the report by the Technological, Economic and Social Development Research Centre at the State Council, in *Price: Theory and Practice*, no. 1, 1986; Zhang Baohua and Dai Guanlai (1986 : 16–23).
23. See Saksena (1986) for the administrative management in India.
24. In November 1985, the government in Anshan City suspended licenses of 116 so-called 'companies' or 'trade centres' and of 104 individual trade units due to illegal trading in steel. 127 other enterprises were also warned to stop trading in steel.
25. Wu Jinglian and Zhao Renwei (1987) claim that 'the volume of steel that was reported sold on the free market was 15–20 per cent of the total steel production in the country, but the proportion of steel consumption said to have been bought on free markets by enterprises was about 40 per cent of the total steel consumption'.

26. This price monitoring for the means of production included 28 monitoring groups with 568 cadres; it covered 27 places including provinces, autonomous regions, and metropolitan cities.
27. This preliminary report covered only 14 of the 27 places monitored (reported by the Price Monitoring Office of the Means-of-Production of the State Council).
28. The essence of the MPM was different from the so-called 'market for the means-of-production', which appeared in 1979 in certain big cities. The main difference was that MPM prices were free, while prices in the market were flexibly controlled by the local governments. See Byrd (1985a) for more detail on the latter system in Shanghai.
29. For example, the Shenyang Material Trading Centre was constructed by the State, Liaoning Province and Shenyang City Material Supply Bureaus (*Jingji Chankao*, 4 June 1985).
30. Medium-Size and large enterprises, who as buyers held state supply quotas yet had to purchase goods from the MTC at high prices, would try to obtain their inputs through barter trade at lower prices.
31. A new policy on dual pricing was announced by the government in 1988. See Chapter 8 for more detail.
32. The central government was highly impressed by Shijiazhang model and decided to adopt it for steel and cement nationwide (*Economic Daily*, 26 September 1987).
33. One of the policies stipulated by the deputy-director of the State Economic Commission, Yuan Baohua (*Economic Daily*, 26 September 1987), was the improvement of administrative management of government shops.
34. In India, dual pricing has been implemented for more than 10 years, and it has fewer drawbacks than total price control. According to Saksena (1986 : 124–6), the superiority of dual pricing includes several aspects. First, it is easier and less expensive to administer. Second, it can achieve a balance between demand and supply by relieving the pressure on the allocation system by allowing output to be sold in the open market. Third, it causes less drain on the limited budgetary resources of the government than total price control. Finally, it benefits deserving sections of the community who need protection against high prices.

7 Price-responsiveness of State Enterprises

1. Lewis Carroll, *Alice's Adventures in Wonderland*.
2. Kornai argues that socialist firms substitute inputs not on a price basis but on a security of input principle. It is therefore a normal phenomenon for a firm to abandon the use of an input which is continually in short supply, even if it is cheaper than a more readily available substitute (Kornai, 1980 : 334).
3. Physical targets are production targets; value targets include finance, cost and profitability.

4. Profit incentives include bonuses paid to a firm's managers based on profit, profit sharing for workers, investment financed from the firm's savings and so on.
5. In Hungary, the demand-pull tendency was concentrated in the investment good and service markets (Kornai, 1980 : 367).
6. Kornai (1980 : 367) says that a high degree of shortage operates to raise prices, but there is no reverse relationship: high prices do not lead to a permanent easing of the tension.
7. Scale varies by industry and is based on annual production capacity or initial value of fixed assets. In 1978, iron and steel complexes with an annual production capacity of at least 1 million tons of steel were classified as large-scale. Those producing from 100,000 to 1 million tons were medium-scale. Those producing less than 100,000 tons were small-scale. Synthetic ammonia plants producing over 150,000 tons per year were large, those producing 45,000 to 150,000 tons were medium, and those producing less than 45,000 tons were small (Xu Dixin *et al.*, 1982 : 132–3).
8. In the pre-reform period, both the input and output of most of the sample firms was strictly controlled by the government. Their inputs were supplied by the government and they handed over their output to related administrative institutions.
9. In the 1960s and 1970s, plan targets included: first, value of total production; second, value of total sale of products; third, quantity of principal products; fourth, quality of products; fifth, labour efficiency; sixth, actual total cost increases; seventh, circulation of working capital; eighth, profit contribution to the State. See Rieman (1967) for more detail on firms' indicators in the 1950s and 1960s.
10. Sample firms admitted that other targets were not important and could be neglected. For instance, the quality target was never strictly enforced by the government at BBF, WCFF, CZSCFF, and AISM. According to the *Economic Daily* (19 July 1985), AISM's poor – quality steel caused three big industrial accidents in 1985.
11. See Chapter 1 for more detail on the Hungarian competitive pricing system.
12. In China, the government did not abolish the command system in a package mode, but instead in an evolutionary mode – that is, a gradual reduction of the scope of mandatory planning. This revolutionary mode created a dual economic system with dual allocation and dual pricing (see also Chapter 6).
13. CESRRI (1986) survey included 279 state-owned firms, 131 collective, and 19 township and village enterprises. According to its report, the majority of its sample firms (78.7 per cent in 1984, 78.44 per cent in the first half of 1985) were mainly dependent on the dual economic system. For example, on the output side, the sample firms (51.4 per cent in 1984, and 45.6 per cent in the first half of 1985) were involved in the dual pricing system engaged in marketing their output.
14. Mixed markets include firms who face a buyers' market for inputs and a sellers' market for output, and vice versa. Here, we deal with the second situation only.

15. See Chapter 3 for more detail.
16. BBF either marketed its products directly to customers at the existing retail price of 165 yuan per set, or sold its bicycles to wholesalers based on the new producer prices of 148 yuan. See Chapter 3 for more details on the formation of these two prices, which involved in institutional conflicts.
17. The local government announced a new policy of quota financial subsidy (*Dinge baogan*) for chemical fertiliser producers. It stipulated that firms which made losses would receive a financial subsidy fixed at the previous year's level regardless of any increases in losses; the potential financial loss would be the firm's responsibility.
18. At the same time, watches and electric fans also faced a buyers' market and their producer prices were reduced. *Dongnan Henchen* (10 January 1985).
19. CZCFF's output capacity was 20 times higher than CZSCFF's.
20. The rapid drop of output in CZCFF in 1983 was due to a sudden cut in its inputs.
21. The total import of chemical fertilisers was 18.35 million tons in 1984. See *China Statistical Yearbook* (1985) : 516, and (1986) : 551. Chemical fertilisers faced a sellers' market again in 1987.
22. In the bicycle industry, the grade system was used only for classifying bicycles; it had nothing to do with price formation.
23. Profit retention and profit contracting policy created the problem of '*panbi*', where workers competed for higher wage payments regardless their economic performance. See Takahara (1988).
24. According to the *Financial Times* (18 December 1987) BBF was closed, and its workers transferred to a nearby food processing plant. CZSCFF stopped manufacturing chemical fertilisers in 1985.
25. In 1985, there was a total of 244,400 state-owned and urban collective firms in China (town and village enterprises excluded). According to the *China Daily* (12 January 1988), nearly 1 million township enterprises had gone bankrupt and closed since the beginning of 1986. They accounted for approximately 7 per cent of the country's rural enterprises.
26. WCFF had to purchase a large portion of coal, about 30,000 tons, from the market after 1984. AISM had to buy 1.95 million tons of ore, 15 per cent of its total input, from the market in 1983 (World Bank, 1983).
27. The annual output of coal at BCM decreased from 6.5 million tons in 1979 to 6.2 million tons in 1980, and to 6 million tons in 1981.
28. Output between 5.9 and 6.2 million tons could be sold in the market at prices 50 per cent higher than fixed prices. Above-quota output beyond 6.2 million tons could be sold at prices 100 per cent higher than fixed prices.
29. The government approved the price increase in 1987.
30. This report says that 6 of the 12 steel mills with self-marketing rates of less than 10 per cent, saw output grow by less than 6 per cent; 2 of the 6 mills actually had negative growth rates of total output. The other 6 mills had self-marketing rates greater than 10 per cent (10 per cent to 34 per cent), and average growth rates of total output of 14.38 per cent (see CESRRI, 1986 : 48–9).

31. The price-responsiveness of total output in AISM was much weaker than in SISM. AISM said that its ratio of self-marketed steel (2 per cent) was too low, it had no motivation for increasing production (World Bank, 1983 : 84). The total output of rolled steel at AISM decreased from 4.42 million tons to 4.14 million tons, a decrease of 6.5 per cent, between 1982 and 1984.
32. It considered converting steel roll to strip steel, but the producer price of the latter increased by only 10 yuan per ton and the extra cost of the processing was 70–80 yuan per ton (World Bank, 1983 : 85).
33. They said that steel supply was tight, and all that was produced had to be sold. They were not worried about making sales. Users had trouble getting steel, so they could hardly demand that Anshan give them specific types of products. If they could get steel, that was good enough (World Bank, 1983 : 83).

8 Summary and Conclusions

1. See chapter 6 for more detail.
2. Liu Su Nian, the Minister of the Materials Allocation, *Economic Daily* (9 June 1988); *Economic Daily* (2 August 1988); *Economic Daily* (8 August 1988).
3. The steel inventory in 1986 was 28 million tons: see *Economic Daily* (2 August 1988).
4. According to *The Economist* (27 August 1988), a policy known as the 'Tentative Plan on the Price and Wage Reform, 1989–1993' was formulated by the Politburo. See also *Renmin Ribao* (19 August 1988).
5. *Economic Daily* (2 and 8 September 1988); *Renmin Ribao* (19 August 1988); *Cheng Ming* (1 September 1988 : 7).
6. *Economic Daily* (2 and 8 August 1988).
7. A proposal of price reform of the means of production in 1987 was postponed because of political reason, according to Liu Guoguang (*People's Daily*, Overseas Edition, 24 August 1988).
8. Called the Materials Allocation Bureau before 1988.

Bibliography

Titles of journals or newspapers cited are translated on pp. xv–xvi.

Books and Articles

AGRICULTURAL ECONOMICS DEPARTMENT, PEOPLE'S UNIVERSITY OF CHINA (1985) *Nong Chanpin Jiage Xue* (Agricultural Product Price Study), Beijing, Agriculture Press.

BAI HONG (1964) 'Further Discussions Concerning Problems of the Basis of Price Formation under the Socialist System', *Jingji Yanjiu*, no. 6, June, 6–15.

BAI QINCAI (1985) *Investigation of Economic Reform*, Shanxi Province Shanxi Renmin Publication Bureau.

BALASSA, B. (1982) *The Hungarian Economic Reform, 1968–81*, Working Paper No. 508, World Bank.

——— (1986a) *China's Economic Reforms in a Comparative Perspective*, International Bank of Reconstruction and Development, Report no. DRD 177, April.

——— (1986b) 'Adjustment Policies in Socialist and Private Market Economics', *Journal of Comparative Economics*, vol. 10, no. 2.

BARAN, P. (1957) *The Political Economy of Growth*, New York, Monthly Review Press, 2nd edn, with a new preface, 1962.

BARNETT, A. D. AND CLOUGH, R. N. (EDS) (1986) *Modernizing China: Post-Mao Reform on Development*, Boulder, Col., Westview.

BERGSON, A. (1949) 'Socialist Economics', in *A Survey of Contemporary Economics*, ed. H. S. Ellis, Philadelphia, Blakiston.

——— (1985) 'A Visit to China's Economic Reforms', *Comparative Economic Studies*, vol. 27, no. 2.

BETTELHEIM, C. (1974) *Cultural Revolution and Industrial Organization in China*, New York, Monthly Review Press.

——— (1978) *The Transition to Socialist Economy*, Sussex, Harvester Press.

BORNSTEIN, M. (1964) 'The Soviet Price Reform Discussions', *Quarterly Journal of Economics*, vol. 78, February, Harvard University : 15–48.

——— (1970) 'Soviet Price Theory and Policy', in Bornstein, M. and Fusfeld, D. R. (eds), *The Soviet Economy*, Homewood, Ill., Richard D. Irwin.

——— AND FUSFELD, D. R. (EDS) (1966) *The Soviet Economy: A Book of Readings*, Homewood, Ill., Richard D. Irwin.

——— AND FUSFELD, D. R. (1970) 'Soviet Price Theory and Policy', in Bornstein, M. and Fusfeld, D. R. (eds), *The Soviet Economy*, Homewood, Illinois, Richard D. Irwin.

BROWN, G. T. (1978) *Agriculture Pricing Policies and Economic Development*, Bloomington, Indiana University Press : 84–9.

BUKHARIN, N. I. (1920) (1970) *Economics of the Transformation Period*, New York, Moscow Berfman Publishers.

BYRD, W. A. (1985a) 'The Shanghai Market for the Means-of-Production; A Case Study of Reform in China's Material Supply System', *Comparative Economic Studies*, vol. 27, no. 4.

——— (1985b) *The Shenyang Smelter: A Case Study of Problems and Reforms in China's Nonferrous Metals Industry*, World Bank Working Papers, no. 766, Washington, D.C., World Bank.

——— (1987a) 'The Impact of the Two-Tier Plan/Market System in Chinese Industry', *Journal of Comparative Economics*, vol. 11, no. 3.

——— (1987b) 'The Role and Impact of Markets', in Tidrick, G. and Chen, J. Y. (eds), *China's Industrial Reform*, New York, Oxford University Press.

——— AND TIDRICK, G. (1987) 'Factor Allocation and Enterprise Incentives', in Tidrick, G. and Chen, J. Y. (eds), *China's Industrial Reform*, New York, Oxford University Press.

CHAI, C. H. (1986) 'Reform of China's Industrial Prices', Paper for Conference on China's System Reforms, no. 36, Center of Asian Studies, University of Hong Kong.

CHEN HONGBO (1986) 'Evaluation of Price Reform in an Earlier Stage and Ideas about Recent Developments', *Jingji Yanjiu*, no. 4 : 60–5.

CHEN HUIJUN (ED.) (1986) 'A Summary of the Symposium on the Problem of Dual Pricing of Producer Goods by the Jiangsu Price Association', *Price: Theory and Practice*, no. 3 : 52.

CHEN NAI-RUENN (1966) 'The Theory of Price Formation in Communist China', *China Quarterly*, July–September : 33–53.

——— (ED.) (1967) *Chinese Economic Statistics*, Chicago, Aldine Publishing Co.

——— and HOU CHI-MING (1986) 'China's Inflation, 1979–1983: Measurement and Analysis', *Economic Development and Cultural Change*, vol. 34, no. 4.

CHENG, C. Y. (1982) *China's Economic Development: Growth and Structural Change*, Boulder, Colorado, Westview Press.

CHINA ECONOMIC SYSTEM REFORM RESEARCH INSTITUTE (1986) (CESRRI Survey), *Reform in China: Challenges and Choices*, Beijing, China Economic Press.

CHINA RECONSTRUCTS (1983) vol. XXXII, no. 10, October : 25.

CHINA STATE STATISTICS BUREAU (1984a) *Zhongguo Maoyi Wujia Tongji Ziliao 1952–1983* (China Trade and Price Statistics 1952–1983), Beijing, China Statistics Press.

——— (1984b) *Zhongguo Nongye De Gonghuai Changjiu 1949–1984* (The Great Achievement of China's Agriculture), Beijing, China Statistics Press.

CHU MINWEI *ET AL.* (1987) 'Financial Effects and the Countermeasures to the Price Reform of Producers Goods', *Caimo Jingji*, no. 1.

CSIKOS-NAGY, B. (1971) 'The New Hungarian Price System', in Friss, I.

(ed.), *Reform of the Economic Mechanism in Hungary*, Budapest, Akademiai Kiado.

——— (1973) *Socialist Economic Policy*, London, Longman.

——— (1975) *Socialist Price Theory and Price Policy*, Budapest, Akademiai Kiado.

——— (1979) *Towards a New Price Revolution*, Budapest, Akademiai Kiado.

DAI GUANLAI (1985) 'The Basic Functions of Price', *Jingji Yanjiu*, no. 6, June.

——— *ET AL.* (1986) 'Strategy of Dealing with the Rapid Price Increases in Producer Goods', *Jingji Guanli*, no. 1, January : 16–23.

DAI YUANCHEN (1986) 'Dual Prices in the Transformation of the Model of the Economic System', *Jingji Yanjiu*, no. 1, January : 43–9.

DENG LEPING (1986) 'Enlivening the Micro-Economy: the Basic Subject of the Reform and Development in the Near Future', *Jingji Yanjiu*, no. 7, July : 22–5.

DENG LIQUN *ET AL.* (EDS) (1984) *Dangdai Zhongguo De Jingji Tizhi Gaige* (Economic System Reform in Contemporary China), Beijing, China Social Science Press.

DIAO XINSHEN (1986) 'Dual Prices in the Transformation of the Model of the Economic System', *Jingji Yanjiu*, no. 1, January : 43–8.

DOBB, M. (1955) *On Economic Theory and Socialism*, London, Routledge; New York, International Publishers.

——— (1961) 'Notes on Recent Economic Discussion', *Soviet Studies*, vol. 12, no. 4.

DONG, FURENG (1986) 'China's Price Reform', *Cambridge Journal of Economics*, vol. 10, no. 3.

——— (1987) 'Increasing the Vitality of Enterprises', in Tidrick, G. and Chen, J. Y. (eds), *China's Industrial Reform*, New York, Oxford University Press.

DONNITHORNE, A. (1978) 'The Control of Inflation in China', *Current Scene*, April–May : 1–12.

DU LIHUI (1986) 'A Summary of the Symposium on Some Theoretical Problems of Reforming Prices on Means of Production', *Price: Theory and Practice*, no. 4 : 3–5.

ECONOMIC COMMISSION FOR EUROPE (1981–1985) *Statistics of World Trade in Steel, 1981–1985*, Geneva, UN.

ELLMAN, M. (1979) *Socialist Planning*, London, Cambridge University Press.

FEUCHTWANG, S. AND HUSSAIN, A. (EDS) (1983) *The Chinese Economic Reforms*, New York, St Martin's Press.

FINDLAY, C. AND XIN, L. (1985) *China's Iron and Steel Industrial Policy: Implications for Australia*, Pacific Economic Papers, no. 127, Research School of Pacific Studies, Australian National University.

FRISS, I. (1971) *Reform of the Economic Mechanism in Hungary*, Akademiai Kiado.

FURUSAWA, K. (1984) 'Pricing China's Industrial Products: Difficulties in the Reform of China's System', *China Newsletter*, JETRO, no. 52 : 2–6.

GAO, S. Q. (1987) 'The Reform of China's Industrial System', in Tidrick, G. and Chen, J. Y. (eds), *China's Industrial Reform*, New York, Oxford University Press.

GAO XIANG (1982) *Lun Wujia Gaige* (On Price Reform), Beijing, China Social Science Press.

——— (1986) *Jingji Tizhi Gaige He Jiage Gaige* (Reform of Economic Structure and Price), Jilin, Hongqi Press.

GRAY, J. AND WHITE, G. (EDS) (1982) *China's New Development Strategy*, London, Academic Press.

GU SHUTANG (ED.) (1986) *Shehui Zhuyi Jiage Xingcheng Wenti Yanjiu* (Study of Problems of the Socialist Price Formation), Beijing, China Social Science Press.

HAMA, K. (1983) 'Systematic Reform and Financial Problems – The "Investment Fever" Mechanism', *China Newsletter*, JETRO, no. 47 : 7–14.

——— (1984) 'New Era in Economic Reform', *China Newsletter*, JETRO, no. 51 : 6–11.

HARE, P. (1983) 'China's System of Industrial Economic Planning', in Feuchtwang, S. and Hussain, A. (eds), *The Chinese Economic Reforms*, New York, St Martin's Press.

HARVEY, C. (ED.) (1988) *Agricultural Pricing Policy in Africa*, Hong Kong, Macmillan.

HAYEK, F. A. (ED.) (1935) *Collectivist Economic Planning*, London: Routledge & Kegan Paul.

HE JIANZHANG AND ZHANG ZHUOYUAN (1981) *Lun Shehui Zhuyi Jingji Zhong De Shengchan Jiage* (Discussion on Production Prices in a Socialist Economy), Harbin, Heilongjiang Press.

HO JIANZHANG AND ZHANG LING (1964) 'A Preliminary Discussion of Production Prices in a Socialist Economy', *Jingji Yanjiu*, no. 5, May, 12–20.

HU CHANGNUAN, (1980) '*Tan Tan Jiandaocha He Jiage Congshuiping Wenti*' (Discussion of the Issue of Price Scissors and the Total Price Level), in Economic Institute of China Social Academy *et al.* (eds), *Problems of Price Formation in Socialism*, Beijing, China Social Science Press.

——— (1982) *Jiage Xue* (Study of Prices), Beijing, China People's University Press.

——— (1986) 'Effects of Price Increases in Raw Materials and Energy on Costs of the Processing Industry's Products in Shanghai', *Social Sciences China*, no. 4 : 27–42.

HUA SHENG *ET AL.* (1985) 'Price Reform With Chinese Characteristics', *Jingji Yanjiu*, no. 2, February : 27–32.

——— *ET AL.* (1986) 'Transfer of Economic Operational Model: Problems and Thought About Reforms of the Economic System', *Jingji Yanjiu*, no. 2, February : 3–11.

HUANG DA (1981) 'Some Problems Concerning Pricing', *Social Sciences in China*, no. 1 : 136–56.

INVESTIGATION SECTION OF NATIONAL ECONOMIC COMMITTEE (1983) '*Woguo Zixingche Gongye Jingji Xiaoyi Fenxi*' (Analysis of Efficiency of the Bicycle Industry), *Jingji Diaocha*, no. 1, Hongqi Press.

ISHIHARA, K. (1983) 'The Price Problem and Economic Reform', *China Newsletter*, JETRO, no. 46 : 2–7.

JIA XIUYAN (ED.) (1984) *Jiage Xue Yunli* (Principles of Prices), Tianjin, Nankai University Press.

——— AND DAI GUANLAI (1985) *Nankai Xuebao*, no. 3 : 73.

JIANG XINGWEI (1980) 'A Discussion on the Issues of the Price Scissors Between Industrial and Agricultural Goods', *Jingji Yanjiu*, no. 4, April, 75.

JING XIAODAO AND ZHU JINFAN (1985) 'Situations, Problems and Suggestions After Relaxing the Control Over the Price of Timber', *Price: Theory and Practice*, no. 5 : 32–4.

KAMBARA, T. (1984) 'China's Energy Development During the Readjustment and Prospects for the Future', *China Quarterly*, no. 100.

KOBAYASHI, H. (1980) 'China Introduces New Pricing System and Market Mechanism', *China Newsletter*, JETRO, no. 25 : 1.

KOJIMA, R. (1985) 'Characteristics of China's Present Agricultural Policy', *China Newsletter*, JETRO, no. 58 : 2–6.

KORNAI, J. (1980) *Economics of Shortage*, vols A, B, Amsterdam, North-Holland.

——— (1983) *Growth, Storage and Efficiency: A Macrodynamic Model of the Socialist Economy*, University of California Press.

——— (1985) 'Comments on Paper Prepared in the World Bank About Socialist Countries', CPD Discussion Paper, no. 1985–10.

——— (1986) *Contradictions and Dilemmas*, Cambridge, Mass., MIT Press.

——— (1987) 'The Dual Dependence of the State-Owned Firm in Hungary', in Tidrick, G. and Chen, J. Y. (eds), *China's Industrial Reform*, New York, Oxford University Press.

KOSHIRO, K. (1981) 'Another Look at the Baoshan Complex', *China Newsletter*, JETRO, no. 32 : 8–13.

KOZIARA, E. C. AND YAN, C. S. (1983) 'The Distribution System for Producers' Goods In China', *China Quarterly*, no. 96.

KRISHNA, R. (1967) *Agricultural Price Policy and Economic Development*, Ithaca, Cornell University Press : 503–17.

LANGE, O. (1936–7) (1972) 'On the Economic Theory of Socialism', in Nove, A. and Nuti, D. M. (eds), *Socialist Economics*, Harmondsworth, Penguin.

——— (1967) (1972) 'The Computer and the Market', in Nove, A. and Nuti, D. M. (eds), *Socialist Economics*, Harmondsworth, Penguin.

LARDY, N. R. (1983a) 'Agricultural Prices in China', *World Bank Staff Working Papers*, no. 606, Washington, D.C., World Bank.

——— (1983b) *Agriculture in China's Modern Economic Development*, New York, Cambridge University Press.

LEEMING, F. (1985) *Rural China Today*, New York, Longman.

LEFTWICH, R. H. AND ECKERT, R. D. (1985) *The Price System and Resources Allocation*, Tokyo, Dryden Press.

LI GUOZHANG (1987) 'On the Guidance Price of Wood in Collective Forest Regions in the Southeast of Guizhou Province', *Price: Theory and Practice*, no. 4 : 34–7.

LI PEILIN (1984) 'On Ways to Develop the Mining Industry Rapidly', *Jinji Guanli*, no. 10.

LI YINING (1986) interview, *China Daily*, 25 June.

LIANG ZHONGXUN (1983) '*Anzhi Lunjia Yu Tigao Shangye Jingji Xiaoyi*' (Price-Setting According to Quality and Increasing Economic Efficiency in Commerce), *Caimao Jingji*, no. 5 : 44.

LIAO YINGMIN AND DAI GUOQING (1987) 'From the Effect of Price Increase on Cement of the State Monopoly for Allocation to Evaluate the Role of Price, *Price: Theory and Practice*, no. 4 : 18–20.

LIN, C. C. (1981) 'The Reinstatement of Economics in China Today', *China Quarterly*, no. 85.

LIN, W. AND CHAO, A. (EDS) (1982) *China's Economic Reforms*, Philadelphia, University of Pennsylvania Press.

LIN WENYI AND JIA LURANG (1981) 'On the Law of Supply and Demand and its Role in the Socialist Economy', *Jingji Yanjiu*, no. 9, September, 30–7.

LIU JUNG-CHAO (1971) *China's Fertiliser Economy*, Edinburgh University Press, Social Science Research Council, Committee on the Economy of China.

LIU FENGCHANG (1981) interview, *Renmin Ribao*, 6 May.

LIU FUSHAN (1987) 'The Consumption of the Market System and Development of a Market for Producer Goods', *Caimao Jingji*, no. 1 : 38–41.

LIU GUOGUANG (1986) 'Price Reform Essential to Growth', *Beijing Review*, vol. 29, no. 33 : 14–18.

——— *ET AL.* (1985) 'The Reform of the Economic System and Macroeconomic Management', *Jingji Yanjiu*, no. 12, December : 3–19.

LIU, T. C. AND YEH, K. C. (1965) *The Economy of the Chinese Mainland: National Income and Economic Development, 1933–1959*, Princeton, Princeton University Press.

LIU ZHUOPU *ET AL.* (1987) *Shehui Zhuyi Jiage Xue* (Socialist Price Theory), Beijing, China Finance Economy Press.

LOCKETT, M. (1983) 'Enterprises Management Moves Towards Democracy?', in Feuchtwang, S. and Hussain, A. (eds), *The Chinese Economic Reforms*, New York, St Martin's Press.

LOU JIWEI AND ZHOU XIAOCHUAN (1984) 'Discussions on The Reform in the Economic System', *Jingji Yanjiu*, no. 10, October, 13–20.

LU NAN (1983) '*Shengchan Yu Shangqu Jiage*' (The Production Price and Two-Tier Price), *Jiage Lunwen Xuanji*, China Price Society, Beijing.

LUO GENGWO (1957) *Problems of Commodities and the Law of Value under the Socialist System*, Beijing, Koxue Zhubanshe.

——— (1985) 'Introduction of the Price Reform in the Soviet Union and East European Countries', Internal Circulation Paper (unpublished).

——— (1986) 'Study of the Problem of Low Prices of Energy and Raw Materials', *Price: Theory and Practice*, no. 3 : 22–7.

MA HONG (1983) *New Strategy for China's Economy*, Beijing, New World Press.

MA KAI (1987) 'A Correct Estimate of the Position and Effect of Price Reform under the Condition of Economic Shortage', *Price: Theory and Practice*, no. 2 : 10–11.

MAXWELL, N. AND MACFARLANE, B. (EDS) (1984) *China's Changed Road to Development*, Oxford, Pergamon Press.

MEIER, G. M. (ED.) (1983) *Pricing Policy For Development Management*, Baltimore, Johns Hopkins University Press.

MILENKORITCH, O. D. (1971) *Plan and Market in Yugoslav Economic Thought*, New Haven, Yale University Press.

MISES, L. V. (1920) (1972) 'Economic Calculation in the Socialist Commonwealth' in Nove, A. and Nuti, D. M. (eds), *Socialist Economics*, Harmondsworth, Penguin.

MOORE, M. AND WHITE, G. (1987) *The Retreat of the State? The Politics of Economic Liberalisation in the Third World*, London, Institute of Development Studies.

MYERS, R. H. (1985) 'Price Reforms and Property Rights in Communist China Since 1978', *Issues and Studies*, vol. 21, no. 10, October : 13–33.

NAKAJIMA, S. (1985) 'The Prospects for Achievement of China's Long-term Economic Target: an Investment Perspective', *China Newsletter*, JETRO, no. 59 : 15–17.

NAMBU, M. (1985) 'Inflation in China', *China Newsletter*, JETRO, no. 59 : 2–6.

NOVE, A. (1983) *The Economics of Feasible Socialism*, London, George Allen & Unwin.

PAIRAULT, T. (1984) 'Chinese Market Mechanism: A Controversial Debate', in Maxwell, N. and McFarlane, B. (eds), *China's Changed Road to Development*, Oxford, Pergamon Press.

PANNELL, C. W. AND MA, J. C. (1983) *China: The Geography of Development and Modernization*, London, Edward Arnold.

PEOPLE'S UNIVERSITY OF CHINA (1979) *Document Collection of the State Purchasing and Selling Policies for Grains, Cotton and Oil-bearing Crops, 1951–1979*, Beijing.

PERKINS, D. H. (1966) *Market Control and Planning in Communist China*, Cambridge, Mass., Harvard University Press.

——— (1986) in Barnett, A. D. and Clough, R, N. (eds), *Modernizing China: Post-Mao Reform and Development*, Boulder, Col., Westview.

——— AND YUSUF, S. (1984) *Rural Development in China*, published for the World Bank, Baltimore, Johns Hopkins University Press.

PERRY, E. J. AND WONG, C. (EDS) (1985) *The Political Economy of Reform in Post-Mao China*, Cambridge, Mass., Harvard University Press.

PROUT, C. (1985) *Market Socialism in Yugoslavia*, Oxford, Oxford University Press.

PRYBYLA, J. S. (1985) 'The Chinese Economy Adjustment of the System or Systematic Reform?', *Asian Survey*, vol. 25, no. 5, May, University of California Press.

QI XIANGDONG (1985) 'Awareness of Problems Resulted from the Reappearance of the Small-Scale Simple Furnaces', *Jingji Guanli*, no. 8 : 10–12.

——— (1986) 'Policies for Resolving the Problems Caused by Small-Scale Rolled Steel Mills', *Jingji Guanli*, no. 3 : 35–7.

QIAO RONGZHANG (1983) 'Price Work Since Liberation', in *Jiage Lunwen Xuanji*, China Price Society.

RIEMAN, B. K. (1967) *More, Faster, Better and Cheaper – A Study of Chinese Industrial Price, Indicators, and Reward Policies 1950–1965*, Michigan, University Microfilms.

RONIMONS, H. E. (1950) *Soviet Planning and Economic Theory*, Vancouver, B.C., University of British Columbia Press.

ROBBINS, L. C. (1934) *The Great Depression*, London: Macmillan, p. 151.

ROBINSON, J. (1964) (1972) 'Consumer's Sovereignty in a Planned Economy', in Nove, A. and Nuti, D. M. (eds), Penguin.

——— (1976) *Economic Management in China*, London, Anglo–Chinese Educational Institute.

ROSARIO LOUISE DO (1987) 'The Power of the Purse', *Far Eastern Economic Review*, 18, June : 75–6.

SAKAKIBARA, J. (1984) 'Demand and Supply Trends in China Trade', *China Newsletter*, JETRO, no. 49 : 16–19.

SAKSENA, K. D. (1986) *Pricing Policy and Price Controls in Developing Countries*, London, Frances Pinter.

SENDER, J. AND SMITH, S. (1987) *The Development of Capitalism in Africa*, London, Routledge Chapman & Hall.

SHANGHAI ECONOMICS INSTITUTE OF THE SHANGHAI ACADEMY OF SCIENCES *ET AL.* (EDS) (1958) *A Collection of Shanghai Price Data and Related Materials Before and After the Liberation (1921–1957)*, Shanghai, Shanghai People's Press.

SHU RONG *ET AL.* (1984) 'Arguments for the Improvement of Enterprise Management Based on the Present Development of the Bicycle Industry', *Jingji Guanli*, no. 9 : 36–9.

SKOLKA, J. (1984) 'Use of Input–Output Models in the Preparation of Price Reform in China', *Industry and Development*, no. 10, UNIDO, New York, UN.

SONG JIANLI (1986) 'Suggestion about Price-Setting for Bicycles Based on Quality', *Henan Price Discussion*, no. 2.

SONG ZE (1986) 'The Dual Price System and its Development Trends', *Caimao Jingji*, no. 8 : 33–7.

STATE COUNCIL (1984) *China's Economic Reform Decision*, Beijing.

STATE COUNCIL EMERGENCY NOTICES (1983) *Price: Theory and Practice*, no. 5.

STATE STATISTICAL BUREAU (PRC) (1985) *China: A Statistical Survey in 1985*, Beijing, New World Press and China Statistical Information and Consultancy Service Center.

——— (1960) *Ten Great Years*, Peking, Foreign Language Press.

——— (1983, 1984, 1985, 1986) *China Statistical Yearbook*, Hong Kong, Oxford University Press.

STONE, B. (1988) 'Relative Prices in the People's Republic of China: Rural Taxation Through Public Monopsony', in Mellor, John R. and Ahmed, R. (eds), *Agricultural Price Policy for Developing Countries*, Baltimore, Johns Hopkins University Press.

SUN YEFANG (1982) *Social Needs Versus Economic Efficiency in China: Sun Yefang's Critique of Socialist Economics*, Fung, K. K., Fr. Lc., M. E. Sharpe.

SUNG, Y. W. AND CHAN, T. M. H. (1987) 'China's Economic Reform, 1: The Debates in China', *Asian–Pacific Economic Literature*, vol. 1, no. 1.

TAKAHARA, AKIO (1988) *The Politics of Wage Reform in Post-revolutionary China*, London, Institute of Development Studies.

TECHNOLOGICAL, ECONOMIC AND SOCIAL DEVELOPMENT RESEARCH CENTRE AT THE STATE COUNCIL (TESDRC) INVESTIGATION TEAM (1986) 'Problems of the Dual Prices of Means-of-Production and Macro-Management Measures', *Price; Theory and Practice*, no. 1 : 9–14.

TIAN JIYUN (1985) 'Price System Due for Reform', *Beijing Review*, vol. 28, no. 4, 28 June.

TIAN YUAN, CHEN DEZUN AND YANG LU (1986) 'A Study of Theoretical Prices and Their Application', *Social Sciences in China*, no. 4.

TIDRICK, G. AND CHEN, J. Y., (EDS) (1987) *China's Industrial Reform*, New York, Oxford University Press.

WALKER, K. R. (1984) 'Chinese Agriculture During the Period of the Readjustment, 1979–1983', *China Quarterly*, no. 100 : 785.

WANG, G. C. (ED.) (1982) *Economic Reform in the PRC*, Boulder, Colorado, Westview Press.

WANG JIYE AND ZHU YUANZHEN (EDS) (1987) *Jingji Tizhi Gaige Shouce* (Handbook for the Reform of the Economic System), Beijing, Economic Daily Press : 936–44.

WANG, K. P. *ET AL.* (1977) 'Mineral Industries of the People's Republic of China', *Mining Annual Review 1977 Issue* US Bureau of Mines.

WANG, T. E. (1980) *Economic Policies and Price Stability in China*, Institute of East Asian Studies, University of California.

WANG TIANHU (1986) 'A Discussion of the Bicycle Market', *Gongchang Guanli*, June : 27–8.

WANG XIAOQIANG *ET AL.* (1987) 'Reform: Results and Lessons From the 1985 CESRRI Survey', *Journal of Comparative Economics*, vol. 11, no. 3.

WANG YONGZHI AND WANG ZHENZHI (1983) 'Jiage Yu Gongqiu' (Price, Supply and Demand), *Jiage Lunwen Xuanji*, China Price Society.

WANG ZHENGPEI *ET AL.* (1987) 'Dual Prices and Two-Track Prices: Comparison of the Price Reforms in China and Hungary', *Young Economists' Forum*, no. 1, January : 64–7.

WANG ZHENZHI *ET AL.* (1982) 'A Summary of the Discussions on Price Theory During the Past Few Years', *Social Sciences in China*, no. 3 : 16–34.

WANG ZHENZHI AND WANG YONGZHI (1986) 'Some Theoretical Problems on Price Reform', *Price: Theory and Practice*, no. 6 : 21–4.

WANG ZHIYE (1962) 'A Preliminary Investigation into Value Measurement Problems under Socialism', *Jingji Yanjiu*, November, 24–32.

WHITE, G. (1985) *The Role of the State in China's Socialist Industrialisation*, London, Institute of Development Studies.

——— (1986) 'State and Market in Post-Mao China', London, Institute of Development Studies.

WHITE, G. AND BOWLES, P. (1987) 'Towards A Capital Market? Reform in the Chinese Banking System', *China Research Report*, no. 6, May, London, Institute of Development Studies.

WHITE, G. *ET AL.* (EDS) (1983) *Revolutionary Socialist Development in the Third World*, University of Kentucky Press.

WILCZYNSKI, J. (1972) *Socialist Economic Development and Reforms*, London, Macmillan.

——— (1973) *Profit, Risk and Incentives Under Socialist Economic Planning*, London, Macmillan.

——— (1982) *The Economics of Socialism*, London, George Allen & Unwin.

WONG, C. P. (1986) 'The Economics of Shortage and Problems of Reform in Chinese Industry', *Journal of Comparative Economics*, vol. 10, no. 4.

WORLD BANK (1983) 'List of Anshan Steel Works Survey Material' (unpublished).

——— (1985a) *China: Long-Term Development Issues and Options*, Washington, D.C., World Bank.

——— (1985b) *China: The Energy Sector*, Annex 3, Washington, D. C., World Bank.

——— (1985c) *China: Agriculture to the Year 2000*, Annex 2, Washington, D. C., World Bank : 11.

WORTZEL, H. V. (1983) 'Equity and Efficiency in the Distribution of Non-Food Consumer Goods: Shanghai as an Example', *Asian Survey*, vol. 23, no. 7, July : 845–57.

WU JINGLIAN (1985) *Renmin Rebou?*, 1 May.

——— AND ZHAO RENWEI (1987) 'The Dual Pricing System in China's Industry', *Journal of Comparative Economics*, vol. 11, no. 3.

WU XUEJUN (1985) 'Market Price Decreases of Coal', *Price: Theory and Practice*, no. 2 : 44.

WU, YUAN-LI (1965) *The Steel Industry in Communist China*, New York, Praeger.

XIAO ZHUOJI (1980) 'The Law of Price Movement in China', *Social Sciences in China*, no. 4.

XU DIXIN *ET AL.* (1982) *China's Search for Economic Growth: The Chinese Economy Since 1949*, Beijing, New World Press.

XU HONGGAO *ET AL.* (1984) 'System Management Applied to Cotton Production', *Nongye Jishu Jingji*, no. 10, October : 17–21.

XU WEN (1985) 'Guiding Ox Needed to Lead Ox's Noses; Analysis of the Problem Between the Pricing System and Steel Output and Supply', *Price: Theory and Practice*, no. 4 : 25–6.

XU YI *ET AL.* (1982) *Socialist Pricing Theory*, Beijing, China's Financial and Economic Publications.

XUE MUQIAO (1981) *China's Socialist Economy*, Beijing, Foreign Languages Press.

——— (1982) *Current Economic Problems in China*, tran. K. K. Fung, Boulder, Colorado, Westview Press.

——— (1985) 'New Lessons of the Reform of the Planning Management Economic System', *Economic Daily*, 12 October.

——— (ED.) (1985) *Almanac of China's Economy*, Hong Kong, Modern Cultural Company and Tai Dao Publishing.

YAMANOUCHI, K. (1985) 'The Chinese Price System and the Thrust of Reform', *China Newsletter*, JETRO, no. 59 : 2–11.

——— (1986) 'The Chinese Price System and the Thrust of Reform', *China Newsletter*, JETRO, no. 60 : 5.

YANG HONGDAO (1983) *Shehui Zhuyi Jiage Gongzuo* (Implementation of Socialist Pricing), Beijing, China's Financial and Economic Publication House.

YANG JIANBAI (1963) 'The Balance of the National Economy and Production Prices', *Jingji Yanjiu*, no. 12, December, 40–56.

YANG SHANGMIN (1980) 'Guanyu Wujia Guanli De Jige Wenti' (Some Issues on the Price Management), in Economic Institute of China Social Academy *et al.* (eds), *Problems of Price Formation in Socialism*, Beijing, China Social Science Press.

YANG ZHONGWEI AND LI BO (1985) 'An Exploration of the Theory of Price Formation and the Policy of Price Transformation', *Jingji Yanjiu*, no. 8, August, 3–10.

——— (1986) 'Pricing and Price Reform', *Social Science in China*, no. 1 : 69–80.

YAO LIN (1985) 'Goal and Model of Price Reform', *Price: Theory and Practice*, no. 6 : 17–21.

YAO XIHONG *ET AL.* (1984) 'On the Marketing Channels of Cotton in Shandong Province', *Nongye Jishu Jingji*, no. 12, December : 29–32.

YE BING (1985) 'Discussion on the Nascent Market of the Means-of-Production', *Young Economists' Forum*, no. 1 : 18.

YE RUIXIANG (1983) '*Nengyuan Jiage Wenti Yanjiu*' (Study of Energy Prices), *Jiage Lunwe Xuanji*, China Price Association.

YU HONGEN (1957) interviews, *Renmin Ribao*, 26 February.

YU XINGFA (1983) 'Guanyu Woguo Jihua Jiage Xingchang De Lilun' (Theories of the Planned Price Formation), *Jiage Lunwen Xuanji*, China Price Society.

——— (ED.) (1984) *Jiage Lilun Taolun Guandian Zengshu* (Summary of Discussions on Price Theory), China Higher Education Research Society on Price.

YUAN BAOHUA (1987) interviews, *Economic Daily*, 26 September.

ZHANG BAOHUA AND DAI GUANLAI (1986) 'Strategies for Resolving the Problem of Sharp Price Increases for Above-Quota Producer Goods', *Jingji Guanli*, no. 1 : 16–23.

ZHANG SHUGUANG (1981) 'Economic Structure and Economic Results: Examining the Process and Models of the Economic Reform by Analysing Economic Structure and Efficiency', *Zhongguo Shehui Kexue*, no. 6 : 41–58.

ZHANG WEIDA (1986) 'Reflecting Upon the Model of the Price System in China', *Jingji Yanjiu*, no. 3, March, 48–53.

——— (1987) 'Development in the Material Market With Economy Shortage', *Jingji Yanjiu*, no. 10, October, 19–24.

ZHANG WEIYING (1985) 'On the Role of Prices', *Social Science in China*, no. 4 : 177–94.

ZHANG XIAOMING AND SONG YAOHUA (1987) 'Contradictions and Directions in the Reform of the Circulation System', *Jingji Yanjiu*, no. 10, October, 24–8.

ZHANG ZERONG (1983) 'The Socialist Economy Requires a Net Value-

Added Price System', *Caimao Jingji*, no. 7 : 17–21.

ZHANG ZHIBIN (1986) 'On the Market of the Means-of-Production', *Caimao Jingji*, no. 3 : 25–31.

ZHANG ZHUOYUAN (1983) *Shehui Zhuyi Jingji Zhong De Jiazhi, Jiage, Chenben He Lirun* (Value, Price, Cost and Profit in Socialist Economy), Beijing, China Social Science Press.

——— (1987) *Shehui Zhuyi Jiage Lilun Yu Jiage Gaige* (Socialist Price Theory and Price Reform), Beijing, China Social Science Press.

ZHAO RENWEI (1986) 'The Dual System Problem in China's Economic Reform', *Jingji Yanjiu*, no. 9, September, 12–23.

ZHAO ZIYANG (1985) 'Report on the 6th Five-Year Plan for National Economic and Social Development', *Chinese Economic Studies*, vol. 18, no. 4 : 3–61.

ZHOU SHULIAN (1986) 'More on the Laws of Enterprise Behaviour', *China's Industrial Economics Journal*, no. 2, June.

——— , WU JINGLIAN AND WANG HAIBO (1979) *Lirun Fanchou He Shehui Zhuyi De Oiye Guanli* (The Concept of Profit and Socialist Enterprise Management), Beijing, People's Press.

ZHOU XIACHUAN AND LOU JIWEI (1984) 'Problems of Socialist Price Formation', *Jingji Yanjiu*, no. 10, October.

ZHU GUANXIANG (1984) 'A Discussion About Bicycle Price-Setting Based on Quality', *Price: Theory and Practice*, no. 4 : 49–50.

Journals, Newspapers and Yearbooks

Almanac of China's Economy: 1984
1985

Beijing Review: 1980
1985

Changzhou Ribao: 25 August 1985

Cheng Ming: 1 September 1988

China Daily: 24 November 1986
11 December 1987
12 January 1988

China's Industrial Economics Journal: 1986

China's Trade and Commercial Statistical Data: 1985

China Reconstructs: October 1983
1981
1983

China Statistical Yearbook: 1984
1985
1986

Donghan Henchen: 10 January 1985

Economic Daily: 9 March 1985
15 March 1985
10 May 1985

16 July 1985
19 July 1985
29 July 1985
13 September 1985
14 September 1985
1 September 1987
15 September 1987
16 September 1987
26 Septenber 1987
9 June 1988
2 August 1988
8 August 1988
2 September 1988
8 September 1988
Economist: 27 October 1984
27 August 1988
Financial Times: 2 November 1984
18 December 1987
28 October 1988
Gongren Ribao: 21 September 1987
The Great Achievement of China's Agriculture: 1984
Guangming Ribao: 21 July 1964
Guowu Yuan Gongbao: 1984
Hongqi: 1983
Jingji Chankao: 13 March 1985
20 March 1985
21 March 1985
6 April 1985
17 April 1985
23 April 1985
29 April 1985
8 May 1985
16 May 1985
18 May 1985
22 May 1985
4 June 1985
25 June 1985
29 June 1985
2 July 1985
3 July 1985
11 July 1985
19 July 1985
22 July 1985
25 August 1985
3 September 1985
11 September 1985
17 September 1985
10 October 1985
20 January 1986

Jingji Diaocha: 1983
Jingji Guanli: 1984
Jingji Ribao: 18 January 1983
24 May 1985
Jingji Xue Zhoubao: 4 May 1986
Jingji Yanjiu: 1984
Ming Bao Yuekan: November 1987
People's Daily: 25 October 1979
17 January 1986
People's Daily (Overseas Edition): 24 August 1988
Price : Theory and Practice: 1983
1984
1985
1986
1987
1988
Reform Decision: 1984
Renmin Ribao: 4 July 1983
13 July 1983
16 July 1983
17 July 1983
Renmin Ribao: 19 July 1983
1 May 1985
20 September 1985
17 January 1986
22 February 1986
1 January 1987
21 February 1987
23 February 1987
26 February 1987
15 March 1987
8 June 1987
11 June 1987
12 June 1987
20 June 1987
9 July 1987
11 July 1987
12 July 1987
15 July 1987
22 July 1987
31 August 1987
4 September 1987
20 October 1987
7 July 1988
19 August 1988
Social Sciences in China: 1985
Zhongguo Shehui Kexue: 1986

Index